M000210087

The Only Planet of Choice

Essential Briefings from Deep Space

The Council of Nine have stated that, while other planets
do have choice, the consciousness is collective. Only on
Earth can a being experience individual choice.

PHYLLIS V. SCHLEMMER
Transceiver

Second Edition
Edited by MARY BENNETT

Foreword by Sir John Whitmore, Bt

GATEWAY BOOKS, BATH

Published by
GATEWAY BOOKS
The Hollies, Wellow,
Bath, BA2 8QJ, U.K.

First edition 1993
Second edition 1994
Revised 1996

Copyright © 1993, 1994 and 1996 Phyllis V. Schlemmer, aka Phyllis Virtue-Carmel

Distributed in the U.S.A.
until 31 December 1995
by ATRIUM PUBLISHERS GROUP
3356 Coffey Lane
Santa Rosa, CA 95403

from 1 January 1996
by NATIONAL BOOK NETWORK
4720 Boston Way
Lanham, MD 20706

All rights reserved. No part of this publication
may be reproduced in any form or by any means,
electronic and mechanical, including photocopy,
recording, or any information storage and retrieval
system, without permission in writing from
the Publishers.

Cover design by Studio B of Kirkbean
Cover photograph courtesy Science Photo Library
Text set in Bembo and Optima, 10 on 12pt by
Oak Press at Castleton
Printed and bound by
Redwood Books of Trowbridge

Library of Congress Cataloguing-in Publication Data:
A catalogue record for this book is
available from the British Library

ISBN 1-85860-023-5

Contents

Dedication

To Tom and the Council of Nine.

Acknowledgments

It has been twenty years of dedicated work by many to bring this book to fruition. It gives me great pleasure to have this opportunity to thank them. Some have funded this book and all have supported me emotionally and intellectually as well as spiritually. I am eternally grateful.

I am particularly indebted to my loving daughters, Phyllis S. Manley and Marilou (Ludi) Long whose support, love and generosity of self and spirit empowered me to do this work. To my wonderfully sensitive granddaughter, Kimberly Ross, this book is for you and future generations. My late parents and grandparents who lovingly helped me, be me. Loving appreciation goes to Sir John Whitmore for his spiritual outlook and constant question 'What if?' as well as his devoted wife Diana and their son Jason; to Dr. Andrija Puharich with whom I have enjoyed working and been privileged and fortunate enough to have done so, for so many years; as to our original group from Ossining, N.Y. Also to Lark von Hugo who took upon herself the monumental task of transcribing eighteen years of tapes. Her commitment was the catalyst that got us all moving. We are forever grateful to you, Lark.

Alick Bartholomew of Gateway Books, our publisher, and Palden Jenkins, for the initial compilation of the communications.

From Austria, Miki and Ingeborg Walleczek, their daughters Sascha and Tini, who often gave me a respite from my hectic life, showered me with love and beauty. Our Austrian friends who gave of themselves and helped the Nine along the way include: Wulf Kruetschnigg, Franzi Lippert and Jane Tilden, also Barbara Lippitt, my 'adoptive daughter' for her loving support and joyful spirit.

From Canada comes Barbara Bronfman, who is always there with love and encouragement, and who provided me with a safe haven and ongoing friendship.

In Norway we have Jan Arne Odegarden, with a new perspective.

The U.K. group for their dedication includes Philip and Rachel Goldman, Susan Kaye, Peter and Teresa Marmot, Funtz Mitchener, Geri

Rogers, Alex Sautelle, Clive and Alyson Sinclair and Ian and Vicki Watson. A special thanks to Cynthia Franklin for indexing the tapes so many years ago, a well as my friend Angela Millburn-Scott.

And a very special 'thank you' to David Hemery and his wife V. for their commitment to bring forth this edition.

From Germany Lore Ritter, who gave me a year of her life, full of joy and humour, and her friend Volker Heim.

In Israel, Avi and Ruti Yasur and all who had the courage to be with me in 'The Course of Miracles'; my partners in 'Shaar Yamin' as well as Rivka Frank, Niva Shapira, Sylvia Sheinbaum, and my many friends, clients and students.

Appreciation to Harriet Abramson and Avi N.Tal, whom I have known from the beginning of time and are always there when needed.

The U.S. contingent includes Henry Belk who started it all. Judith Skutch Witson and her husband Bill, who provided us with *Miracles*. The late Brendan O'Regan, a scientist who never rejected my reality, Jo and Bob Pease for the many years of friendship and loyalty, my friend Bette Davis who believes in me. Ileen Maisel who sees directly into the heart of things and is my friend and sounding board as well as my confidante. Ivor and Ronnie Witson, who lovingly gave of their expertise and provided us with the software necessary to do the transcriptions. Desiree and Jim Hurtak (*The Keys of Enoch*) for their commitment to the Universe and their help in getting us through difficult times.

The late Gene Roddenberry, creator of *Star Trek* for his courage, curiosity and desire to communicate with the Nine, and the semi-autobiographical film script he created for us called 'The Nine'.

I am immensely grateful to Mary Bennett, our editor - she is a 'gift' from the Nine - for her dedication in bringing this book into form.

To all who sat with the Nine and believed or disbelieved.

Finally, to my husband Israel Carmel, who lived through my doubts, my pain and often unerringly put me back on course, who never doubted for one second the existence of Tom and the Nine.

If it be true that 'By their works you shall know them', then these are truly light beings and healers of the Planet.

I thank all of you.

Phyllis V. Schlemmer.
Flagler Beach, Florida & Pardes Hanna, Israel

One person with courage is a majority.
Andrew Jackson.

Foreword

by John Whitmore

The Search for Extra Terrestrial Intelligence (SETI) is now a serious business. In 1992 NASA invested much effort, money and new technology in searching the stars, or rather their planets, for radio signals which might indicate the presence of intelligent life forms. On a recent British TV programme entitled 'ET, Please Phone Earth' several eminent professors involved with the project expressed little doubt that such life exists and were anxious for Earth to keep listening for signs of it.

However they were not all in agreement about the wisdom of us Earthlings revealing our presence to the wider Universe. As one luminary pointed out, we all know what we humans did to societies that we deemed to be more primitive when we discovered them, so what might more advanced life forms do to us? That fear is based on the contradictory assumption that these 'advanced' beings would be as aggressive, thoughtless, uncompassionate and primitive as human beings!

It is too late now anyway, for we have been sending out radio messages for many decades, the first of which have already sped past neighbouring solar systems. However, the bizarre nature of the more powerful signals that follow those first dots and dashes, from soap operas to evangelist preachers, might cause an alien to wonder whether intelligent life does exist on Earth after all! When Mahatma Gandhi was asked what he thought about western civilization, he said 'it would be a good idea'. Such might be the view of Earth from afar!

The threat posed to us by travellers from other worlds which was fostered by early science fiction books, Orson Welles' famous broadcast and many films, is today reinforced by strange stories of cattle mutilations and UFO abductions. However more recently, perhaps initiated by Gene Roddenberry's *Star Trek*, there have been several cinematic attempts to present extraterrestrial life as benign, culminating with Steven Spielberg's endearing ET.

In most science fiction stories the beings, good or bad, are humanoid in appearance, but have the capacity to pass instantly through time and space. The cynic would dismiss both as convenient devices to assist the story teller to bring aliens down to Earth. Humanoid actors are certainly the easiest ones to come by, and we now know that in reality it would take ETs too long to travel here by conventional physical spacecraft, but can we be so sure that these fictions are not fact?

Years ago, physicist John Wheeler postulated many interlocking Universes, and other pioneers have gone past his limits of speculation to their limits of credibility. Other universes suggest other dimensions based on laws beyond the comprehension of our scientists and beyond detection by our technology. Anything operating in this realm would appear to be magic to us and would of course be dismissed as a non-event or an illusion by those who hold tenaciously to the limitations of existing science. Only a century ago were not electric light, radio, television, and flight, let alone space flight, in the realm of magic to all but the foolhardy? Are we so arrogant, and Earth-chauvinistic to think that our science, a mere hundred years on, is the only science of the Universe?

While Wheeler was theorizing about other realms, Uri Geller was bending spoons by other means. Predictably he was dismissed by defenders of the scientific faith such as magician James Randi, SETI seeker Carl Sagan and science fiction maestro Isaac Azimov. Nevertheless, some reputable scientists validated his work and Geller himself went on to make a fortune locating oil and minerals for multinational commercial enterprises who were less sensitive about the scientific correctness of his powers.

We find plenty of occurrences that defy our scientific reason in religion, of course, and they have strong symmetry with the types of events in which psychics like Geller engage. In our Bible alone there are many examples of clairvoyance, clairaudience, channelling, telekinesis, healing and dowsing. It is profoundly illogical of us to accept our biblical stories on faith and yet to deny that these things can or do occur today. The passage of time lionises historical people and events, in the same way as television does now, making it hard for us to find a balanced perspective of distant times, and to find their modern parallels.

Of course religion, at least the Christian religion, has been overtaken by science as the guardian of the truth for us lesser mortals. We look to the high priests of science for knowledge and understanding, robes have yielded to the white coat, the chalice to the test tube.

Science has the advantage of not being obliged to define good and evil, though I believe we would all be better off if it was. At first glance, even on moral grounds, science can make a good case for its ascendancy because the track record of religion is deplorable. Both in biblical times and today, examples of sheer evil carried out in the name of God and religion abound. From time to time psychics too, are revealed as frauds or use their powers for evil purposes. What is new, surprising or different? Wherever there is good, there is evil to oppose or distort it. Has not science created its monsters too? Of course neither science nor religion are inherently evil, but what some people will do in the pursuit of them is horrendous.

The Christian view of the coexistence of good and evil may not be too far off the mark, but people often find comfort in a more one-sided interpretation of this concept where extraterrestrials are concerned. While some deify and rush to embrace all forms of cosmic experience to help them escape our material existence, others see all alien acts or contacts as the work of the devil. However, it may not be that clear cut. Is it not reasonable to speculate that technologically advanced beings might exist in other dimensions, beings who are not evil but who regard us as a laboratory of lower life forms for them to experiment upon? We have few scruples about what we do to mundane animals in the interests of scientific advancement. Might they not do the same, hence the abductions and cattle mutilations?

Such occurrences could easily lead us to believe that all extra terrestrial life forms are evil. Certainly they would, unless we are able to recognise just how many different types of alien exist, and how many of them may be around us at all times. This idea directly challenges the scientists' notion of physical ETs developing along rare chance evolutionary parallels to ourselves on a few distant planets, but it readily fits with religious beliefs. Yes, beings of white light, dark forces and the greys in between could be here now, though for the most part in another dimension undetectable to us. It is only our blind logic that asks 'Why don't they come and land on the White House lawn? Why don't they come and sort out the mess we are in? Why would they bother with a little planet like ours?' It may be up to each of us individually to discover them for ourselves and make our own allegiances. Is that not what some religions suggest?

In our eagerness to embrace the wonders of science and acquire the new technological luxuries, we have elevated scientists to undeserved heights of infallibility and have not considered whether they are looking in the right place for extraterrestrial life. That life is here amongst us now, and has been ever since that brief moment, in universal time, of what we call recorded history, began. If 'angels' and other cosmic beings exist in another dimension, I'm sure they would appear and disappear as if by magic, and is that not exactly what they do? Might they not come in 'Chariots of the Gods' which would defy our laws of gravity and common sense, the way that UFOs are reported to?

If we read between the lines of religion and science fiction, and look a little less to science for the understanding of extraterrestrial intelligence, we might be more successful. I suggest that NASA's array of radio telescopes cannot see the wood for the trees. They are looking out there, and it is right here! It is even willing to talk to us, if we are willing to listen. Perhaps if we were to ask ETs about their existence and purpose, they might tell us, and also spell out why they do not make their presence globally known. The problem is that religion invites us to talk to God and his cohorts, but if we dare to claim that they have answered us back, we are considered crazy.

For nearly twenty years now, I have been talking with a group of beings, non-human and invisible, who have, with great love and patience, told me and several colleagues much about the structure of intelligent life forms in the Universe, where Earth fits into the scheme, what our purpose is, and that of our planet, how our misuse of religion and science has distorted our understanding to the point of blindness, and what we can do about it. My partners in this venture included Dr. Andrija Puharich (identified in the text as 'Andrew'), other scientists, religionists and Gene Roddenberry of *Star Trek* who obtained a detailed description of beings from elsewhere in the Universe. Gene and Andrija have passed on, but most of the others are still with us.

The Only Planet of Choice is a selection of our conversations with our friends from space. I hope it will help to clear up, for some people at least, the huge gulf of understanding that divides religions from each other, religions from science, and scientists from psychics. Sadly we also have to contend with certain powerful earthly authorities who have in their folly or wisdom, depending on your point of view, chosen to protect us (by the judicious use of disinformation and ridicule) from their more complete knowledge about extra-terrestrial life. One wonders if they really know with which level of the cosmic hierarchy they are dealing, and who needs protecting from whom.

This book along with other books, with crop circles, the new genre of Sci Fi films, a few global crises, whistle blowers, paranormal events, controlled leaks and not so controlled ones, are all part of the essential awakening of Earth. That awakening demands that we move beyond the present structures of both science and religion. The challenge for science is that the essence of religion is true, the challenge for religion is that there is but one truth. All that any one religion possesses is a perspective of that truth, and by now a fairly distorted one at that. There is no authority for real understanding but ourselves. We need to be bold, but very discriminating.

I don't expect that my particular logic expressed in these few pages will be sufficient fully to open the mind of the more skeptical reader. Some of us, will, not without good reason, balk at any messages that purports to emanate from a cosmic source, especially if it is delivered by or transmitted through a fallible human being. We may shield ourselves from that which we do not understand or cannot believe, with the assumption, or even the accusation of fraud. Fraud, however, only occurs where there is a perceived or actual pecuniary gain or power to be had. This is certainly not applicable to Phyllis.

The role of a go-between at the interface between Earthly and Universal consciousness is fraught with difficulties, loneliness and stress and is often both physically and emotionally painful. Phyllis has experienced that and more. She is an ordinary American lady, nutritionist, mother and grandmother, with extraordinary gifts as a teacher, healer and channel, who tells about herself and how it all began in her own words in "Briefing". To understand more about the channelling process, I recommend a reading of Briefing Part Two before embarking on the main text.

There will still be those who reject channelling or have an unshakable aversion to it. I have a lot of empathy with their position myself, but are we dependent upon knowing the source of a message in order to recognise or accept the wisdom contained therein? Does a good quotation only acquire its power when attributed to Abraham Lincoln, William James or Shakespeare? If we need the name or the fame of the sayer to validate a quotation, are we not abdicating our discrimination and choice? *The Only Planet of Choice* suggests just how important our individual choice may be in the years to come, for ourselves and for the Universe. Neither do you have to, nor can you, decide now if the wisdom offered stands on its own merit, nor are you able to determine whether the information contained in this book holds together as a reasonable hypothesis until you have read it. Then make your choice. Read on.

I

THE UNIVERSE AND ITS BEINGS

1

Prelude

"We are here. This is Tom. We come in love and peace. Greetings, blessings, joy."

This is how many of the transmissions from The Council of Nine begin. They are transmitted via Tom, their spokesman. This edition of *The Only Planet of Choice* has grown out of the need to prepare the original text for translation into other languages. Also, with the success of the previous edition it became clear that there was a need for more material from the Nine. So the original text has been expanded from the archives and new transmissions (given in May 1994) have been added. To this end it has been necessary to keep the editorial input to a minimum, the Nine texts will speak for themselves, for as Tom has said in a transmission in 1991: "The energy of these positive understandings enables lives to be changed. It is of vital importance that this Cosmology is available for humankind. To give them the opportunity to know the truth, for when it is exposed to them it will bring forth that code within, to make them aware."

So my editorial decision has been to keep a light hand on the wheel. It is quite possible that we do not understand all the meanings of all Tom's sentences – but it is also possible that with inner growth, what is unclear today will be shining with clarity tomorrow. It is this sort of book that stretches and helps us expand.

This book is very different from both *Prelude To The Landing On Planet Earth* and its first edition. It does not have the narrative style of the former, nor the commentaries of the latter. It requires that the reader simply 'be'. It is a reflection of the rapidly changing times, of our increasing capacity to assimilate extraordinary ideas into our lives and act upon them. Very often Tom makes a statement and then repeats it, with the alteration of just one or two words. He is stretching our minds and gradually a large concept is fed into our minds in easy, spiralling stages. This is another way of nudging our coding, allowing us to absorb information which we will access when it is needed.

I would also recommend reading "Briefing," Parts 1 and 2 before settling down to the main text, as that information would be most helpful in understanding the processes involved. For my part, while working on these transmissions, I have felt them become as a great crystal, reflecting light from all its facets. And I have been, and still am, elated by the tangible energy emanating from these sentences.

It must be said that my task would have been far more difficult without the skills of Palden Jenkins, who compiled the transcripts for the first edition. And Tom also requested that Palden be thanked: "As spokesman for the Nine, I convey from the Council of Nine, our great gratitude and joyfulness for the task that you accomplished."

My thanks also go to Lab Nine Ltd. for permission to use extracts from *Prelude to the Landing on Planet Earth* which includes the extract from *Uninvited visitors* by Ivan T. Sanderson.

I have left Tom's speech patterns as close to the original as is possible without rendering them uncomfortable to read. The words are all exactly where they are meant to be, even if that can feel 'odd' by our modern standards. Many of the sentences have several meanings, and each will find their own truths. I have been with these texts for many months now, and have found several layers of meaning in each paragraph. He often uses the word 'Yes' at the end of his sentences. Sometimes this is to affirm the point that he has just made. Often it is to advise the listener that he is ready for another question. Sometimes he appears unable to pronounce a word, and has several attempts at it, but I have spared the reader such sentences as: "That is a probable-ness...a probabab...a prob...a probability!" This last pronounced with an air of triumph. He likes to ask why words are the same sound but not the same meaning, and such diversions are usually cut short by the Council asking him to get on with the matter in hand. He enjoys wordplay, and the reader should look out for double meanings, though amusing, their content will usually have serious implications for the text. He is delightful to be with, and if that is an odd thing to say of a non-corporeal being, I can only say that through all my exchanges with Tom, I have found him immensely responsive and I have grown very fond of him.

The Council of Nine only transmit through Phyllis Schlemmer, and this is worth repeating, at a time when channelling is becoming increasingly popular. As Tom explains: "When you open yourself for communication with other dimensional beings, it is of great importance to have understanding of purpose and motive. For there are those who come forward proclaiming one thing yet being another and there may be a slipping through of information that may be truth, but may also be a method of manipulation and control. We come only through Our Being [Phyllis]. I am the only spokesman for the Nine and I do not speak through any other". The text from which this quote has been taken can be found in "Briefing".

Tom has also said that it is not necessary to go on "in wind of longness"! So I shall leave you with these transmissions. They have given me great joy to work with for which I shall be forever grateful. If, from reading this book you receive as many blessings as I have done, then truly you will be enriched. I leave you with this quote :

"We imbue you with our energy. We awaken you, as you awaken us. We wish you to know that we love you. We wish you to know who you are and we wish you not to make gods of us or of yourselves. We thank you."

2

The Council of Nine

Apart from the replies given in the following chapter, one very striking aspect of these transmissions is the ability that Tom has for accurate and total recall of the content of earlier conversations. He has often said "Look to your transcriptions of two years ago" and has also acknowledged that what for us might take months of research, they can do in seconds. The understanding of the origins of the Nine would seem to be bounded by the inner development of the individual, (be it the questioner or the reader). For as Tom has said: "if there is one who would ask of questions that cannot assimilate and cannot in truth understand, we do not answer until they are in that moment when they can". This is why the chapter starts off with several different people asking the same sorts of question.

Tom once replied: "We are in truth Aeons" in reference to the Gnostic philosphers, and that very conversation appears later in the book. An Aeon is a term commonly used to describe a period of time, an eternity. However it also describes the highest form of Celestial power, spiritual entities formed from the Divine Presence.

This first exchange, which took place in 1975 is between Gene Roddenberry (of *Star Trek* fame). Gene had some very long sessions with Tom, and more of them will be found later on in this section.

GENE: *To whom am I talking? Do you have a name?*

TOM: I am Tom. I am the spokesman for the Council of Nine. In truth I am Tehuti. Yes. I am also Hamarkos, I am also Herenkar, I am known as Thomas and I am known as Atum.

GENE: *Are you one of the Nine or are you a separate being?*

TOM: I sit in the Council of Nine, yes. I am one that is in wisdom that speaks to you. But the Council has said that, in communications, at times I sound not wisdom! Yes.

This is the reply that Tom gave to another questioner in 1977 on the same subject:

GUEST: *I would like to ask what is it that greets me?*

TOM: I am the spokesman. I am known as Tom for the Council of Nine. I am of the Nine.

GUEST: *Whom do you represent? A higher authority above you that commands you and directs your ways?*

TOM: This is difficult to explain, for the world has no similar situation. But we would say to you – yes, we are in connection with one that is higher, but in totality together we are one, as all the Universe is one.

GUEST: *Do you have any purpose in our world, any major message?*

TOM: We wish you to know firstly that we are not physical beings. Your world is the manifestation of creation and of the Creator manifest in your world – in the form of humankind. You ask if we have a message for you?

GUEST: *Yes, I do.*

TOM: We say to you: You have been created in the image of the Creator. This world has lost its identity with creation. What is, of necessity to understand is the going forth and creating action and deed that brings you to completion in who you are. It is not enough to pray, it is not enough to gather groups of humankind for meditation. What is important is to act.

GUEST: *Thank you very much, Tom.*

ANDREW: *I was particularly interested in 'Hamarkos'. Could you tell us...*

TOM: I am the day, and I am the evening, and I am the mid-noon.

ANDREW: *How did the Egyptians come to build and name the Sphinx after you?*

TOM: You found the secret, the true knowledge of that will be related another time. But the original time that I was on the Planet Earth or identified with your Planet Earth was 34,000 of your years ago. I am the balance. And when I say 'I' – I mean because I am an emissary for the Nine. It is not I, but it is the group. And the principle of the Nine is infinite intelligence, and what we try to bring to this planet is this type of intelligence. We are of nine principles of the Universe, yet together we are one. We are separate and one at the same time. Each represents a portion of energy, knowledge, wisdom, love, kindness, technology, and in continuity it goes on until each portion of a spiral is composed of all that is important to bring complete understanding to each atom, until it becomes one with us. There are in actuality multiplications and more, but in principle there are nine.

We are what is identified [in the Hebraic tradition] as the Elohim. We wish you to know we are not God. We are collective and become one. We wish you to know that we are you as you are we. You created us, and out of that creation you were created. Do not underestimate who you are, and your ability.

Know that all people are pure, that you are perfect, and that all things are possible with you. Know also that we cannot exist without you and all souls, and neither can Planet Earth nor the Universe. When you understand that, you will understand your own life. At times in your world people create confusion, for the density of it is a density of darkness. But always hold the light of truth of your own being, who you are, in your heart. We are with you always. We give you love, we bring you peace.

ANDREW: If I may just give you my conception of what you are like: I gather that you are pure light-beings, in a sense that we don't even understand, because you exist at a velocity beyond light...

TOM: It is beyond your comprehension.

ANDREW: Yes, but essentially you would be of that nature rather than anything   substantive...

TOM: That is true.

ANDREW: ...something beyond photons, beyond tachyons [the least divisible known quanta or subdivisions of light]. And secondly I would assume that you are more of the nature of what we call 'soul' than any other thing we can imagine...

TOM: We are soul.

ANDREW: You are soul. Now, in your relationship to the Nine for example — are the Nine of the same nature as you are?

TOM: We are one and the same.

ANDREW: I see. And then could you explain the profound mystery: why there are nine basic manifestations of, I guess we should use the word 'God,' for lack of a better term?

Tom: I will try to explain it in a manner in which you may understand. Nine is complete. Everything is nine. In your world you have said seven so many times, when everything is truly nine. There are nine chakras, which are the nine principles and nine elements of what you call God. There are nine bands around this planet Earth. There are nine etheric bodies, and the purpose of growing your etheric bodies or going through your transformations and transitions is to attain the nine etheric bodies. Nine is a complete number, it is whole. When you go over a nine it cancels, it becomes one, and a nine is complete. This does not change. But remember this: we ourselves are not God. All of you and all of us make God.

then came a discussion on language:

Andrew: Have you some method of producing your language so that we could hear the quality of it.

Tom: When we speak of what our language is, it comes from deep within. It reaches different degrees but it is a tonal language. In your languages on Earth you speak in a box and then you throw it out.

John: Yes. Our language is produced in the vocal chords.

Tom: We speak in this box and then we push air and throw it out, do you understand that?

Andrew: Yes.

Tom: And our language, it is within. It vibrates from the body, do you understand?

Andrew: Then it does not come out the way ours does at all.

Tom: No, it does not.

Andrew: Does it produce a sound which another ear can hear?

Tom: It produces a sound that you may hear but it is inside.

Andrew: In other words, it is produced inside my head rather than my ears? Is that why you mean that the tonal range of your language is in 98.6 megacycles?

Tom: That is correct.

Andrew: In other words, it is what we would call a radio wave?

Tom: That is also correct.

In this next transmission, one questioner names various Biblical characters from Genesis (Chapters 4 and 5), descendants of Adam, asking whether any of these were members of the Nine.

TOM: In totality of understanding we are not any of those. There are hints of us upon your planet. There are many who try to understand who we are. In your earthliness, it is difficult for you to accept that that you do not understand! At times the attempt to understand colours the truth of the Universe. There are only keys for unlocking portions, for the human mind cannot totally comprehend. There are many interpretations and also many conflicts about who we are. Yes. In a future time we will attempt to explain ourselves on another level of consciousness, but first Planet Earth must reach that state of evolutionary consciousness where we may be understood, yes. The Council has said do not try to put us into a box, we do not exist in that form, yes.

JOHN: Is it true to say that there are several dimensions between us and yourselves?

TOM: That would be an understatement. There are many. Within, in your mind, visualise your Earth. Then from your Earth visualise that there are waves spiralling outward. And one wave creates another, and as it circulates, it grows. And it creates more and more. And it is heavy in the beginning, and if it has a sound it is loud of sound. And as it radiates out it becomes refined, it becomes more expansive, and all of those irritants that exist within the physical planet Earth are eliminated as it becomes a pure sound and a pure wave. And if you would have it in the colour of browns or blacks, as it is radiating out it is also being purified, until it becomes in truth the colour of colourless, which is in truth a golden light. We are at the extent of that. We are — how may we say to you? As you can take a sound until it becomes the purest, and as you can take a colour until it becomes the purest, and if you can take all vibrations until their level has raised until the pitch is of a pure nature — that is where we are.

JOHN: I see. That's a beautiful picture. Thank you.

TOM: It is as if you would take all that was spiritual within the Universe, and all that was of the intellect within the Universe, and take all of the physicalness that has been refined, and blend it together to make one pureness. It is a like a crystal.

ANDREW: What we would like to know is something of your natural

*history. We would like to know what you look like, how you repro-
duce, what you do for nourishment, what is your role in the Universe, what is your interest in the Earth, and so on? I think it would
help all of us enormously if you could just give us some idea of who
you are in the more descriptive sense.*

TOM: We do not have a physical body. Although we may put on the
mantle of a physical body when it is necessary. It would be difficult
for us to describe to you exactly what we appear like. We appear in
many forms, when that is necessary. And in your thought-process we
may appear as a human, we may appear as an energy ball, we may
appear as a very bright light. We have evolved beyond the point of
needing a physical-type body, as many souls need. We are always
here, but you do not always see us. When I say we, I do not mean
me, but I mean all of us. We are often observing. There are particular
times in your life when we do not observe, and that is when you are
involved with your desires. We do not understand this, and it is none
of our affair.

*ANDREW: I see. So assuming you had certain physical energies to
draw upon, you could mould into something that would manifest in
our world. Is that the idea?*

TOM: It would be similar to that, but you would not understand our
technology. We are in our mind what we think we are at that time.
Do you understand this? We exist in the zone of cold. Because of this
we have no problem in manifesting in any manner in which we
desire. As far as our reproduction is concerned, we do not need
reproduction. You must remember that those of us that live in this
zone have come a very long way in evolving. It is not necessary to
reproduce as it is in your place. We are soul.

*ANDREW: What part of the Universe do you work in, or what is your
management...*

TOM: We are the Universe.

*ANDREW: Now, in this Universe, there are worlds of matter, anti-
matter, photons, rays, energies, particles and more. Which part of
this domain do you exist in, or is it beyond our comprehension?*

TOM: It is beyond your comprehension. We come from the zone that
is cold. This is perfection.

ANDREW: You know, on Earth we are just beginning to understand, very feebly, the zone of cold or superconductivity, and we know that there is no resistance there, no friction, in other words, in our simple notion, it is the area of perpetual motion. Is that not essentially true?

TOM: This is true and this is perfection. We are in the centre. And we do not wish to sound as if we are perfect or as if we are egotistical, but on either side of us there is the positive and there is the negative. And when I say this I mean there is the positive that is not balanced, and there is the negative that is not balanced. We are in the centre, and we are balanced. We are trying to bring those other forces into balance. We have never been out of balance. It is other things in the Universe that are not in balance. We exist at the pivotal point of the Universe. There is a balance. Within each of you there is all of the positive and all of the negative of the Universe. Do you understand?

ANDREW: No, I don't. Because you told us once that you were neither on the good nor bad side, you were the pivot in between.

TOM: Yes. But do you understand that you are the balance of this?

JOHN: We have all of the good and all of the bad....?

TOM: That's why you are the balance. And why we are the balance. You understand matter and anti-matter?

ANDREW: We never have in our world any fusion of matter and anti-matter – you are telling us something quite foreign. Matter and anti-matter exist independently. If they get together there is a gigantic explosion...

TOM: What is Armageddon?

ANDREW: I don't know. Just a word in the Bible.

TOM: Is it not a giant explosion?

ANDREW: That's not matter and anti-matter, is it?

TOM: I am making an analogy. How may we explain?

ANDREW: I don't know, it's very difficult because the Earth concept does not fit the one that you are trying to explain.

TOM: We will begin at the beginning. In each of you, as in each of us, there is completeness. Completeness is a perfect harmony and balance between what you call 'good' and 'evil.' This is what keeps us in the pivotal point. This is why we are the pivot, because we are in balance. When we are together we are one and we are the pivot.

Assume that we live in a world of matter – it is not true, but imagine that. Now the Council of Nine is in the centre. And on our right would be the world of matter and on our left the world of anti-matter, you understand this? If the two came together we would have an explosion.

ANDREW: *But the reason I have difficulty is that you said we are a composite of both sides of polarity, so how could there be another side when we are a composite already?*

TOM: You have not understood what we have said.

ANDREW: *If you're a composite, you don't have two sides, see? If you have black and white you can have two sides, but black and white is not a composite, grey is the composite. I'm having difficulty...*

TOM: You are explaining in your world, we are explaining in ours. Shall we say, in essence....?

ANDREW: *In essence, okay. That makes it easier to deal with, if it's the essence rather than the actual substance, whatever that maybe...*

TOM: It is the essence.

ANDREW: *All right.*

TOM: There is balance within all. What causes the great dissension is a similar situation to putting together matter and anti-matter. They cannot mingle, they cannot mix in harmony, they cannot blend, they become destructive to each other.

Here again, Andrew has another exchange with Tom on duality: and Tom takes several attempts to clarify the picture for him:

ANDREW: *We do have difficulty understanding what is negative and what is positive, in respect of what is called 'good'and 'bad' on the human level.*

TOM: It is difficult in your physical world for you to truly understand the importance of both. I will try to explain in a manner in which you may understand. It would be similar to a giant scale. We are in the pivot of this giant scale. Visualise the Universe with the pivot being us. On one side of the Universe, visualise that all is negative, and all on the other side is positive. And as you see this, you know that there is a complete out-of-balance situation. It is difficult for us to explain this so that you may understand. Within each of the sides there are many...I will explain it in earthly terms: As each of the galaxies and solar systems within the galaxies.....first I must clarify: The Universe, with the Nine in the centre, has four sides, the side opposite that in which you exist and the other two are all in balance. Do you understand?

ANDREW: *Yes, I'm following.*

TOM: It is in perfect balance. On this side we will now place your solar systems within your galaxies and the galaxies. If you would take a stone for each of these galaxies, if they were in perfect weight and perfect proportion to the rest of the three sides, then this would be also in balance. But if one of those stones were of a porous substance, and if you placed it in oil, and it absorbed the oil, and became weighted with the oil, then in turn it would upset the balance and pull the balance and the scale out of calibration, and would upset the other side of the Universe. Your Planet is accomplishing that. The negative is the heavy oil. Remember: the other sides are balanced, but this imbalance can in turn topple the rest. That is not correct. In actuality there is no good and there is no bad. It is only when one of them becomes sour or rotten that it then contaminates the rest, be it good or bad. Because of the ignorance of the peoples of Planet Earth, and because their religious leaders have taught ignorance, your negative forces, which do not truly appear as you see them, manifest in that way in order to instil fear. But what is truly negative – listen carefully – what has created the upset, besides the desires and the greed, is the complete denial and misinterpretation of the existence of ultimate reality. Your over-population is because of the trapping of spirits, because of reincarnation. So the Earth people, the souls and spirits that surround your Earth need to release themselves of greed and desire, because that is the trap. Your religious leaders do not understand this and do not teach the people.

Remember that in you is a seed of purity and beauty, and that if you do not maintain a balance, ugliness or an ugly part may appear. But remember forgiveness. We hold no animosity within us, and you should not do so either. Even though you exist upon a physical planet and the densest of all the planets in the Universe, remember that all souls may be saved. The only thing of which we are unforgiving is in the denunciation of God...

ANDREW: *Yes, I understand. I think at times there have been occasions we have been guilty of that attitude.*

TOM: This is a truth. But remember to forgive when there is true acknowledgement. May we say to you, to voice what you feel is one thing, but it is the act that is important. There are many actors upon the world's stage that play a different part than what they feel. It is when they begin to feel they are that part, not themselves, that it makes a big difference. They may say they love God, and they may say that they have understanding, but if they do not act in that way, then that is a graver problem, because it is not done in ignorance. It is the same as when you give to another because you believe it obligates the other to give back, then what you give is not gold, it is black and putrid. We wish you also to know that we do not have the need to be worshipped. Our need from you is to be loved. Do you know who is God?

ANDREW: I know who is God in the abstract sense.

TOM: Do you know truly who is God?

ANDREW: Not truly, no.

TOM: Are you prepared to know who God is?

ANDREW: I would be prepared, yes. I do not know what that means in terms of consequences, but yes, I would be prepared.

TOM: Love is God. And it is love that creates the energy which feeds God – and makes God. In your world there are religious groups that say that God is within. And this is true because there is a portion of divinity within each individual. But what we have told you is not the same.

ANDREW: It took me a long time to square up with this, the notion that the Nine collectively are God, and that we all collectively are God...

TOM: Remember that as God we all carry a heavy burden but also we carry joy.

ANDREW: Well, being in the centre, can you go on further to indicate how we stand between the negative and the positive?

TOM: Remember this: that the position that you have chosen in your physical world is limited. But remember who you are. Never lose sight of who you are. And remember that in God all things are possible and will be done. The problem is the limits of the physical mind and understanding. And also remember that as God, in order to maintain the balance in your physical world, you must at times be detached. Gently you must detach. Because the work that conscious people on Earth have to do does not involve one or two individuals or the multiplication of those individuals. The work you humans have to do involves the Universe. And remember: God never fails. In your physical world, you as God are being tested. Not that God can be tested, but your physical limitations to yourselves as God are being tested. And though we know that this may sound a contradiction to you, in being God and having a problem in the physical world, you must come to understand these problems of the physical world. There are some of us who have never had this problem, and it's difficult for those of us that have not had it to understand. God is all-knowing and is all-seeing but there are parts of God, as there are parts of every atom. The whole together makes one, but not all parts experience the same. Do you understand this?

ANDREW: *Okay. We are beginning to get questions about the Nine. Not only do people ask 'who are they?' but also 'are they good or evil?' This is a problematic question to answer.*

TOM: You are aware that difficulties have arisen because of the religions that have been perpetrated upon the peoples of Earth. So may we say to you, when people ask 'are they good or are they evil?' you know who you are and you know who we are, so you can happily, without doubt, say that the Nine are good and they wish to help. And if there are those that say 'But we have seen evil beings', then we would ask you to ask them to look within themselves. To see what you call evil does not mean that you must be evil to perceive it, but this is a way of helping those who believe in evil to look within themselves, to help themselves. Have we talked in riddles?

In 1991, another guest asked Tom the following question.

GUEST: *What is the relationship of the Nine to God and to the Devil?*

TOM: You cannot use that terminology of God and the opposite in the same sentence, for there is not of any equal to what you call God. For what you call God is the all-knowing, the total creation, all that is. That that you call by the name that you have used, we speak of as the opposition. You cannot equate that together. You ask us what is our relationship? We tell you now: We are not God. We have no relationship to the opposition. We are the Council of Nine that are in service to the Creator. The Creator is not destructive. The opposition is destructive.

and before that transmission, in the '70s, Andrew had had this conversation:

ANDREW: What do you say to those people who tend to think in terms of absolute good and evil, who use figures like Ahriman and Satan and so on..?

TOM: Ask them to look within themselves, and to understand that within each physical being there are all the elements of good and all the elements of what they call evil. We do not like that word 'evil.'

ANDREW: I don't either. It has the wrong connotation. But you know, many people are very pious.

TOM: They are not in truth pious, for they do not understand truth. They are in truth fanatics, they have doubt.

ANDREW: Yes, and they are the most difficult ones to ask to look into themselves; some of our most pious friends have become very anti the Nine's basic teachings.

TOM: Walk gently away from those, and the truth will come eventually. It is important that you do not start, may we say, pounding at them, but say 'You have your belief and I have mine.'

ANDREW: Yes, I think we've all learned that lesson.

TOM: You must be of great gentleness, but firm, do you understand? Keep to the purity within you, and know who you are, and do not contaminate your purity with other influences that will try to weaken you.

ANDREW: We have many physical and human weaknesses.

TOM: Not as many as you wish to believe.

ANDREW: But is doubt one of the prominent things?

TOM: Yes it is. It is as prominent as fear.

ANDREW: For myself, I do not really know fear – that is almost foreign to me.

TOM: But you have doubt.

ANDREW: I have doubt.

TOM: And that is the same.

ANDREW: I have scepticism. But I am learning. We have been reviewing our communications with you, and we are quite astounded at how much we have grown, and are kind of embarrassed to hear some of the things we said earlier! So I think to some extent we feel that we have made some progress in growing.

TOM: Remember we have grown with you, because when you grow we also grow.

ANDREW: That surprises me. Growth-potential still exists at the level of the Nine?

TOM: Yes. Because you are in the physical, and we are communicating directly with you, we are growing and coming to understand the physical, and that is important. We are not of the physical, and yet the paradox is that we are ahead of all that is physical. So do you understand how we grow with you?

ANDREW: Hmm, that's a difficult one, do you mean ahead in time? I don't quite understand that idea.

TOM: What has happened with us is that we have learned through you because we have attached to you, and we are now living your emotion and we are beginning to understand. The Council has said I should use the word 'beyond' and not the word 'ahead.'

ANDREW: I didn't realise that you were getting a refresher course in Earth experience.

TOM: It is not just Earth, it is physical, do you understand?

ANDREW: I only know Earth-physical, I don't know the physical throughout the Universe.

TOM: The Earth is the densest of all physical. And so what better place can we learn?

JOHN: One thing about doubt: I feel that blind faith is also a dangerous thing, and the fine line between the two must be found.

TOM: We never ask you for blind faith. Has there been a time in your entire existence upon Earth when suddenly you came upon something that made you become paralysed with fear?

ANDREW: I think when I was a child I had a fear of snakes, but I overcame that...

TOM: But you had that. Do you recall the moment?

ANDREW: Oh yes, I recall the moment when suddenly there was a rattler in front of me, and I just froze in fear, not knowing what to do.

TOM: That is something that we are beginning now to understand, but that is also the same as a doubt.

ANDREW: I see, that's very instructive.

TOM: But we do not ask you to follow in blind faith. You must at all times ask for clarification. You must never simply accept.

3

God and Creation

While this chapter needs no introduction, there are many people who do not relate to any concept of God. Reading this could be an enlightening process leading us to review our own ideas of creation, sometimes unquestioned since first receiving them ...

TOM: It was necessary in the beginning to have a structured form of religion. The error was with those religionists who began to have control over others, and to make themselves important instead of the understanding. Humankind is now revolting against this, and at this time there are those who are attempting to form a new religion. It is the old attempting to take the new and mould it in its own dimension. This is out of doubt and fear. Remember that this is the only planet of complete and total free will.

JOHN: We are likely to be asked in the future the question "What is God?" Now we have some idea ourselves, but we would like to present a consistent and understandable answer to those who ask.

TOM: What is God to you?

JOHN: Well, there's many ways I could answer that. I could say that God is the Ultimate, or Love, or.....

TOM: It is unified, infinite intelligence, supported with pure love. And it grows with pure love. It is absolute faith and absolute love. That is God.

If you have doubts that we exist we do understand. But remember that in each of you there is God, and in each of us there is God, because God is love, and love is with us all. And if you doubt our existence at times, then remember what I have said to you: with God all things are possible, and God is love. And keep your love pure, because through this, then this planet and this Universe will be evolved, and we will all become one with God. You are witnesses to him, to the Being that is the Universe. And remember this: you are also the Universe, because you are one with God.

When you understand that you hold within each of you the total power to change all, and you accept that, you truly become a divine being. Also when you understand that what you term 'religions' have in reality emanated from those of physical civilisations then you must also begin to understand more about the Supreme One that is Un-known.

Do not create gods from physical beings, do not give power to physical beings – except inasmuch as you consider yourselves equal to them.

Understand that your planet Earth is on a precipice – if the pollu-tionary direction is not abated, it can contaminate your planet Earth to the degree that physical beings may not exist upon it. It would not destroy it, but a physical being would not be able to live. Most important: be joyful, and know that you hold within your core, your centre, your hand, the ability to create transformation. You are not here by coincidence, you are here because you asked and chose to be. Know that because of you we exist also, and we love you for that. Yes. May we explain to you the one God?

ANDREW: *Yes, I would be most anxious to know.*

TOM: Imagine an umbrella and each of the spokes of the umbrella, of which there are twelve, would then feed to the top. It is the top that is one God and it is actually of twelve.

ANDREW: *Is there a little point on the top – geometrically?*

TOM: Yes. The energy is fed and becomes the one. All the twelve feed to the one that becomes One. But the One cannot exist without the twelve. It is the balance and the harmony and it is what keeps the Universe in harmony. It is this system by which there is not one that is in more control than another but in unision together. Do you understand?

ANDREW: *Yes. Except for one point: does the One who is made of the twelve, indeed have an individuality of his own? Can he, so to speak, talk back to some of the twelve, or is he the summation?*

TOM: He is a summation but he may speak. Do you understand? You do not understand.

ANDREW: *Yes I do. I think I understand. It's a very complex, sophisti-cated notion.*

Tom: In the beginning there was one that understood that he needed to be of twelve. So all the Twelve is in truth the One, do you understand?

ANDREW: Yes, I see they became parts of him in the beginning.

Tom: Yes.

While the number twelve is vital to the above conversation, during the communications of May 1994, Tom asked me to make it quite clear that this use of the number twelve does not refer to the Council, nor should it be used by humankind as a 'cultist' number and finally to be aware "that there could be some 'output' [channellings, information] from civilisations not comprehending and saying that they are the Twelve".

GUEST: I wonder if you could comment on the Big Bang Theory – recent satellite research [1992] seems to have strengthened this theory.

Tom: Altea has said it is this way: You know of the Creator? You know that what the Creator created was an energy. You know that energy was in aloneness, in a void; and then in that aloneness that which created, intelligent, had only itself – which was all knowing, all wonder, all creativeness encompassing all. But it is a truism that in the mind one can create a thought of expanding the mind with self. That which created came to the realisation that expansion of all knowingness, of created intelligence, of forward expansion, would give more joyfulness, more quintessence.....

We do not know how to explain. It is knowing and not knowing at the same time. Over a period of time – if you play a game with your mind in your head- you reach a point in your mind where you know every game, is that not so? Therefore to create a game in which all parts of you had a choice to do as that part wished, but were connected, it would then create a game in which you did not know the results. Would that not be more jollyful?

Then the supposition came, how do we create that game? Not *we*, you understand, the Creator thought this. It is we and all. It is you and all. So what is the best way to create that game? You can put it in a sphere and jumble it around but then you would recognise every part within the sphere, would you not? Therefore is it not better to release those energies to the most distant arenas? That is what happened. It was the releasing of the energy of the Creator that created. The intelligence that said, 'I know all I do, now I do not know all I do and I do know all I do'. If you were to tell humankind it is a game, they would not understand.

JOHN: *Maybe it can be explained, because it is a beautiful concept, that the Big Bang is the greatest game in town.*

TOM: Universe. Is a town a universe? Yes. Council has said a town is a universe, yes.

GUEST: *So you are confirming that the Big Bang astronomical theory of the beginning of the physical Universe, is the right kind of direction for scientists to follow?*

TOM: That is correct.

GUEST: *There is a question related to this, which is to do with a statement you have made several times. That is: 'You created us, and out of that creation you were created.' Can you explain this a bit more?*

TOM: Do you understand creation?

GUEST: *I don't know whether I fully understand it, but I believe I basically understand it.*

TOM: Without you we do not exist. Without us you do not exist.

GUEST: *The thing which concerns humans, is that we get the sense that the Creator created us, in a sequence of cause-and-effect.*

TOM: It is this way: did we not explain that we are part of the created?

GUEST: *Certainly you have.*

TOM: So the Creator, without all cells and particles, is not complete. So when all cells and particles came together, that was the creation of infinite-intelligence-Creator. Example: there is a forest. In this forest there are many trees, and there are no humans, and there are no animals in it. Those trees begin to fall, and there is none to prove that there was a tree. For without the observation, there was nothing happening, is that not so? Without the ears to hear, there was no sound, is that not so? Therefore, without those necessary ingredients for creation, there was not creation. It is an exchange. Then that which was Created out of its own creation – which is all that is created – got bored. That is simple, is it not? Then what did that-which-got-bored do? It exploded and sent all particles and so on to the far ends... there are no ends in the Universe. Therefore all that is there knows all that all knows. It only does not know that it knows that all knows.

We say this to humankind: each human knows in its innermost knowing that it is a part of the Creator, the one that is called 'God' upon Planet Earth. They know they have come from the Creator. Therefore if you come from the Creator, are you not part of it? If a mother births a child, can you say that child does not contain part of that mother? Even a mother who is implanted, that child still has the blood supply of the implanted mother, is that not so? Then why is humankind not intelligent to understand that? That which Created did not remove intelligence. Does humankind prefer to remain ignorant, so there is no responsibility?

GUEST: *Often we behave like that, but at heart I think we don't.*

TOM: We know they do not. Yes. Do you understand that under us there are those that you humans call 'gods'?

JOHN: *Yes. As I understand it, although they are not in reality gods, they have often been called gods on Earth, is that correct?*

ANDREW: *I think the best example we can think of is Yehovah, who is called 'God' by many on Earth...*

TOM: That is true, he is not a god, and in a sense he is a god, do you understand the difference? We too are God.

ANDREW: *Then there are lesser gods, you say?*

TOM: Yes.

JOHN: *It would be perhaps helpful to have a definition of the word 'God' in that sense. You say there are lesser gods, I'm trying to see what the word 'God' means. In that sense.*

TOM: We must explain. We as a total are 'God'. One, do you understand? 'gods' that is different, do you understand?

JOHN: *There is one God over other gods. The other gods are the representatives of the one God?*

TOM: Yes. We are not representatives, but gods. There are gods of light and gods of darkness. Do you know why they are called gods?

ANDREW: *I presume because they have extraordinary powers that are something like those of God.*

Tom: Of which we are. Yes.

John: What I'd like to try to find is what would be the dividing line, because in a sense...

Tom: We in truth are 'Aeons' [spiritual entities formed from the divine presence] We do not call them gods, you call them gods. You understand that in your physical world, anyone who is better than you is a god?

Andrew: (Laughing) Yes, that's the general idea. We have sports gods and love gods and all kinds of gods.

Miki: Could you give us an understanding of God the Creator?

Tom: When you speak of God, do you mean the one that creates all?

Miki: Yes.

Tom: There are those that are called 'God' that are appendages to God, that also create. But there is One, the highest, that is of the purest light, that is a composite of all, that creates all. Each soul in the whole Universe came directly from the true Creator, so each soul is imbued with this energy. There is a collection of beings that generate outward points of this source, but when they come together as one pure energy of collectiveness then that energy becomes what you call 'God' that creates all. Each of these entities has individual knowledge or principle, but not of the whole. There is only one that has the whole. When those energies that you call negative upon your planet Earth attempt to destroy, attempt to control others, it is because they are in competition with God, the one Creator. For in their cells they know the divinity within them, and their personality takes hold, and they then attempt to be God. It is sad, yes.

Miki: Thank you. So in my understanding 'God' also represents the negative side.

Tom: That is not so. God created all, and that which became the negative went in competition with God: he does not represent them. I will attempt to explain. The Council has said I must try.

There are gardeners who have been to this planet Earth. They are those who seeded this planet. You are a gardener, we will explain it in this way: as you know in your planting, you plant each seed with equal love, with equal nurture, with all that is necessary for it to grow strong and straight, in a manner of purity, there are some that are weak and some that are strong. There are those that you plant that become stronger to the point that they then may strangle others, is this not so? Then you must remove, weed, transplant. But the Creator does not weed, does not interfere in free will, as you do with your plants. Then those who attempt to strangle and to take over others are fed by the energies of what you call negative, as we are fed by love, and they then begin to strangle all. They go in competition with that that planted them, that that created them. Is this some clarity for you?

MIKI: Yes. So originally, what is now the negative once came from the Creator – but did God leave them?

TOM: When you say 'Did God leave them,' we understand not. Do you mean did he forsake them? Do you mean he threw them out?

MIKI: Yes.

TOM: No one can compete with God, for they have not truth within, for God is a collection of purity which means only goodness for all the Universe. They threw themselves out by going in competition and having the desire to become all that is. That is not possible, for in order to do that you must return to God. That is the sadness: they had not patience for understanding. They are attempting to disrupt the work of the Universe.

If you have one that you have loved, nurtured, fed, and have transferred great love to, and all you wished from it was for it to grow in beauty, straightness, flexibility, and love, giving as it has been given to, but it chooses not to do that, then there comes a time when you come to a realisation, that it must find for itself that it may not destroy others – and so in the Universe it is not discarded, but it is also not fed and supported, for that which loves it, it attempts to destroy. What we are attempting to say is that God did not discard, but he does not help, for the negative refuses help. Is that clear?

DAVID: Can you tell me how you, as the Nine, relate to what we would call the Holy Spirit?

TOM: It is the Holy Spirit that governs us. There is the Son, the Father and the Holy Spirit, is that not so? Dare we say to you, you are the sons and through us emanates the one of Holy Spirit? And then there is the Father.

JOHN: I'd like to ask now about a biblical statement: "In the begin-

ning there was the Word." Can you explain this in a way that we can begin to really understand what that means?

Tom: "In the beginning there was the Word" – that is a translation error. But if you take it to mean that the Creator came forth and said: "That that is, that that I am, will be". First, before the manifestation of any method or any creation, there was the communication of Being.

John: Yes, I think I understand: what we would call the 'intentionality' is explicit and thought precedes action.

Tom: That is exactness, yes. By adding communication it is strengthened.

Miki: I was thinking of the statement 'God created man in his own image'. Can you comment on that?

Tom: That is correct. Which means that all that He is you are; all that He knows you know; all that is good is contained within you; all that is pure is contained within you. And know this: that God knows that in order to manifest the spirit of God and soul within you, it is necessary to be in a physical form for that soul to function upon a physical vehicle [a Planet]. A physical form that has evolved to the stage of having two arms and two legs, and the senses to see, or feel, or touch, or hear. And you also have the sense of knowing.

Miki: Thank you. Can you comment on the importance of consciousness?

Tom: Consciousness is that elevation of humankind into a sphere of connection with that that they created. You know that you created God, and that God created you. Do you know that?

Miki: No.

Tom: Do you know that God could not exist without your creation, and that you could not exist without His creation of you?

Miki: Yes, I get it now.

Tom: Yes. That is the importance of consciousness.

The following exchange introduces the Civilisations, which will be examined in greater detail in the next chapter.

Tom: We understand the Earth plane, its entrapment, its density and its illusionary factor, yes.

IRENE: It'd be fun to have you here.

TOM: The time will come when all of us will be in togetherness, at the time of the elevation and transformational density of Planet Earth, in its rightful place of existence as the paradise of glory, yes.

JOHN: Where is that going to be?

TOM: Upon Planet Earth.

JOHN: Whereabouts? (Laughs) I don't ask when.

IRENE: Your backyard! [laughter]

TOM: You speak of an exact location: in that time all Planet Earth will be the exact location, for it will not be necessary to have those elements of mechanical.

JOHN: Communication, you mean, won't be necessary mechanically?

TOM: Not with that physical industrial mechanism. You may flip your hair and you will go.

IRENE: Great! We're ready! Now specifically, I would like to go back to the creation and the Twenty-Four civilisations. Who created the Twenty-Four? Or were they in fact a creation? Or were they in fact elements and particles that were brought together by you, but in fact they already had existence and you gave them order?

TOM: That is a large question. It was in this nature: there was one Creator, one energy, one pure light, one pure-being Self that contained all components of all that is. It is extremely complicated, but in simplification, it came into that Being the knowledge, and wisdom to begin to divide the components of which it consisted, not to remove them but to build a structure. For in its aloneness it had only self for companion.

That was not wrong, but it was more valuable to create a situation whereby there was a separate element – to create a situation that would then have the structure to give the cells that would be populating different environmental existences, those portions necessary for its attainment of its choosing.

For it was found, in the creating by that that was created out of nothing, that there would be the necessity to expand this creating. Now what would be the purpose of creating nothing out of nothing? It was important to have created something.

So the Twenty-Four universal civilisations were created, as guides, elements of direction, elements of purpose and also to know that there would be some areas of civilisation (such as that of Altea) which would govern and rule that element of their existence all over the Universe, as Ashan does with colour, sound and arts.

It was a way for the Creator to expand and provide and begin those elements necessary for expansion, because once that was created, then the expansion would continue and it would go on and on. Therefore it needed the different elements that would make expansion purposeful. If the expansion continued with only the creating of Universes, with no purpose, then it would have served no purpose. Now have we confused you completely?

IRENE: No, not only does it not confuse, this is the most brilliant thing I've ever heard!

This was a communication made in 1975 to a group of three people:

TOM: It is important now for us to pray together, because it is the beginning now of a sequence, in which, if everything goes right, the result will be the saving of the planet Earth, and the understanding and awakening of the souls of Planet Earth. As the twelve of us are together – remember that many times we have spoken to you and explained that with twelve, and today it is Nine of us and the three of you, all things are possible.

If the planet can be saved, and will be saved, the entire Universe will be raised to a level that all souls will have gained the nature of what they have searched for from the beginning of time. And remember that when the souls of the Universe have calmness and joy and peace within their hearts, and generate this love, it overtakes even those souls that are negative and dark, and brings life and love to them. And can you imagine that what you have come to this planet to do, when you accomplish it the entire Universe will be glowing with a light that will be blinding, because it will be a light of pure love. And all will become one, and that is what all have striven for:

ANDREW: I was trying to define your existence, and then our exist-ence, and then the relationship between the two. And I might just prompt you with a question, for example: are the Nine considered the ultimate source of knowledge, wisdom, and power, and so on in the Universe?

TOM: You are asking your relationship to us, is this not so? It is what you would call infinite intelligence. It is not of twenty-four. It is of twelve. (Nine of us and three humans in a triangle).

ANDREW: *All right. And, if this is the fountainhead, or 'the unmoved mover', if that be a correct definition,then all your thoughts and actions somehow must be put into effect through other peoples, or groups of beings...*

TOM: Universal Civilisations.

ANDREW: *Ah, right. Do you yourself initiate the intelligence, the thought, but the action is always carried out by others?*

TOM: By the civilisations.

ANDREW: *And then at one time you hinted there were twenty-four major civilisations through which you acted?*

TOM: When you say major, there are many. But there are twenty-four heads of civilisations.

ANDREW: *I see. They themselves are part of those many civilisations, or just heads of large groups of civilisations?*

TOM: They are heads of civilisations.

ANDREW: *And these are what the Bible calls a 'Council of the Twenty-Four' and 'The Elders' and so on?*

TOM: It would be the Congress.

JOHN: *One question about that: these are all working on the same side, the positive side, or as the twenty-four?*

TOM: The positive and the negative must be blended to make it whole. It is as we have explained to you: to be positive with no sense is not as good. They are balanced civilisations. Do you have that in clearness?

ANDREW: *I think we do now.*

TOM: When you speak of positive, remember: refer to it as a balanced-positive.

ANDREW: *Now, under those Twenty-Four, could you give us an example of one civilisation? Let us say – Hoova. Where does it fit in under the Twenty-Four?*

TOM: When you speak of the Twenty-Four, you speak of the heads of the civilisations. There is one you know of as 'Jehovah'.

ANDREW: Jehovah? And then under him is his civilisation? So the Jehovah is one of the Twenty-Four.

TOM: Yes. It is known as Hoova. But he would have as a pyramid many under that.

ANDREW: I see, there would be many civilisations, right. Okay, now that clarifies that part. Now take our existence as ordinary human beings. Where do ordinary people come from, and why do they come here, and where do they go? This is one of the great mysteries to us.

TOM: All beings, all species come from us. There is a question that is asked by all beings and all species, and it is what you have asked: 'Who am I, where did I come from?' and 'Where am I going?' Is that not so?

ANDREW: That is the question, yes.

TOM: All species and all beings are particles of us. There is not a way for you to have this understanding. How may we explain?

ANDREW: Well, I have the understanding that they are part of you but they go through many cycles of existence before they reach Earth, is that not so?

TOM: Remember that the planet Earth is not that evolved. We are looking for an analogy to give you...

ANDREW: Well, could you say for example, that those who come to Earth all come from another given civilisation or planet or something like that? Or state of existence? That is, is there a regular sequence or place through which they go before they come to the planet Earth?

TOM: Not in a particular planet. Depending on the needs of that soul. Some souls need more than some other souls. There are levels of intelligence, there are levels of consciousness. Not all are equal.

Remember this: it is not true that all are equal. There is a soul. The soul is a particle of us. If you have a giant electric spark, and you put two together that would cause a giant electric spot, there would be sparks that would come off it. Those sparks would be part of us – but each of those sparks would either die out or continue to grow. Some may create a fire, and some may grow slowly, but it would depend upon the ambition of the spark.

ANDREW: Yes. Now, when that spark cycles through Earth, and achieves its full growth, does it go through other civilisations............?

TOM: It must.

ANDREW: It doesn't return directly to you?

TOM: It will continue for millions of years. But it cannot continue if it stays upon the planet Earth. If you will recall, in a previous communication we had explained to you that the planet Earth is the only planet within the Universe that has the variety of animals and plants. It is the most beautiful of all planets, because of the different varieties. This in a sense, attracts the souls, and they have desires to remain upon it. In other civilisations, the souls feel, and they have all the qualifications which you have, but it is more physical upon the planet Earth.

JOHN: There is a very large question: what is the purpose of a soul? In existing on all its civilisations and so on?

TOM: If a soul becomes what you call perfect, then it is... if we could explain this to you, in your mind you may feel that we are cannibals!

ANDREW: Well, we want the truth, and I think you know us well enough to know that we would not jump to that kind of erroneous conclusion. What we're really asking is: if we had to tell a human being what the purpose of life is, what is the most succinct answer?

TOM: You may tell what has been told to humans many times, but was not given to them in clear understanding: that the purpose of their existence and the purpose of their living is to return to whence they came.

ANDREW: Yes. And how can they, while they are on this Earth with all its problems? What is it that they can best do in order to return to the source?

TOM: If they would treat all as they have desire to be treated. If they would walk in dignity and permit no one to remove their dignity, and if they would have love for all their fellow humans, and for all those that touch them – for this in turn sends love to us. We ask not that they have a total understanding of us.

ANDREW: Yes. But in essence then, God feeds on this kind of nectar, so to say.

TOM: Yes.

ANDREW: *I think that people would love that idea.*

TOM: We have the creation, we have created this, but it in truth has created us.

ANDREW: *Now that part which, let us say, you feed on, is it totally immaterial, that nature of love — something that has no material or physical existence? Since you are not material in any way, you must feed on something immaterial..?*

TOM: It is an energy. It is not something you may hold in your hand. It is a spark that is a glow that emanates, and it grows, and becomes a shining sun, and then it returns to us.

ANDREW: *Yes. I find that very beautiful and very satisfying, don't you John?*

JOHN: *Yes, this is the upward spiral, I imagine. Then it's sent out again, on a higher level again, is that so?*

TOM: Yes. It is integrated.

ANDREW: *Now, how do the other creatures on Earth fit into this plan? And I speak of birds and fish and cattle and so on...*

TOM: They have more love for us than the humans. They have a greater understanding of us.

ANDREW: *And when they live this way, do they also come back as sparks directly, without having to go through our human form?*

TOM: They are not a human form. They are planted and they have been brought to the planet Earth to give to the souls upon the planet Earth — how may we say? — for them to cause humans to ask in their mind: what created this? How did this come to be? It is to jog their mind. Do you understand that?

ANDREW: *I think so, for example we were watching two hawks today, and they were incredible and beautiful, and they were mating, as it is the season for mating, and we wondered about their span. They live in such freedom, and apparently, love and dignity...*

TOM: It is the purest love.

ANDREW: *And we wondered for example, whether their souls would spark too? If they achieved perfection would they go directly back to you?*

TOM: They feed to us.

ANDREW: And bees, for example, that collect honey, and are in tune with each other and their environment, do they feed you too?

TOM: Remember this, your planet is the only one in existence with this nature.

4

The Universal Civilisations

In the mid-90s, it would at first appear that there is perhaps a greater acceptance of the idea that 'We are not alone'. However, while more people are prepared to acknowledge the subject, when faced with a Crop Glyph, anomalous lights in the sky or an account of a close encounter with an extraterrestrial, a glazed look comes into some people's eyes. We could call this the 'shutters down' phenomenon. As if the conceptual envelope of that person had been stretched to a maximum and the safety mechanisms ordered a 'stop'. Government and defence organisations continue to ignore the subject publicly, while rumours abound concerning official interaction with E.T. and various alleged ex-government employees publish books, while implying that they are under pressure to desist. This chapter explores some of the civilisations mentioned by Tom and it is as well to remember that he does not always mean this word literally. He has been known to allude to the civilisations in terms of consciousness. Please read on with a flexible brain. Tom also points out that each planetary civilisation has, in its midst or around it, a spirit plane or numerous spirit planes. Also that there is a difference between Aeons and those of the Spirit planes. ....

Tom: The Council of Nine has asked that I, the spokesman, Tom, explain a little to you of the structure and relationships in the Universe.

We are nine that exist independently and exist in wholeness in the Universe, in a place that you could identify as the zone of cold. We are not physical, as you are physical or as Altea or Hoova are physical (and this again is not the same manner as yours but it is also physical). If need be, we may manifest but we are pure energy.

Together we oversee and I, Tom, relate all that we wish to convey to Planet Earth from the Council of the Nine, of which I am one.

In relationship to us there are Twenty-Four physical civilisations, in another dimensional realm. Each is a total collective consciousness that oversees and from these civilisations, physical beings have incarnated upon your Planet Earth, and at times have intervened, when necessary. These physical civilisations, the Twenty-Four, each in its own dimension, are total and complete units of one collective consciousness that have agreed to be in that collective consciousness. They have evolved to that form of action to oversee, to pass through information of great importance, and help other physical civilisations in their evolutionary process.

An example would be the civilisation of Altea; as we are in another realm of existence, we depend upon Altea for communicating with you. They guard the body of our being while you are in communication with us, and they provide the technology for us to communicate. Altea was also the head of what you know as the physical civilisation that manifested upon Planet Earth as Atlantis.

There are other civilisations – and there are amongst you incarnate souls from those civilisations who have come to help Planet Earth. One of these civilisations, Hoova, was the civilisation that originally seeded Planet Earth, as did some of the others, but Hoova re-seeded Planet Earth on three occasions. Hoova is the civilisation from which the Hebrews derive: hence the importance of the Hebrews. Hoova is the civilisation that brought forth the Nazarene.

GENE: *I understand that the Nine are not physical entities, but do I understand correctly that those of Hoova, and Altea and other civilisations are physical beings?*

TOM: They are physical civilisations, but not in the same dimension as Planet Earth. They also have physical limitations but not to the extent of those on Earth.

ANDREW: *Could you amplify that and indicate which dimension, for example, Hoova exists in?*

TOM: When you speak of dimensions?

ANDREW: *I mean fourth, fifth, sixth... for example we live in a four-dimensional world [height, breadth, depth, time] in our physical world.*

TOM: We understand the different, as you would call, dimensions. But in truth they are not dimensions.

ANDREW: *Well, when it was explained to me before, dimensions were said to consist of various velocity-envelopes.*

TOM: Yes, speed.

ANDREW: *Right. And relative to the speed of light, what is the speed of Hoova?*

TOM: I am consulting... Altea is giving us his numbers. Yes. Altea has said it is not exactly a dimension, but it would be fifty-six times the speed of light, as you know it on Earth.

GENE: *Thank you. What about the rest of our galaxy and the Universe? Are any of the visitors we seem to get on Earth coming from there?*

TOM: There are those within your galaxy that are not within what you call the dimension of your Earth, but those that come to benefit Planet Earth come from galaxies not within your galaxy. Altea, for example, is what you might call fifty million light-years away.

JOHN: *But from our perspective on Earth, these other civilisations like Altea or Hoova, could in a sense be existing in or around us, and we would not perceive them..?*

TOM: They are in a different reality-frequency. Because of the speeds.

JOHN: *But, is it possible to talk of them as existing close or far from us in our terms at all?*

TOM: If you are asking in the terms of the physical Planet Earth, and you are asking about a length or a space of time, it would be a great distance. They are not of this galaxy.

JOHN: *And we would not be able to see them, even if we were there where they are, in our present condition, would we?*

TOM: In the dimension in which you are, you would not be able to see them with your eyes – if you were able to transport yourself to that area. But they can come to reach you within your area.

JOHN: *But they experience themselves as physical, even though we wouldn't experience them as physical.*

TOM: In the dimension in which they have existence they have a similar sense of physicalness that you have within this area in which you exist. But they are not physical in the sense that you know on Planet Earth.

JOHN: *And is it true to say that there are several dimensions between us and yourselves, for example?*

TOM: That would be an understatement. There are many.

GENE: *Are there any civilisations or races within our galaxy visiting us at present?*

TOM: Yes. There are civilisations of different dimensions, different intelligence, different evolving, that are working with the Twenty-Four civilisations. There are those within your galaxy that are in service to those that are attempting to salvage the Planet Earth. But they are not the primaries (the Twenty-Four).

GENE: *If the Alteans, the Hoovids and others were to visit Earth, would they be in the same physical body as they are in their own dimension?*

TOM: When those of Altea manifest upon Earth, they have a similarity of appearance to those that exist upon the Planet Earth. They have a higher rate of vibration, but they may bring it into the rate of vibration which is correct for the Planet Earth. There are others, such as those of the civilisation of Ashan, who do not look like the people of Planet Earth. Should the civilisations land on Earth, those that would appear in the beginning will have similar appearance to those of the Planet Earth, or they will manifest in the manners of Earth people – such as Hoova has done. Those of the other civilisations that follow would come in the form which they have. We wish to reassure you that those who exist on Planet Earth will find that those visitors that do not have what you call beauty, will have within them the essence of beauty. There will be many appearances. A diversity of appearances, yes.

Years later, the following exchange brought out another perspective on the physicality of the beings of the Universal Civilisations:

JOHN: *Do civilisations like Altea and others of the Twenty-Four exist on a physical planet that is in our understanding of physical – we know they have form in their own time-space envelope, but do they have a physical planet we could locate in our time and space?*

TOM: You mean does it have density?

JOHN: *Does it have the same density as us?*

TOM: You cannot have the same density as Planet Earth.

JOHN: *Right. So it wouldn't be recognisable from Planet Earth in that sense.*

Tom: You do not have a telescope large enough. It is not anywhere in the closeness of Planet Earth.

John: But even if it were, it couldn't be seen by our physical means — it would be detected by means perhaps undeveloped yet on Earth, is that correct?

Tom: Not correct. If a device were designed that could see to the furthermost reaches of the Universe, then you would see also different levels of densities. Within their civilisations the Twenty-Four have attained perfection, unity of oneness, complete obedience to the Creator, so therefore they understand their physical world, and are not tricked by physicalness. You know that this place you sit upon is made of billions of trillions of molecules, is that not so? You do not see that, therefore you would think it doesn't exist like that, yes? If you were to see the civilisation Altea, you would see it is physical in movement.

John: So it has a form, but a kind of form we could not comprehend, because we do not have experience of that form in our lives?

Tom: It is physical. It has evolved to the point where the physical and spiritual are in harmony and balance, and that is what you must achieve, so you can enter with the Twenty-Four.

John: Now when the Twenty-Four interact with our solar system, I believe you said once that they may use other physical planets as a way of stepping down towards us, so there may be physical planets in our solar system that are used by individual civilisations..?

Tom: Not by the Twenty-Four. By Sub-civilisations. The Twenty-Four have no need.

Gene: There's a question that I cannot avoid asking: why you do not give strong and definite signs of your existence or proximity, on top of approaching humanity by indirect means such as these channellings, or other ways? Obviously you have your reasons, but this question does matter to me.

Tom: It is of great importance for you to understand that the governments of your world of Earth have refused to believe, or to convey to the people, our existence. If there were an attempt by the civilisations to land upon Planet Earth in a mass situation, which in truth will come to pass in the course of time, the people upon Planet Earth would panic, for they have not the understanding, the knowledge, that we would mean no harm to them.

Remember this: there are also certain civilisations, not of the Twenty-Four or their helper civilisations, that have a great desire to control Earth, to keep souls in bondage. And these civilisations have landed at times upon Planet Earth and have created difficulty, which they forced on Earth people. It is important that there is no panic amongst those that exist on the Planet Earth: that the knowledge be brought to them in gentleness, that those of the Twenty-Four civilisations mean no harm to them. This is of great importance, for if there were panic, humans may then attempt to end their own life, and also the lives of their families and neighbours, which would not serve any purpose.

The governments of your world have refused to accept that there are others of a higher intelligence, and in truth of a more spiritual intelligence than those that exist upon the Planet Earth. We need to convey to the people that there are others that mean them no harm, but have an interest in saving Planet Earth. For in truth, if there are no other civilisations to help Planet Earth, it will bring destruction to itself. We do not come to control, we do not come to hold in bondage, we will come with love and patience and understanding – but since there is the denial of our existence, how can those of Planet Earth accept the fact that the civilisations of Altea, Hoova, Ashan, and the rest of the Twenty-Four, mean well?

GENE: I have another question that I think people will wonder about: on previous tapes of your conversations I heard you explain that you constantly know the thoughts of either all of us or those who communicate with you. Am I correct in this assumption?

TOM: If we have the wish to help you, yes. But we wish you to understand that we do not invade the mind, we do not control the will, we do not interfere with freedom: we do not interfere. It would not be of service. Altea, Hoova, Ashan and Aragon have asked to convey to you that they may have the abilities within them, but it would not benefit Planet Earth to use them – nor would it benefit them. That would be an invasion of a soul.

GENE: I have been most impressed by the communications, the expressions and atmosphere of love and peace that surround all the people here, but I do have some difficulties in understanding why, if you are in the minds of humans at times, and your representatives have visited Earth, and you have a knowledge of human affairs... I find it difficult to understand how you have difficulty speaking with

*us, and understanding our basic colloquial English? Could you help
me with that?*

Tom: We will explain that. The civilisations have indeed visited Earth,
but do you understand that when you have communication with your
mind, it is not necessary to have words? It is difficult from where we
are to give explanations in your words. We have concepts that cannot
be explained in your language, for you do not have the words to
explain. If you could read our mind... if we could communicate with
your mind in the essence of pure telepathy, then we could convey to
you what we are trying to transmit. Also, within the mind of the
channel, as also within your mind, there is only a certain vocabulary
that we can use.

*Gene: Thank you. You mentioned that at some stage there might be a
large-scale landing of the civilisations. I think the next questions
involve who and where, how and why; the first such question most
people would ask is 'how?' In other words what method of transportation would be used in such a landing: are we referring to physical
vehicles?*

Tom: Yes. They would be in the nature of what you would call a
physical vehicle. If you have the desire to go and touch it, as you have
with an automobile, you would be able to touch it.

*Gene: Can you tell me anything about the relative size and shape and
so on? Will they hold a large number of people, or...*

Tom: There would be vehicles of different sizes and different de-
signs. There would be some with the appearance of a glass top, but it
is not in truth a top, it will just have its appearance. There will also be
those that will remain in your atmosphere that are very large, that will
then send out smaller ones... you have, upon your oceans, carriers
that send out ships that fly, is that not so?

Gene: That is correct.

Tom: It would be similar, but instead of being upon your oceans, it
will be in your sky.

*Gene: You're saying that smaller craft will exit and come down to
Earth from this carrier craft?*

Tom: Yes. There will also be those that have the appearance of what
you call saucers. There will be those that are pointed, as with a 'V'.

Gene: Will these vehicles pass through the time dimension, or other dimension in order to arrive here at Earth?

TOM: The intelligences that exist in the civilisations have the ability to come into your dimension – they have that technology, yes.

GENE: A very common Earth question would be how these vehicles are powered? By what method?

TOM: It resembles the reversal of a spinning top.

GENE: Would these vehicles remain on Earth after such a landing, and would humans be permitted to inspect them?

TOM: They would have permission to visit the interior. The craft would remain for a period of time. Not a great length of time – not for years, for example.

GENE: Because of many stories we have of flying saucers, people will be interested to know if humans would be permitted to travel in any of these vehicles?

TOM: It would be necessary, before they could travel in a vehicle, to have a vehicle around them.

GENE: Does this mean that the atmosphere within your vehicles will be different, or that the stress of the movement would be dangerous?

TOM: The stress of the movement. It would be possible to move within your Earth atmosphere, but to take them out would require another vehicle inside a vehicle. But it could be done.

GENE: Landings would undoubtedly be judged by humans and governments in a variety of ways, which includes the almost certainty that some would view your landings as a threat. Do you have a method of defending yourself from attack?

TOM: We wish you to know that we are talking about the civilisations, not us, the Council of Nine. We do not need to manifest in the physical. There would be a method to stop people from attempting to destroy those of the civilisations. It would be done with love and gentleness. Those of the civilisations that are in service to us will not attempt to destroy, nor harm in any manner, any physical being on Earth. We will have a way of preventing them from attempting to destroy us. But we would wish not to come without giving some prior knowledge, for otherwise people would begin to believe that we would seek to control them. We have not the desire nor the need to control, we come only to benefit. If an Altean were to appear at an entrance of his vehicle, and were stepping onto Planet Earth, and if there were a group that attempted to destroy that Altean, he has only to hold out his hand in an upright manner, and not in great extension, to bring calmness, and also to render them into a state in which they would not have the desire to harm, and would put down their weapons. Hoovids would operate in a different manner: if they were in the same situation, and they came out and raised their arms, those humans with weapons would become totally stationary for a period of time. So there are different methods. But none of these methods would harm a physical being. Do you understand?

GENE: *Yes, I understand, and I certainly understand why you would not want to land showing force, because this would create great fear.*

TOM: Yes.

GENE: *Can you describe the ones from the civilisations who have something like human shape – something as to their size and colour and features and so on?*

TOM: Alteans have the tallness of you. The colour of their eyes is a shade of blue, as that of your clear sky. They have a translucent appearance; they are very fair in their colouring. They are in erectness. When we say translucent, it is that their vibration is of translucence. Do you understand?

GENE: *No, I'm afraid I don't quite understand that.*

TOM: People upon Planet Earth have many different sizes, do you not? Those of Altea have one size. They have a glowing that gives the appearance of being translucent. It is their vibration. They have a silverness about them. You have automobiles that have a translucent appearance... they say I am using the wrong term: it is an iridescent appearance.

ANDREW: *Do they have any hair on them?*

TOM: No.

GENE: *Other than the hairlessness and iridescence, is the spacing of their features like ours?*

TOM: They are similar in appearance to those that exist upon the physical Planet Earth. Do you understand that the physical human seed upon Planet Earth came from Altea?

GENE: It is my understanding that there are some of us here on Earth who are of Altean blood...

TOM: Yes.

GENE: ...or genetic features...

TOM: Yes.

GENE: ...mixed with our basic Earth features..?

TOM: Yes. The Hoovids are smaller. They manifest small, and dark of skin, not as fair as Alteans. They have hair, straightness of hair. It is also dark, yes.

GENE: And are there other features, again nose, mouth, eyes, hands and so on, Earth-like?

TOM: Yes. Those of Ashan are not.

JOHN: May I just say: do any of these have vocal cords at all? Do they make sound?

TOM: Alteans do not. Hoovids have vocal ability, but not similar to you on Planet Earth.

ANDREW: How long does an average Hoovid live, for example?

TOM: If we placed it in your Earth time, it would be in the realm of 500,000 to 1,500,000 of your years.

GENE: Are you saying they would live at least half a million years?

TOM: That would be in relation to your time. Their time is not the same: your time goes in great slowness because of your density.

GENE: I see. You spoke of Hoovids who have vocal cords – will they speak Earth languages so that we may communicate with them?

TOM: They have the ability to convert, Hoovids have a method of speaking which will be transmitted; while Alteans will have it in a computer-box, so that what they think will come as a sound.

GENE: While talking of those who are humanoid, will they be male and female, as we recognise the sexes here?

TOM: Alteans are of two polarities blended in togetherness. They do not have what you would call male and female. There are tri-polarities in Hoovids.

GENE: Yes, I am acquainted with the possibilities of three genders, if

*that's what you're trying to say, and I believe you're describing the
Alteans as a unisexual race, is that correct?*

TOM: Yes. That is correct, yes.

*   *   *

It is of interest to note here, an incident that occurred several years
earlier when Phyllis was waiting for a client, who had an appointment
for a reading at three o'clock at her school in Orlando. At ten to three
she checked with her secretary who told her that her client was a
woman named Mary – in fact a 'regular' who was always on time.
Seated in the reception area was a stranger, a dark man about five feet
six inches high. He was wearing a dark suit and looked Italian or
Jewish, except that, according to Phyllis, he had almond–shaped eyes.
The stranger said to her "I want to see you at three." Phyllis explained
that she had a client at that time to which he replied: "She won't be
here." Phyllis returned to her office to wait for Mary, who still hadn't
turned up by ten past three. Phyllis wondered how the stranger had
known that her client was a woman. She returned to the reception area
and asked him this, and also how he had known that she would not
show up. He told her that Mary's car had stalled on the Parkway.
Intrigued, Phyllis invited him into her office and asked him what he
wanted. "I want you to give me a reading", he replied. Phyllis
touched his hand and in an instant she knew that he wasn't from
Earth. She told him her impression. He said, "That's right. Give me a
reading anyway." Phyllis said, "This isn't why you came, is it? Why
did you?" He said "You've been asking for signs since 1953." Phyllis
thought that she would test him and said: "If you are who you say,
then bring in one of your people". She had scarcely spoken the words
when a being materialised before her eyes. He was about six feet four
inches high, well–built, with blond hair and blue eyes and was wearing a silver–blue jump suit. He didn't speak, but communicated telepathically that his name was Altima, that he and others were coming
to help the planet and that in future she would be able to call on him in
any emergency. He remained in the office for less than five minutes
then dematerialised. The dark man left and Phyllis watched from her
window as he got into a white Cadillac with Miami number plates and
drove away. One Friday afternoon about two months later, just as
Phyllis was about to leave and go home, he suddenly reappeared, put
his head around the door, and said: "Hi, Phyllis, everything okay? Just
checking on you". While this story can seem to be preposterous,

Phyllis remembers the incident vividly and swears that this is precisely what happened.....

*   *   *

GENE: *How would we be able to explain to people, and to our scientists, how people from varying dimensions have so similar a humanoid form?*

TOM: Man made those of the civilisations into their gods... When they have the saying that man was created in the likeness of God that referred to the civilisation that had that appearance. Planet Earth does however have the independent capacity to develop human-type beings on it. Alteans have, as we explained earlier, a manifestation that appears to be very similar to yours. They also have the ability to manifest in a different manner, but they would have... I will ask Altea how he would choose to appear... Altea has said that they would choose to appear in their usual form, which is what you would call humanoid. Hoovids have that appearance. Ashans do not, Zeneels do not.

GENE: *Did the Alteans and Hoovans as well as others develop and evolve in the same way that we evolved? Were they planted as seeds, and did they evolve somehow on their planets naturally? With the geography and atmosphere and all of that?*

TOM: Not in terms of atmosphere and geography. But they did go through a process of evolution. But they perhaps had a more fortunate manner, in that they were not trapped − although as you are aware, there were some from the civilisation of Altea that were of Atlantis − Remember that Earth is the planet of balance, to learn to balance the ethereal with the physical. This was what trapped many of the souls.

When you speak about Planet Earth evolving, remember this, that all the souls that exist in the Universe have had, at one time or another, the necessity to manifest on the physical Planet Earth, for the lessons to be learned. So those that have existed upon Altea have also lived at least one of their lives upon Planet Earth. It gets very complicated trying to explain that, when you have not the words to explain the concepts of the Universe. I am sorry, they are saying I am not explaining it rightly... Souls with the desire or necessity to learn balance do come to live on Planet Earth, to understand how to refine the physical in relation to the spiritual. Many Alteans − the greater majority – have lived on Planet Earth: that is why they have a great wish to help Planet Earth.

There are the Twenty-Four civilisations that are in direct service to us. There are in truth Twelve of two. The Twenty-Four civilisations also are physical. At this present time, the civilisations are working with each other to move into balance, and to resolve all residues of difficulty. Because the Twenty-Four are in a form of physicalness, they also have some of the difficulties associated with physicalness – not to the extent of the Earth, but nevertheless to the degree that they have. If they had reached perfection, they would have merged with us. Among the Twenty-Four civilisations, not all have manifested upon the physical Earth. There are those that have seeded Planet Earth, but there are also those that have not – such as those that have been to Earth but have not been involved with the work of the other civilisations. Each of those civilisations – in particular those involved with Planet Earth, and those that have not been involved with it but have sent a representative – need to be brought into balance.

GUEST: *What is Ramtha? Why does Ramtha speak so definitely about September 1988?*

TOM: Why was it said that the end would come in 1914 and again in the '50s? The different civilisations have different measures of understanding. Let me explain:

The members of the Council of Nine are not, and have never been, in physical form. There are the Twenty-Four civilisations that are in physical form, and then there are what we could call helper-civilisations that are in more physicalness than the Twenty-Four. Example: Altea is a civilisation of the Twenty-Four. That civilisation has one thought, one being. In other words it is a collective consciousness of a very high calibre and is of millions of souls that support, create and survive with each other. They know all in their location and in their knowledge. They in turn have underneath them other civilisations, that you would term workers or helpers of ...we do not wish to use term 'sub-civilisation' but there are those that filter down.

Now if humans on Planet Earth have communication with a helper or a lesser civilisation that does not understand the workings of all, then they are liable to receive misinterpretations. Example: in a corporation, there is the chairman of the board, there is the board of directors, and there are the departments within all the corporation. The department of purchase does not understand the department of selling, and the department of management knows more than both the departments of purchase and selling. So if one communicates with one department within their realm of understanding, they can speak on that but outside their realm they do not understand. They can hold views which are valid only within their frame of reference. What that means is this: perhaps there is a communicating being in a civilisation who sees that, if the Planet Earth continues upon its present path, then it can bring about destruction. What that being does not see is the ability for humankind to change that. Planet Earth is unique in the Universe, for upon this Planet Earth there is freedom of will.

GUEST: *It is generally understood esoterically that the four etheric sub-planes of the cosmic plane can be the highest possible spiritual influences as far as humanity is concerned. I'd like to know if that is correct.*

TOM: You have received this information from one of the civilisations, you understand?

GUEST: *I thought this was generally esoterically understood, and that it was coming from the channelling of Alice Bailey which I thought was...*

TOM: You understand that that was not from us, it was from one of the civilisations. You understand that the Twenty-Four civilisations are the highest of all beings in the physical, that they are next to us? But you also understand that information is from a physical civilisation?

JOHN: *Yes, could you say which of the civilisations it came from?*

TOM: I will ask for permission... It is the partner civilisation of Myrex, called Mora-Triomne. It is not necessary to explain all the Twenty-Four. It is best to speak of Hoova, Ashan, Altea and Aragon.

ANDREW: *Can we clearly state at this time, that the civilisation of Hoova is that which identified in the Bible........?*

TOM: Hoova is Jehovah. Yes.

ANDREW: *And as far as Altea is concerned, can we... ?*

TOM: It was from the time of Atlantis and before.

ANDREW: *Right. And Ashan, can you give us some historical reference for Ashan's role in the past?*

TOM: Ashan was the beginning of the great composers, the Renaissance, the greatness of art upon the Planet Earth. It began in a small portion in the time of Egypt in its working with gold, and in its beauty of architectural environments. Ashan is simply a civilisation of great creativity. It has brought to the Planet Earth great music, great art, and great literature. Yes.

Remember: there will be those who will have great difficulty in accepting this. There will be no difficulty from heads of government or security services of government, for they will publicly pretend that this does not exist, while quietly they will send people to find out. For they know they need communication.

ANDREW: What would you suggest is the principal reason that you are coming here to help mankind, and what is the primary problem of man that needs help?

TOM: The Council has said to explain it in a twofold manner: that if it continues in the manner which it is now, around or after your year 2000 Planet Earth will no longer be able to exist as it is now. So the civilisations are attempting to cleanse it and to bring it back into balance by using their technology, not only for the saving of those that exist on Earth, but also because Earth is under the guidance of the civilisations that initially colonised it, and it is thus partly their responsibility. Then there is the entrapment and the recycling of souls. The necessity of coming at this time is because man in his dominion over animals and flowers and plants, is now trying to control all of humanity, and we cannot have it.

In the following transmission, Tom announced the presence of other beings:

TOM: With us today we have individuals that are observing what is transpiring. They are in service or in study to us. We are preparing them to go and do the work and perform the service that is necessary for this planet to raise its level of vibration, to evolve, in order to help this Universe.

ANDREW: Well, we welcome their presence, and I hope we can be of some use in their education...

TOM: They are beings from civilisations other than yours.

JOHN: Could you clarify what you mean in this case?

TOM: When we speak of civilisations, we speak of levels of conscious-ness. In order to raise the level of this Planet Earth, by which that also raises the level of the Universe, there are many different beings and civilisations that must learn to work in peace and harmony. As you have many millions of plants on your planet and many millions of species of animals, also in the Universe there are many. Those that observe us on this day are observing the technique, and at the same time we are trying to show them the way to generate love and peace and harmony. They are observing the vibration of love.

JOHN: Could you perhaps explain what happened when these people came in?

TOM: These beings from space, from other different systems, became curious. Our primary concern is with the Earth, because it is import-ant to raise its level, since it is holding back some of the evolution of the Universe. But, as you know in your world too, at times inquisitive beings can create a problem. At times it is better to tell them a little, and this is what we are doing, although we have had a conference of many of the major groups and civilisations. This erases fear. It is our affair to help raise those from other different civilisations, other levels, also.

JOHN: Are any of these inquisitive ones with you now?

TOM: No, these are their leaders.

ANDREW: Could we enter into an exercise with you to help show them the evolution or the awakening of love?

TOM: They are observing this because when we bring you peace and love we put a band around you, and we link that band with us. It is a vibration that is also like an electrical band. This is the only way I can describe it. They are very tiny atoms that link you with us. They are not molecules, they are atoms. I was told to clarify that.

ANDREW: That's very interesting, we didn't know that.

JOHN: I'm interested to know whether that can exist as a feeling on some levels.

TOM: The chair that you are sitting on is tangible. This is not a tangible product, it is a vibration. It is what we would imagine an emotion to be like.

JOHN: We always feel good in our sessions with you and I imagine that is our experience....

Tom: That is your emotion. We cannot explain this easily, it does not exist in your world. But what this generates to you is love and peace. The two words 'love' and 'peace' mean the same in our world as in your world but the vibration (or feeling) is experienced differently. It gives you peace, with peace you can then love, and love is necessary for the evolution of all the beings on this planet. It is also necessary for raising the level of consciousness and the collective consciousness of this universe. When you are serene and peaceful within, and know in which direction you must go, and are solid in your convictions, this helps these beings who are observing. These other beings are observing the vibration of your commitment. It does generate a vibration, and in their observing this, then they in turn can tell, in the case of those with whom they are working, whether they are truthful or absolute in their convictions and in their commitments, or if it is just desire or ego.

IAN: Roughly what proportion of our society is open to the possibility of the existence of intelligent beings from space?

Tom: It fluctuates between – in your developed world – 68% to 71%.

JOHN: Now that there is a change under way [1991], is there a likelihood of any direct contact with the civilisations?

Tom: When it is transformed there would be no reason not to, would there?

JOHN: That's true.

Tom: Part of that transformation will be a greeting of each other.

JOHN: Hm, that would be nice.

Tom: However, know in fullness also there are others than ours.

ANDREW: Is it possible for you to give us a brief idea of where the Alteans come from, in terms of distance, the size of their planet, the atmosphere, what special problems they have entering our atmosphere; just so we have a thumbnail sketch of their characteristics?

Tom: As you know we come from the zone of cold. The area of Altea is on the fringe of the area of cold. It has no sun as you have a sun... We speak of a dimension...

ANDREW: Yes, is it a large planet, or a small planet? For example I was told that Hoova was 16,000 times the size of the Earth. What is the size of their planet relative to the Earth?

TOM: Fifty-two times the size of Earth. Yes.

ANDREW: Now, the reason I ask these questions is: we were thinking about how the Hoovids and the Alteans would adapt to the Earth's atmosphere if they landed here, and it seems to me both would have to undergo considerable transformations in order to enter our atmosphere. Then by the same token Phyllis told us that she had the feeling that particular people could be physically transported, one of these days, to either of these two planets in order to communicate, and so on.

TOM: The transport would not be to the planet, it would be to a vehicle.

ANDREW: Aha, so we would be dealing with our own atmosphere in the vehicle?

TOM: Yes.

ANDREW: I see, and we would not have to undergo major transformation in order to enter their zone?

TOM: No.

JOHN: We don't know whether a civilisation might be only ten souls or it might be many millions. Can you give us a general idea about that?

TOM: Within Altea, as stated in your Bible, there is the figure 144,000. Hoova would be within the realm of five million.

JOHN: And those civilisations, are they what we would call eternal? I mean do they last indefinitely in terms of our Earth time?

TOM: If you lived a million years in Earth time, you would feel you were eternal, is that not so?

JOHN: (Laughing) Yes.

TOM: Then we would say it is eternal.

JOHN: (Laughs) Yes, okay, I understand that.

TOM: Altea, we will say to you, is eternal.

A Hoovid would live approximately one million of your years. The civilisation of Hoova is the one that brought forth the nation of the

Hebrews. They came to Planet Earth for this in the time of Sumer (whence Abraham came), and at the time when it is said in your books about 'the sons of the gods merging with the daughters of the Earth' and they came one other time also. As they were the one civilisation that had sustained energy and were determined to survive, they elected to play a central historical role on Planet Earth — their descendants represent a microcosm on Earth.

Ashan communicates through the artistic. You understand that those of Ashan are not always capable of discipline? May we just say to you that for the millions of Hoovids there are only a handful of Ashans. They come through by their own means. They are of creativity — if you will look into the culture of the Chinese, you will see the effects of their influence. Ashan is the creator of music, it is the creator of the beauty upon the Earth, it is the civilisation that creates muses. The Scandinavians were of Ashan as were the Phoenicians.

JOHN: *They were very artistic with glass, I understand.*

TOM: Yes. They were bohemians. Ashan is lithe of body, and light as the wind, and as the sounding of crystal, do you understand?

JOHN: *Yes, that's very graphic.*

TOM: They are what you would call the surrealists of the Universe. Involved particularly with Earth, you have Hoova, Ashan and Altea.

JOHN: *Yes. Hoova works with the physical?*

TOM: Yes.

JOHN: *And the astral, the creative, the emotional is Ashan?*

TOM: Yes. And Altea works with the mental. It is the blending of three primaries, Altea, Hoova and Ashan, which brings together the connection and the coupling of Planet Earth with the Universe.

All involved with Aragon (Jose Arigo the Brazilian Healer for example) are involved in healing. It is different from Ancore, Ancore works under Aragon. They work in conjunction towards perfecting the health of humankind. They work together, as Spectra works for Hoova. Zeneel represents a similar principle to a computer but not just like a computer... we know not how to express it... Zeneel works with interplay, interchange. Zeemed and Zenthorp are worker civilisations of Zeneel. They give a specialised structure of understanding and ability in the bringing forth of the energy of Zeneel. Zeneel is light and joyful and orderly. When we say 'orderly' we mean the creating of order in the colour energy. Zeneel is the alchemist of the civilisations.

This chapter finishes with an exchange between Irene and Tom concerning civilisations on this Planet:

IRENE: I want to ask about the Chinese and the Buddhist Tibetans. How far back does this unhappy relationship go? What needs to be understood about it and what is there that is not known in humankind's history about it?

TOM: In the beginning China was one seeding and the Tibetans were direct descendants from another civilisation, which was the soul of the Chinese. You know the importance of bringing forth the material with the spiritual? The Chinese represent the material......

IRENE: symbolically.

TOM: Yes and the Tibetans represent the spiritual.

IRENE: But somewhere in the history of China and Tibet, they used the Tibetan Lamas to teach the Chinese emperors their spiritual teachings – and yet even before that there was some imbalance that is still playing itself out now..?

TOM: You know that the priests of Tibet are in a direct relationship to what is called in the nation of Israel 'the sons of gods merging with the daughters of men'.

IAN: So, at which point in the evolution of man did the Tibetans appear and begin mingling?

TOM: They were teachers. As Ioannes came out of the sea to teach those of Ur – they were the teachers to teach the Chinese, you understand? Now China wishes to consume Tibet, for in the consuming they believe they know best.

IRENE: So the Chinese unconsciously felt that they should have had the divinity that the Tibetans had.

TOM: That is correct, but they did not have the ability.

IRENE: So, knowing they lacked the ability, they sought to remove the Tibetans from sight? In more peaceful times they made them their teachers, thinking that if they learned better than their teachers they would assume that place of divinity.

Tom: That is exact. As in ancient times the Bedouins ate the porpoise thinking they would receive its knowledge.

Irene: Okay, and when the Chinese saw that this transfer didn't happen, they turned toward violence.

Tom: And bondage, for then if they could bondage this soul-knowledge, they then could own it, control it, you understand? It is similar with the Jewish people, who hold a valuable place in the matrix, which others would take from them.

Ian: So which of the civilisations did the Tibetans come from?

Tom: It is one of the Twenty-Four.

Ian: And which one of the Twenty-Four?

Tom: I will ask for permission to tell to you the name... They are peoples that represent in the Universe the principle of humility. They are of the civilisation that, in total togetherness, are the principles of inner knowledge – not for expansion of self but for service... Now in this time, they are the only peoples, apart from the Hoovids, who have inherent knowledge of their purpose as a collectivity in their coding. That is why they are cohesive, and why now, in this time when the Twenty-Four are emerging, they are expressing themselves, in their humanness. For they understand that they can bring to an end the elimination of threatened human groups.

John: Could you give us the name of the civilisation?

Tom: ...

Irene: I understand your apprehension. I know it takes Buddhists and Lamas many, many years of studying and transformation to be able to obtain their knowledge, but I do think it's important.

Tom: You have brought the Council of Nine into a wrangle!

Irene: I understand that the Council might think this is a short cut to peoples' commitment of faith and spirituality.

Tom: That is correct. We choose not to tell at this time. We apologise.

5

Visitations

Many people use the word 'Alien' to describe a visitor from outer space. Extra terrestrial is another word, which is rather more user friendly. For the sake of the question and answer format, the word used by the questioner has been left, though even Tom questions our use of 'Alien'. Should we wish to foster openess between all beings of the Universe perhaps we should also look at our vocabulary?

In a discussion between Andrew and Tom many years earlier, Andrew had asked Tom about UFOs and whether they were created manifestations. Tom had replied: "Many of the flying things that you call UFOs come from our place, but they come from other places also, and they do come in physical form. But many of them are not physical. They are like your movie screen".

This chapter begins with a conversation between Tom and two guests, in 1991.

Tom: Elarthin is one of the Twenty-Four civilisations responsible for unifying the energies of the Twenty-Four with those of your Planet for its evolution into greatness; and this in bringing to humankind information in a form of communication that registers in the ground.

Others on Planet Earth have come from different civilisations in the Universe – those from Hoova have come and have been implanted on three occasions. Others have come from other civilisations. And then there are some from civilisations not evolved to the same level as that of those with collective consciousness. The origins of humankind did not evolve from the animals of Earth matter. There was one group which emerged by itself- all others were colonised and merged to create species.

Guest: *Do we have any particular connection with those of the constellation of Lyra, who moved to the Pleiades?*

Tom: Those that have been seeded on this planet Earth have also been seeded in other systems in your galaxy. The Pleiades are in your Earth galaxy. Know that there are some of them in that arena that have great negativity. Do you know that?

JOHN: Are you saying that the beings in the Pleiades are also cousins of ours? That they have been seeded as we have?

TOM: That is correct. Yes.

GUEST/2: Is one of the governments of Planet Earth working in conjunction with a group from another source, from Reticulum, which is thirty-seven light years from Earth?

TOM: That is also within this galaxy. There are government agencies upon this planet Earth that have awareness of other species within your galaxy. There are many. Elarthin does not come from your galaxy, neither do we. Those within this galaxy could be said to be working within a corporation. If you have a mega-corporation which has many divisions within it, then within these divisions there will be units that manufacture or sell or service, without necessarily knowing who owns them. If you go into an individual unit, you would find a manager of that unit. But this person would not be the general manager of the whole corporation. That is the order of this galaxy. Do not limit yourself or tie yourself only to the solar systems of your own galaxy.

GUEST: Can I ask if the current phenomenon we call 'crop circles' that are being formed in England are being created from outside Planet Earth?

TOM: That is so. When anything takes place within your solar system, it is imprinted and then is manifested on Earth.

GUEST: Could you please explain a bit about the thinking behind the messages that are coded within the corn circles? What is the purpose?

TOM: It is of great importance for humankind to have the understanding of other realities of existence within your universe, of other systems of energy with the capability of bringing these into reality from great extensions of time, forms and matter; for your humankind to question their origins, their expansion of mind, and the time of now.

Those of the Twenty-Four have come to this your planet Earth. Those of other civilisations have often visited, since the beginning of humankind's history. Visits have been made by others very frequently. Please see your historical records. To date, this has not made an impression on humankind, for these other realities have been mostly eliminated from humankind's programming.

As this planet Earth is moving towards its evolutionary importance, and the reason for its existence, (for it is, as you know, the only planet with freedom of choice), those civilisations are attempting to bring to humankind information concerning other beings, other species, other energy forms, so that humankind may look on this, question it, and then probe into it. The challenge is to present an alternative. One to question, is it not? You have now been alerted to those energy fields that are in existence.

GUEST: *Are there any specific ideas behind the patterns that are formed in the crop circles? Is there an intended programme to help us build a picture of what is being represented within the crop circles?*

TOM: Now, reason, investigate and contemplate this thoroughly. All that has been sent into space from Earth is being reflected back, so that those of Earth may understand that when you create a situation that might be catastrophic, it may then impress upon the minds of the people the effect that one unit can make on all.

JOHN: *How many scientific and governmental organisations have made the connections, or made such interpretations yet?*

TOM: Are you not the forerunners?

JOHN: *We are wondering if they have reached a conclusion on their own or whether this project is one that is going to release that information.*

TOM: Yes. However be aware that there are many groups creating them, to distort the real purpose. It is not possible to speak about these at this time. For humankind could not comprehend, for the disbelief would then add no credibility. Some circles are from civilisations who wish of the most high, and there are others who wish to confuse and add their appendix too. It is timely to create a shaking brain in humankind, to question, as you now are questioning.

GUEST/2: *Is it possible to give any clues for circle researchers so that they can distinguish which is a genuine crop formation worth looking at, and what are the others there to confuse?*

TOM: The ones of confusion have brokens... It is a type of damage.

GUEST: *Damage of the stems of the corn in the field?*

TOM: Yes.

GUEST/2: *So the circles which have stems which are neatly bent, those are the ones which are not damaged, just bent, those are the ones which are...*

TOM: They are twirled. There are many civilisations, not all... they are sub-civilisations. What is important is not what is done by whom. What is important is the observation of other realities. Let the per-sonalities of humans move their own hair out of their own eyes... There will be more, and there will be less. In some areas there will be more, and where there were more, there will be less, yes. It is not just humankind that attemps to confuse.

GUEST/2: *In a couple of the circles last year [1991], some researchers detected radioactivity of a particular kind which is not found on Planet Earth.*

TOM: Does it not make sense that the vehicles that are able to go through space-time envelope dimensions radiate differently?

GUEST/2: *Yes.*

TOM: We wonder why humankind is as dense as its planet. [Laughter]

GUEST/2: *Well, we're slowly awakening. And certainly the crop forma-tions are adding to the awakening of those who are focusing on them.*

TOM: Think about this also. As atmospheric damage is done and created, it creates fields of energy that can upset the vegetation upon Planet Earth. You understand that this atmosphere that encircles Planet Earth is a protective device? You understand that there is influence from other planetary positions? And when there are mouse-holes in the atmosphere, then there are, from other planetary positions, energy-fields that may affect vegetation. Yes.

GUEST/2: *When you talk about planetary positions, do you mean planets in our solar system or in a larger spectrum?*

TOM: In your system, planets that have devices upon them, left in times past. We wish not at this time to go into detail, our being [Phyllis] is in weakness. Therefore we ask you only to ask urgent questions. Yes.

The latter part of that transmission, which ended there, took place in

1992. Here is another exchange from the early '90s: with particular emphasis on technology:

BRIAN: *I wanted to ask some questions about a recent ['90-'91] series of statements made in the United States concerning the presence of extra-terrestrial vehicles in the Nevada area. Is there any general comment you could make about the authenticity of those statements?*

TOM: As many are aware, the reality of lesser civilisations in physical-ness upon this planet Earth is a fact. As they have technologies and information, do not create the mistake of believing their higher motivation at all times, in visiting your planet Earth. A portion of this motivation is indeed prepared for utilising, if necessary, Earth species for their own environments, on their own planets. Not all are here for the betterment of Planet Earth, although there are those who do work for the betterment of Planet Earth. They have physical exist-ence.

BRIAN: *Are you saying that there is more than one group involved in the experiments at the Nevada test site?*

TOM: There exists at this time a totality of twelve different groups – physical civilisations – that have come to Planet Earth for investigation of the environment. Not all are well-meaning. The Council has said I must be clear to you. Not all are creating experiments.

BRIAN: *It would appear that some of the technology involved in the vehicles they have brought here is on the verge of being discovered by people here on Earth. Will there be an attempt to prevent those discoveries from being utilised and developed?*

TOM: Do you mean by other civilisations, or by those of the anti-peoples on planet Earth?

BRIAN: *I'm speaking of discoveries being made by physicists here on Earth. I'm wondering will their efforts be prevented in any way by the aliens?*

TOM: That is not the purpose of those that you call 'aliens'. Why are they aliens?

JOHN: *Well, it's just a word we use for anything that does not come from Earth.*

TOM: Yes.

JOHN: You say that is not their purpose, could you state what their purpose is specifically?

TOM: There are several purposes. Those that have well-meaning are working for prevention of total destruction of Planet Earth, and to oversee it and, if necessary, prevent a totality of ending. For in the ending of it, it would take so much time to start over again that it is not possible to start again. The situation of Planet Earth also is that its destructiveness would then create an energy that then could affect other systems of the Universe. There are those also who would wish to come here because they have begun the destruction of their own home physical planet and are looking for a place to relocate themselves. Therefore they are experimenting upon humankind and animalkind for testing available possibilities.

BRIAN: What will happen to the man who has told us about this, will he be punished in some way?

TOM: As you know upon your planet Earth, the country of USA, has created a secret situation among its people that cannot be revealed – they have not revealed the facts. Therefore all attempts will be made to create injustice to him. If there comes a time upon your planet Earth when people function as a unified force against those philosophical beliefs that are not correct – such as destruction of truth-telling people – then people will involve themselves, and if enough people do so, they cannot punish all people.

JOHN: If enough people know about it, that will be a protection to him, in a sense.

TOM: In protest. Yes.

JOHN: Now the American people who are working where he was working, what is their motive for working with these aliens – as we are calling them?

TOM: You speak of leadership, not of others?

JOHN: I'm talking of the people in Nevada, the scientists and the leadership there: presumably they're interested for military purposes, or what?

TOM: There are those who have interest in the betterment of humankind, and there are those who have the greatest concern about other 'aliens' approaching Planet Earth, therefore they seek technological information for stopping their arrival.

BRIAN: *I see. Will the efforts to understand the alien technology be successful?*

TOM: They are but a small percentage away from completion.

BRIAN: *Is the technology in the alien vehicles the same as the condensed charge technology that I'm aware of?*

TOM: It is in that realm. It is two polarities which exactly overlap and overlay, and each charges the other. It is 'as above, so below' as with the emblem of Hoova – the six-pointed star, do you understand?

JOHN: *Yes, the Star of David is two triangles.*

TOM: Instead of repulsion by magnetic charge, it is attraction by magnetic charge.

BRIAN: *Well, the alien vehicles operate by controlling gravity, it seems.*

TOM: Which has to do with the discharge of magnetics. It has to do with creating a magnetic field. That is the discharge, when you release the magnetic. When you function with the magnetic you draw all things to you. When you know how to discharge then the propulsion is reversed. To operate and release gravitational fields is related to magnetic fields.

BRIAN: *Well all the descriptions say nothing about magnetic fields, they talk about gravitational fields, which are different, and they say it requires a special element, element 115. Do you know what 115 is?*

TOM: That releases the magnetic attraction.

JOHN: *Are you saying that when you use the word 'magnetic' it is the same as when we're using the term 'gravitational' here?*

TOM: If you have attraction, an energy field that holds upon your Planet Earth, that is magnetic.

JOHN: *O.K. We used different terms.*

BRIAN: *One of the things that happened was when they put a burning candle flame in the field...*

TOM: It created a vacuum.

JOHN: *A time vacuum.*

TOM: Do you understand that in this movement it is possible to move quickly? For non-friction is created.

BRIAN: *So there is no action/reaction?*

TOM: There is freedom.

BRIAN: *How soon do you think there will be more information re-leased about these vehicles and about...*

TOM: Do you speak of information release? They will not release the information.

JOHN: *Have they been asked by the aliens to keep it secret also?*

TOM: That is correct, they are working in conjunction with them.

JOHN: *So it is a fully co-operative venture.*

TOM: In some ways, in others it is not.

JOHN: *So there's some holding back by both sides. Are you saying that the aliens are also holding back the different motives that you already mentioned with the people in Nevada?*

TOM: There are those who were working in conjunction with these lesser civilisations, and these civilisations began to control them. There are other civilisations that do not co-operate with this, and are in effect eliminated in physicalness. You understand that?

JOHN: *Yes.*

TOM: Out of fear the government of USA and others are in co-operation.

JOHN: *Well, that was the next question: are there other groups of aliens working with any other governments in a similar way? In other parts of the world?*

TOM: There have been many visitations, physical appearances and accidents that have been funnelled to the USA, and there are also attempts in Russia in investigations in cooperation with USA.

JOHN: *So is that project continuing at this moment in Russia, or is that something that happened in the past and is no longer in existence?*

TOM: There is informational exchange with USA.

BRIAN: *Are the alien people involved in the Nevada experiments – are they involved in any genetic experiments on human beings?*

TOM: Those are ones who wish to know if they may exist upon Planet

Earth by taking samples of tissue for culturing.

BRIAN: *So this same group that has provided the vehicles is also involved in genetic research?*

TOM: If you would use that terminology, yes. We would say to you, be in great caution.

BRIAN: *Well, that was my next question. Is it dangerous to persist in trying to learn more about this?*

TOM: It is important to assimilate, to be in a form of observation, but to be in great caution. And move in great caution when getting involved in information from others. And be in caution of any from what you call Reticulum, in your Milky Way. Be careful of those who say they are from there.

JOHN: *At what level in the United States is this project controlled ?*

TOM: The highest level.

JOHN: *So it is from the President down, is it?*

TOM: He is not the one who controls, but the head of state was involved in the past, this is an exceptional matter. [This conversation took place in 1990.]

JOHN: *So it is the C.I.A. who control the project?*

TOM: That term is not correct. It is not in a form. This is the creation of an element that is above that. What is important is that you begin to understand the implications.

In times past humanity did not comprehend the information we have given about the civilisations and the Council of Nine. Now it is important to comprehend, and know that what was begun in times past does exist, and continues, and it is time for humankind to know the importance of this information, but in a time when there can be directness, without interference from the governments of human-kind.

STEVE: *I would like you to speak about the emphasis you were giving in the mid-1970s: there was at that time a great emphasis on the appearance of beings to intervene in the critical world situation, and this did not occur. Perhaps some brief explanation of why it was so much stressed at the time and whether it might still be an option?*

TOM: There have been sightings of other civilisations, not all helpful to Planet Earth, and there has also been contact with several people that have authority in different countries of your planet Earth. There was also agreement between several countries not to permit information about this to be released in public, and also to eliminate portions of their destructive devices against each other, for fear of other civilisations permeating Planet Earth. Those who do not at all times have benefit towards this Planet Earth have also made agreement with some countries of Planet Earth, out of fear of reprisal.

JOHN & STEVE: Reprisal?

TOM: Reprisal: the Twenty-Four civilisations, and those that are in conjunction with them, would arrive if Planet Earth were on the brink of destruction from those lesser civilisations. These wish to maintain Planet Earth in its state of being, for they also have looked upon it as a vehicle for themselves. The Twenty-Four civilisations also will not permit a complete take-over, but humankind must have awareness of the existence of the Twenty-Four, and those working in conjunction, and of these others. Then there can be a correct sense of judgement when information about extraterrestrials is received. Those of the other lesser civilisations also bide time for they are playing wait-and-see. You have asked about the landing which we mentioned in your year 1976: it was not appropriate for the Twenty-Four, for we wished not to have the responsibility for physical interactions which would create more pollutionary destruction of Earth: humankind already creates enough pollution destruction. Is that clear?

STEVE: Much of it is but I am not very clear about how pollution would be caused by intervention...

TOM: Those lesser civilisations who have been viewing Planet Earth, who have made contacts with governments, and who are in portion in beings upon Planet Earth and are in this realm as well, would have warlike conflict with the Twenty-Four civilisations or those who work with them: therefore that would mean a destructive device in the atmosphere of Planet Earth. Humankind in its great fear would not have acknowledged or understood that there were those of goodness also.

JOHN: Because they would only see two groups...

TOM: Destruction

JOHN: ....destroying each other.

TOM: That is correct, and that would then create nightmarish pollution destructiveness of portions of Planet Earth. We must find another way of removing these others at this time.

STEVE: *There seems to be an implication that several landings had in fact occurred...*

TOM: That is correct, it is known by Russia, by the government of USA, and in other countries where there is communication with these two countries. Also it helped bring about the end of the non-speaking to each other for they knew that they must now begin to be with each other. We speak of the, you call them 'biggies'.

JOHN: *The two super-powers [this was 1990].*

TOM: For they knew that if they stayed in separateness they then could not survive.

STEVE: *Is this because they interpreted their findings as being dangerous to Earth?*

TOM: Yes.

STEVE: *They regarded the alien civilisations as the enemy.*

TOM: Those that have been inter-playing, yes.

JOHN: *So what you're saying is that the civilisations that have come to Earth, have not come and allowed themselves to be.....to interact willingly. It has been done with some tension and conflict for example in the United States?*

TOM: That is not what we meant. Those that have been in contact with these governments, and with those vehicles which governments have got hold of: some of these incidents have been accidental, some have been intentional, but in giving they have attempted to ingratiate, and the 'biggies' have decided they must align, for they are not sure of the motives of these civilisations. Their motives are not in goodness, and they also have abductions.

JOHN: *They have taken away, abducted some people.*

TOM: That is correct. The 'biggies' of Planet Earth decided to align with each other so that they might keep a cohesive front.

JOHN: *Yes, so basically what you're saying is that the Twenty-Four civilisations decided to stay away so as not to get mixed up with these other forces, either in people's minds, or in fact in a conflict.*

TOM: That is correct.

JOHN: Yes, OK. Well so what next?

TOM: If they can influence the Crescent [the Islamic countries] – that is why the country of USA is attempting to change that situation – if they can activate the Crescent or cause irritation they then create a situation upon Planet Earth which is divisive. And the lesser civilisations then move into a position that may create more devastation.

We of the Council of Nine, you must understand that we must function in a manner that does not bring fear of devastation. It is important for humankind to know that there are others who mean well for them and wish only to help the elevation of Planet Earth. We will not permit the destruction of Planet Earth, but humankind must begin to help itself and make decisions based on the survival of Planet Earth.

STEVE: What you are saying is good news and bad news, because we had thought in 1988 that the 'rapprochement' between the great powers signified a development and heightening of awareness and consciousness, and perhaps a coming of rationality into international affairs...

TOM: That time the threat of force brought that rapprochement: though it does not matter if it was force or willingness, for in the togetherness they have become partners against another threat that may bring destructiveness, and in togetherness they see each other as humans – so that benefited Planet Earth.

MIKI: Could you tell us about the circumstances in which a major landing of the Twenty-Four civilisations on Earth would be carried out?

TOM: If there were an imperative to land because of major destruction upon Planet Earth, then the civilisations would amass over the major cities to cause those in power to stop the destruction. There are those in the atmosphere of Earth, and those in closeness to your planet Earth that would make themselves quickly visible if there were the necessity. Altea has said to tell you that plans for a landing are currently on hold, for at this time it would create great chaos – for the percentage of humans accepting the civilisations' existence is insufficient, and also because we do not want to cause warlike attack by humans on the visitors of the civilisations. However, we assure you that if Planet Earth were near major destruction, the civilisations would arrive and stop it.

MIKI: Is it only in case of big danger for this world that a landing would happen?

TOM: It would happen when those of the planet Earth do not feel a need to attack, or if there were great danger on Planet Earth — then in any consequence it will happen. But currently they are on hold, yes. I will explain about the landing, and what it means to your planet. Our technology first of all will help you to understand how to raise your vegetables, your cattle, to purify your water, and to raise the vibration of souls — to bring them out of darkness. When we say 'darkness' we do not mean negativity, but true darkness, in which people do not see and do not understand the cosmic. And they also do not understand that when they hate and have anger, this creates a problem for the Universe. Only by raising the level of this planet and the level of consciousness of this planet, perfecting the love and perfecting the core that is inside each human, can we then go on and perfect other planets in the galaxies. This planet is one of the lowest that a soul comes to, in order to learn a lesson. The tragedy is the density of this planet — it is like a mire, it is sticky, and these beings get trapped in this stickiness. We are going to raise the level of this planet with your help, which will make this planet a lighter planet. The energy then coming from this planet will be sent into the Universe, and will help raise the level of consciousness and the levels of other planets. Do you understand that principle?

ANDREW: Yes. Now I take it that this will all come out in the new science that you once said you are giving us?

TOM: This is true. There will be mutations. Also your planet will be raised to that type of vibration where there will be physical relationships, but it will not be the primary concern. This energy will be put to use to preserve this planet. We do not object to sex, and it is none of our business as far as your physical relationships are concerned — we realise the necessity of physical relationships. But we are speaking of raising the level of the vibration, so the energy is not dissipated in physical relationships. These new beings that are coming to your planet and are being born on your planet, and the children that have the 'sonars' in them .... I was going to try to give you the names of the different galaxies and planets that these beings come from to help the Earth, but the names are so difficult in your language.

ANDREW: Uh, thank...

TOM: You are disturbed about something..?

ANDREW: No, not really. I simply know what you're saying is beautiful and rings clear, and it's like getting zapped!

TOM: Yes. I understand.

ANDREW: Could you just give a simple description of what a landing would be like?

TOM: A landing would not take place all at one time. It would start and for nine days there would be landings taking place all over this planet. There would be a visual landing, with many different types of craft, but before we landed we would radiate out a beam that would nullify the fear in people. Films and books have planted a seed of recognition of us, and people will remember. And this energy, the beam that we send out, will come from this seed-energy that is already planted.

JOHN: I understand that the major spiritual events that take place from time to time on Earth can happen in many different forms. Is the form of a landing chosen because of the sort of beliefs and understandings that people have at this particular time, in the space age..?

TOM: Humanity is now coming out of the true dark ages of this planet, and is now becoming aware of the existence of other life-forms in other parts of this universe. And humanity is now beginning to understand that there is more than themselves. People have always assumed that there was someone sitting up there taking care of all their problems. But they also assumed through their egos that they were the only existence that mattered to that which they called God, and that God was only concerned with them. Humans now have to look within, and begin to understand that there are other forms of life, and that the Universe does not revolve just around humanity.

JOHN: The beings that might come in such a landing, would they remain on the Earth to be teachers among people..?

TOM: There will be some that would remain, and there would be those of ours that would continue on, because this planet then will begin to evolve in its truest sense. We will then be able to go on and to work in other areas. This has been a major project, and it has taken many hundreds and thousands of your years, and much energy.

JOHN: The beings that would remain, would they collectively represent the Christ, or will the Christ be one of them?

TOM: You must remember that all of you and all of us have the Christ within us. It will be a collective consciousness.

ANDREW: *Yes, there would be no great single figures that would...*

TOM: You are all leaders and we are all leaders.

In the following transmission, Tom uses the word 'catastrophe' and – as with many words in our language – the meaning has become limited. Apart from the usual interpretation of 'disaster', the Oxford English Dictionary informs us that catastrophe can also mean: 'overturning' or 'a sudden turn' or 'the change which produces the final event of a drama'. In geological terms it can mean 'a sudden and violent physical change'; 'an event producing a subversion of the order or system of things'. So this transmission becomes rather different in meaning when all the shadings of the word are remembered. Tom may have difficulties with pronounciation sometimes, but he never chooses the wrong word and should there be a vocabulary problem, he always indicates when a word is not as descriptive as he would like it to be.

TOM: The preparation of the Twenty-Four civilisations in gathering forces is to make people upon Planet Earth aware and alert, to bring the prevention of greater difficulties. Apocalyptic prophecies are not necessary to be fulfilled, if those that exist upon Planet Earth have awareness and understanding. But also what is in prophecies – such as the Book of Revelations – may only be modified by the souls that exist upon the planet Earth. Remember this: without meditation, without love for humanity, without prayers, without love for Planet Earth, there could be many serious catastrophes. But with prayer and love it is possible to release the pressure. When the time of decision on Planet Earth comes, all the Universe will be working in conjunction with humanity to release the pressures upon Planet Earth. But if within you humans, and we speak to you all, if you generate great fear, then this negates part of that which the civilisations are trying to do – to prevent catastrophe. It is possible to prevent catastrophe completely, and we would hope that could be done. But there is a possibility that catastrophe will not be negated totally. For there are those that oppose you, that are functioning to control the planet Earth.

ANDREW: *What in the Book of Revelations would correspond to what is happening right now in the world?*

Tom: It is the beginning of the last of the seals, yes. It could imply destruction if what the civilisations and conscious people on Earth are doing is not accomplished, but on the other side, it implies that blessings are coming from the civilisations to Planet Earth. Do you understand?

ANDREW: Yes, I understand the dual implications – it depends on how everything works out, in terms of the energy we put into it...

Tom: We are sure that what we wish will be accomplished. So that your angel in the Book of Hoova will shower blessings from the civilisations, so your government leaders, the leaders of your societies and your religions will then have to ask questions about whence this comes, this shower of energy. Yes.

If the Twenty-Four civilisations come in a mass landing on your planet Earth, there will be not any that would doubt the teachings they bring. There will not be any person who would have a question, for they will have the understanding that comes from what you call God. That is positive and of benefit. But... If humanity causes its own extinction, then billions of souls are trapped within the Earth spheres for millions upon millions of your years.

The bottlenecking has already stopped the growth of the Universe. It is necessary for the civilisations to have an influence, for there is not time for humanity to come to a solution within itself, alone without help. So the civilisations come with great love to help people upon Planet Earth. To help them help themselves. Yes.

IAN: Could you tell me how they plan to effect this? To help man arise and grow spiritually? What do they plan to do if they should come?

Tom: There is in each civilisation a different manifestation of love. Altea will proceed with technology, to bring forth knowledge of non-destructive technologies, which work in unison with the nature of Planet Earth – to help with production without destruction.

Aragon will come with knowledge and wisdom, and the ability to release disruption and pain within a physical body, for it is Aragon's concern to relieve humans of bondage, arising from the influence of physical pain – such relief can free the mind. That does not mean there will not be suffering, for there will be those that choose to suffer, but those upon whom suffering and disease have been inflicted by mankind, not by their soul's choice, can then be helped, to give such souls an opportunity to perform what was their true choosing.

Ashan will awaken the creativity in humans upon Planet Earth, and through great music and great art will educate in the ways of the Universe.

With great love Hoova of the Nazarene comes to bring love to the planet Earth. They will set down a system to begin, to teach humans what they must do for themselves to help Planet Earth and the souls that are trapped. They will explain the systems of the Universe. But most importantly, they will make humans aware that they alone are not in control of the Universe, that they are not alone as beings, and that they must be responsible not only for themselves, and for the Planet but also for the Universe. For if humanity causes destruction of its planet, it is then responsible for millions of souls. And again most important: they will instil in humans that life does not cease upon the death of the physical body, so you cannot escape the consequences of what you have done. That is the most important.

IAN: Okay. So, should the civilisations land, would they do this in conjunction with each other as a unit working together or would they work separately? And if they worked directly with people, would people be conscious of their working with them on this dimensional level?

TOM: There are the civilisations of Twenty-Four, and there are those that work in service to the Twenty-Four. They would work in harmony, together, to show man the necessity of nations and civilisations working together. There would be some that would come first, then others later, and then they would work together. Those that do not work together, that is a clue for you, for they are not from us. You are aware that there would be those of the opposition that would also attempt to come as well, do you understand?

IAN: I think so, but I'd like some clarification. Are they of other civilisations or can they also be of the same Twenty-Four civilisations?

TOM: They are not the Twenty-Four. They are others. In answer to your question – we have not completed your answer – people will be conscious of those of the civilisations. In many cases in the beginning people will not know, but there will be those that do know, and through them, all will know to know who and what we are.

And again, on another occasion…

MIKI: If there should be a landing of the Others, by that I mean the opposition, is there a way for us to recognise them immediately?

Tom: There will be a method. If there were a landing that is not in good motivation, it would be negative in its outcome. Remember this: by their works you shall know them. In each situation you will know, for they cannot hide their attempts to gain authority and superiority. They come not in gentleness, they come in superiority.

Miki: Is there a way for us to protect ourselves from negative energies?

Tom: If each person, together with others, in each family, group and community, thinks of others with love, with devotion, with the wish for goodness for each other, that is your protection — for then that energy becomes like a ball, as all energy that is collective becomes a ball, that is your protection from negative influence. You are a circle of light: we observe, we see your motive. Your motivation is your protection always, yes.

Ian: I want to ask about Hoova. I asked you earlier to define what different areas of work the civilisations would do if they came, and the statement was made that Hoova would be bringing love. I was wondering if you could give more of a specific definition of what you meant by that love, and what they would do to that end?

Tom: You understand the nature of love in your human world? There is love that is possession, of convenience. In the case of Hoova, those people that come in contact will not be able at first to recognise the true strength and energy of love. For this contact will bring to them awakeness, and the opening of their heart, to understand that love is all-giving, is not selfish, has no possession, has no ego, and arises from the wish to give, to bring peace to all. Hoova will accomplish that. When those who are in contact experience the releasing of love, they in turn will be able to release others' love. You have had experience in your existence of the purest love, but for you it stays but a moment. Hoova will bring it to stay not a moment but for all existence. Love is the only thing, it overcomes. We speak of the true love of all.

This is about knowledge and wisdom, for there is a difference between them. Wisdom cannot be communicated, for on many occasions wisdom sounds like foolishness, for there are not words to communicate wisdom — it is but a knowing. That is nearly the same as love. It is difficult to communicate what love is, or what feeling is in combination with wisdom and knowing. The Hoovids will bring that.

But love also means to not give for satisfaction of self: love is also strength, it is discipline, for the benefit of yourself and others, but it is always love.

IAN: *How would they effect this?*

TOM: There is a radiation that generates from those of the civilisation Hoova, but it will also come from your brothers of the sea [dolphins] for their energy is the greatest, and in water it may be released. Do you understand that love is the most powerful energy of all?

IAN: *Yes, I do. One last question: if they come, will it be in a form that is like our humanoid form? Or will they be recognisable as other than human in body?*

TOM: They will be recognisable as other than human in body. For there is that which glows from them, which will be seen by everyone. All civilisations of physicalness have a form of body similar to what you call your human form, for in all civilisations it is natural to have forms of legs and arms and torso, for as a physical form it is easier to be able to function on a physical planet. But it is the degree of the glow that is of great strength: it does not dissipate in your density but it elevates your density, yes.

IAN: *Yes. Am I to understand that that glow is like the glow that one has seen on pictures of Jesus?*

TOM: Jesus is of Hoova, is he not?

JOHN: *I understand now [1979] that the landing which could have been a possibility in 1976 has diminished in importance. I'd like to clarify with you what your mission is now.*

TOM: There has not in truth been a vast change. In the beginning, we brought news to you that it was important for those on your planet Earth to have the knowledge of the existence of other civilisations, and an understanding, even belief, that there are those that are in great readiness to help them. It has not changed that your planet Earth is a great bottleneck, neither that those that exist on Earth have contaminated it greatly: if you will recall we always maintained the importance of the civilised world having acceptance of this, in order to prevent great catastrophes and disaster for you, and for the civilisations that would come upon your Earth.

We want to tell you about the importance of the nation of Israel, not for its own importance, but because it is a microcosm: until they can come to peace within, understanding and openness, then Planet Earth cannot come to a breakthrough. Our purpose, and the civilisations' purpose, has not changed.

JOHN: When you say that it's important that people know of the existence of other beings, is it important that they should expect the arrival of those beings?

TOM: It is in truth inevitable that at some time there will be a visitation to your planet Earth. We would wish that it may come with arms opened for greeting. We have explained that if it is needed because of a major disaster, particularly in warlikeness, a landing would happen to prevent that. But we would prefer that such a landing would take place in openness, yes. When there is acceptance by the mass, so that governments of the world could not attempt to attack the civilisations, the acceleration of evolution would grow.

Again, in 1980, the question of a landing was brought up.

JOHN: One more question on the time you planned to intervene with a landing...

TOM: We explained the necessity of having the civilised world understand and accept the possibility of existence of other beings in other parts of the Universe, in order not to create disaster, war, panic, destruction of self. Do you remember?

JOHN: Absolutely, yes.

TOM: If there were an attempt to destroy your planet Earth, we would not permit it, but until you humans have at least a marginal comprehension, coming to Planet Earth would not have value, for humans would feel in captivity or destructive towards those whom they assume are captors.

When it reaches the point that the planet Earth – which in reality is a spaceship – is in perfection, and those that live upon it keep it in balance, the Twenty-Four civilisations will then be seen, and they would land visibly in their vehicles. Humankind is not ready to accept us without creating destruction. If you will remember we said to you that we would intervene if there were imminent total destruction of Planet Earth by nuclear forces, did we not? The governments of humankind are not yet ready to accept us without extreme confrontation. In the shift of consciousness necessary for making Planet Earth a light vehicle, this acceptance and understanding of other civilisations will come about. We have recognised that a premature landing would create great animosity as well as aggression, because of lack of understanding. Yes.

JOHN: *The preparation at that time then was in case you had to intervene in the event of nuclear destruction, and since we are now past that time, as I understand, you will not intervene until 75% of the people are awake, is that correct?*

TOM: That may change, given a situation of destruction. However there is a figure of close to 60% in the country of USA, who believe in the possibility of the existence of other civilisations. The critical issue is that people need to understand that the civilisations will come without   confrontation.

JOHN: *But if most of the people of the Earth are already that awake, then it surely will not be necessary to make a landing, because they will then be able to change things on Earth of their own free will?*

TOM: That is correct. But is it not beneficial for one evolved soul to meet   another?

MIKI: *Well, yes. Why has there not been any proof of any possible landing? If there were so many UFOs so close, why wasn't it possible to give proof, so that people know for sure?*

TOM: There is proof in your USA, there is proof in the country of Swiss. If you mean the capture of an entity and capture of a ship as proof – for that would probably be the only acceptable proof for the nations of the world...?

MIKI: *Yes.*

TOM: If one came from the heart, with love into a nation, and if one walked out with open arms, then there would be destruction of that entity, is that not so?

JOHN: *Yes, I think so.*

TOM: That then creates another set of circumstances of debt the planet must then work from. Is that clarity?

MIKI & JOHN: *Yes.*

TOM: May I ask you a question? Do you believe in the Creator called God?

MIKI: Yes.

TOM: Can you prove God exists?

MIKI: No.

TOM: Thank you.

MIKI: We were joking today... we would love it if you landed in front of this house tonight... (laughs)

TOM: We would love it also, but if we did all that, you would all have...

ISRAEL: Wet our pants.

TOM: Yes.

ALL: (Laugh)

MIKI: Yes, well, I guess that too!

TOM: That would be permissible.

ALL: (Laughter)

6

The Others

In the previous edition this chapter was called "The Opposition" but in a communication of May 1994 Tom relayed the information that it would be better to use the term "The Others" as it carried a less significant energy imprint. And while awareness is required, the less thought that is given, the less power is available for negativity.

There are many insights in this chapter, turning a potentially unpleasant subject into an extremely useful exercise.

Tom: There are those groups, those organisations, those religions and all forms of government that set rules on paper to control both humankind and their souls. Yet humankind has rebelled against the laws. When we speak of laws, we mean the laws that govern the Universe. It is a form of natural law, what you might call a 'gentleman's agreement'. This agreement applies on Planet Earth, as well as in the whole Universe. The Others do not adhere to laws. They are what you would call the rule-breakers of the Universe. They do not adhere to natural law, but there are natural laws that are in essence a form of discipline for those who exist upon Earth. They have been instituted in the Universe because they bring the greatest benefit to all, and because working with these rules is also a learning process for the soul. For, in truth, the spirit has no rules or laws set upon it to guide it – yet without them it would be as a ship at sea without a rudder. The Others, knowing that Earth is a place of free will, do not adhere to natural law on this Planet. We cannot give to you our guarantee that you will therefore be in total protection from the influence of the Others, for we do not interfere in the free will of humans.

ANDREW: Could you give us some idea what the Others' forces are like, their anatomy, their physiology, their distribution, their presence. See, we know nothing about them, and it would help us a great deal to understand what they are, and who they are, and how they operate.

Tom: First let us explain to you how they operate in the physical body. All that is not good in a physical body is used by the negative forces. The objective is to be positive-balanced, not positive-imbalanced. When you re-balance the positive and the negative, or when the physical body is tired or weakened, the negative forces may attempt to use your physical being, even if balanced, to create disharmony, to upset and unbalance. So this is how they attempt to use those beings who are working with us: Your physical body, because of its density and heaviness, has certain things that it must keep in balance. Even over-exposure to your electrical equipment can bring imbalance. Desire, greed and unbalanced emotions can be used to upset the balance and they become trapped, so that they then reincarnate over and over. In the other worlds of the Universe they attempt to do the same, but it is only on Planet Earth, because of its density, they are able to accomplish this. You would like to know if they are the counterpart of us, is this not correct?

Andrew: Yes.

Tom: No, they are not the counterpart of us. We are in the centre. And we do not wish to sound as if we are perfect or if we are egotistical, but on either side of us there is the positive and the negative. By this I mean there is the positive that is not balanced. and the negative that is not balanced. We are in the centre and we are balanced. We are trying to bring those other forces into balance.

Andrew: Right.

Tom: Remember: those that are so positive in their approach that they have no sense, create just as many problems as those that live on greed, anger, frustrations and fears.

Andrew: Well, what is the nature of the negative and the positive? We do not understand clearly what their nature is.

Tom: We will try and explain so that you will understand, but we are not sure that we would find the words to explain the entire truth: you are a physical being and you have a left and you have a right side. And without that left you would be unbalanced with your right, and without your right you would be unbalanced with your left. This is the situation. They are part but they are not all, and they are not complete. Does this answer your question?

ANDREW: *Just one further point: the negative forces of the nature of beings – are they aware, do they live?*

TOM: They live as you live and we live.

ANDREW: *Well, I understand that one of the names of the leader of the Others is Satan. Is that correct?*

TOM: May we say to you that the word that you have just spoken is a very powerful word, and it is unfortunate that people on your planet do not understand that the use of this word creates much difficulty for all that are around. Nevertheless, it is true what you have said, it is the most horrible of all: the Beast.

ANDREW: *I see. My real question was not really that, but what is the opposite of that Beast?*

TOM: Do we not speak to you? Remember there is a balance. The Beast is in oppostion to us but it is not the counterpart of us, as an 'equal-and-opposite'. Do you know what causes 'Satan'?

ANDREW: *No, I have no idea, to me it's just a meaningless word. I have no feeling for it. You're telling me it really has meaning in the world.*

TOM: It has great meaning because of the power of the word... It is the temptations of the world.

ANDREW: *That means for Earth specifically, or for the Universe*

TOM: The Universe.

ANDREW: *I take it when you say 'temptations' that means something not desirable in evolution?*

TOM: That is correct.

ANDREW: *What would be examples of temptation on a cosmological scale?*

TOM: For example, mis-representing us, with a false picture, or using our name in falsehood or deception. The Nazarene was very sad about the things that had been done in his name. We are also sad about the things that have been done in his name and for the use of his name.

And we are also sad about the things that have been done in our name. When we say this, we say it for you to understand that the temptations of Satan to feed egos, to control individuals, is the most serious problem upon your planet: it is the one thing that will destroy, it is the craving for power and the craving for control. And the craving is so strong that when it cannot be fulfilled one way, they will find another. But when they use the name of the Nazarene or they misrepresent us, and they say 'In the name of God I do this' that is the worst. We know what is in their hearts, and it is Satan that tempts them to do this, for the control and the power it gives them over other beings. Satan is the unbalanced negative. Now does that help you?

ANDREW: Yes, it does. I take it for example that these evangelical preachers who are always talking about Satan, evil, sin and power and such matters.

TOM: They feed Satan. Look at the money, the business that falls into their pockets for controlling the masses.

ANDREW: They seem to appeal to one's guilt, in order that you pay them in some way or another.

TOM: You cannot pay your way to us, and someone should have informed humanity. We do not need your 10%.

GUEST: Can you tell me what are the rules or agreements that you and the Twenty-Four have with the Others?

TOM: We do not agree with them. We have rules of the Universe, they do not always abide by them

GUEST: Yes but what are they supposed to be?

TOM: How can we convey that? We will try to find an analogy: as there are rules of war and peace within your world, it is the same with the civilisations.

GUEST: Yes, I understand. I'm asking if it's possible to communicate what these rules are – specifically?

TOM: They are not to bring about physical harm, destruction, insidiousness; they are not to use the strengths. Yes.

GUEST: I don't quite understand because I find that completely unrealistic. All the things that you just mentioned, it seems to me, are exactly what their existence is based on.

TOM: They are to use the weaknessses – not the strengths.

IRENE: On thinking about the Others, it came to me that the opposi-

tion's need to bottleneck souls is not just about the destruction of humankind but is in fact a much larger issue and has to do with many Universes. Is that correct?

TOM: That is correct, yes.

IRENE: What is the nature of the Others?

TOM: All that comes from creation.... there is not really the language to explain this properly. I will try again: of all matter that is created from creation, that of the opposition is like anti-matter. The Universe must have an element of both for complete balance. If one is out of balance or in negative control then the Universe is not in balance for evolutionary development. The Others are the opposite of life, the anathema of life.

ANDREW: Is the composition and nature of the Others in some way equal and opposite to your existence as the Nine?

TOM: Correct, you understand that.

STEVE: I've now come across two separate statements in the communications about the Others. One statement was: "the Others are not the counterpart of us". Much later you said: "Satan is the opposite side of the coin to us". I find these two statements difficult to understand and reconcile.

TOM: We will try to explain. If you recall, we explained ourselves as being a pivot. And we explained about the positive and the negative, did we not? What in your world you call 'evil' is not a counterpart to us. When we speak of Satan being the other side of the coin, are you prepared to hear what we have to say? As we are in force, then on the opposing pole is Satan. We are attempting to bring what is negative and what is positive into perfection and balance. For it is necessary to have both to make a perfect whole. But on the opposite pole, what you call Satan, wishes not to bring it into balance, for if by bringing it into balance a soul becomes perfect and may live in freedom, Satan cannot live. It only exists and lives from souls that have desire for power, control, manipulation and greed.

IRENE: When were the Others created and why?

TOM: If you could not challenge your own mind, would you be bored?

IRENE: Yes.

Tom: Therefore first there was the thought. Then the necessity to challenge the thought, do you understand?

IRENE: Yes.

Tom: There is your answer.

IRENE: Oh, there's more to it than that. Isn't there? But you want me to find out, what's in my self first, don't you?

Tom: Together in slowness we find out.

IRENE: I want to ask about angels. When you once spoke about angels not having choice, are angels messengers of one of the Twenty-Four?

Tom: Each side has angels.

IRENE: You mean the Others also?

Tom: Yes. There are different appearances of angel.

IRENE: How can we recognise on whose side they are?

Tom: Always look for the golden light. Those angels working for evolution always radiate a golden light. They are messengers from the Creator, they are messengers from the civilisations, and they do not have free choice.

IRENE: Why?

Tom: For they have given their free will to the Creator.

IRENE: So it's another form of service?

Tom: Yes. Much truth has been destroyed to keep the masses in control. People, organisations of government and religion do not suppress any manner of thing unless it is a threat to them, or unless it is truth. Is that not so?

This is the Others at work, since they understand the energies of all creation, and how to use it to make themselves look like God, in order to keep humankind in bondage.

JOHN: In these days of accelerating changes, it seems that on Earth there is a negative reaction against change as well as a positive movement: what is your assessment of this?

Tom: When there is movement in forwardness, all that has been wishes to remain as it was. That is an element within humankind: a portion of humankind has fear, not knowing the future, and also wishes not to give up the known factor. Therefore you have that aspect of negativity. You also have the aspect of negativity from those in power who wish to maintain control and manipulation over others. However, in our assessment it is a remnant that appears to be holding firm, and when its life is being threatened it maintains a stranglehold.

RON: *I would like to find out about the energy of the Others, in distinction to our own negativities that arise within ourselves : is it important to be able to distinguish where this negative energy is coming from, or is there a different way of dealing with it, as it arises?*

TOM: There is within you – which there is in all upon Planet Earth, in different degrees – an amount of negativity. Let us say that if you had a black spot of negativity on the all-white of purity, and then you permitted it to grow such that the white deteriorated, if you looked at the spot as being negativity within you, and accepted it, and permitted it to be dispersed with recognition, and if you thereby came to know your fears, this would be useful negativity. But if it grew out of proportion to your fear, then the Others are attempting to unbalance you. If you are aware of this, remember this: you have a greater power, because you are in a physical existence, but also if you are consciously connected with us, you have an even greater power. When you come into knowledge, wisdom and truth, when all that is in the Universe is slowly beginning to be revealed, then those that desire to control Earth, in order to control the Universe, begin to create great difficulty for you. Coming into knowledge and truth does not make your path easier.

Remember this: to be in service is to pay for that service. For in truth, there are those that would like to remove your awareness and your knowledge. Respect them, do not laugh at them, but be firm in your faith, and they cannot deter you, nor harm you. If they create difficulty for you, then, with your mind, see yourself being swept from the ground to your head with our love, our light, and our joy in you. Do not hesitate to ask for help. Do not proudly do all by yourself. We cannot help if you do not ask. We do not interfere in your free will. But even with all our love for those that are in service to us, and for the sake of all the souls upon Planet Earth, without your asking we cannot help. Be not as proud as Planet Earth has been, for much of its existence, acting independently and wishing to do so on its own. It is in togetherness that the planet Earth will come out of its bondage – togetherness with us, the civilisations in service and the souls in service upon Planet Earth.

JOHN: *If people were left alone and there were no opposing forces, would they tend to do the right thing?*

TOM: Yes. Humanity could overcome its own weaknesses, but these are exploited and increased by the opposing forces. There is temptation, greed and desire.

JOHN: *How did this problem start in the first place, and how was it not checked earlier?*

TOM: It happened because we were not aware of the problems that the physical would create, and we were unaware of the implications of feeling of heaviness and pleasure. We never interfere in free will, so we choose not to intervene, if possible, in what has developed. We were not aware of this because this is the only planet in the Universe that has the physical qualities that create this problem. It does not have a sister planet nor a brother planet. The problem is created within the soul of the individual. The planet is a dense planet, and it in turn then gives a different feeling to the body, but it is actually within the soul of the individual. It feels pain, it feels pleasure, it feels sorrow, it feels happiness. The physical body has different feeling than in all the other planets and in all the other souls that exist. In other systems, other galaxies, there are other physical beings that do not have the density of this planet. Here the soul begins to feel in a different way from the way it felt before, and it has the feel of desire. It has pleasure and pain. Yet this has become very important for the evolutionary growth of the planet, because it was originally the planet of balance.

Here is a very important point illustrated by the Sino–Tibetan conflict:

IRENE: *I realise how important it is that the systematic genocide of Tibetans by Chinese not be allowed; because if the Chinese were allowed to wipe out the Tibetans, that surely becomes an imbalance that could never be balanced again.*

TOM: That is correct. It is important, in your meditations, to work to stop it, for when you permit extinction through deliberate elimination, as also with the extinction of an animal species, it can never be replaced. And then that portion of the matrix becomes a portion where the Others may superimpose.

IRENE: *So it's more than just disappearing, it's allowing the Others to take a stronger hold.*

TOM: That is correct, yes.

IRENE: Well, then we just won't let it happen!

TOM: We thank you, yes. It is necessary to bring into the consciousness of humankind the necessity for worldwide protest over elimination of peoples on Planet Earth. The Others act to attempt elimination through genocidal methods, just as they seek removal of different strains of animal and plant species upon Planet Earth. You humans dedicate yourself to stopping elimination of those endangered species of animal but you do not protest the danger of extinction of endangered species of human-kind. Include exposure of these issues in your meditations. What is of importance is bringing forth that knowledge about genocide and extinction into the conscious viewing eyes of humankind – then they cannot turn away. When it is not spoken of, or when it is pretended that elimination is non-existent, then many negative developments can take place under this decoy.

IRENE: It feels that things are moving quickly, [1989]. There is a balance being affected that those of us who live in the third dimension can't see. What's happening?

TOM: Do you understand the concept that if the awakening comes in its own time there is total destruction and if it comes with acceleration then there is salvation. You have begun the acceleration. It must continue. You also noticed that there is more fanaticism?

JOHN: Yeah.

TOM: That is slowly being dissipated. Yes. The most important thing is for it to be released, for in suppressing it, it grows more violent. Yes.

IRENE: But isn't it also true that as we move forward, the Others...

TOM: Are moving in forwardness towards you, yes.

IRENE: They are attempting to do whatever they can to maintain the imbalance on their side. Fanaticism is one of the tools that they are using..

TOM: That is correct. We have been with you in your sorrows and despairs and agony. And we have also been with you in your joys and your laughs.

At times, in your conscious mind there were doubts that perhaps you would not be able to complete your task, nor benefit those you wish to benefit, nor sustain an emotion to help and serve. We will explain one more thing necessary for your complete understanding. You have doubted yourself, you have doubted your ability and you have doubted that you have the power to accomplish what your soul prompts you to accomplish. From this moment we ask you to remove your doubts. You have the power and love and strength to prevent chaos, tragedy, and loss of life upon your planet – we mean this with all that we are, and we ask you to remove your doubt.

ANDREW: Thank you for that strong reassurance. We do live with doubts, questions, and it is based on the fact that we cannot see the results of our work. For example in our meditations we do everything we can to respond to the needs you describe, but at this moment we have no way of knowing whether we are indeed effective or not. And that is the basis of our doubts, I would say.

TOM: We understand, but there will come a time when even that doubt will be removed. But may we ask you to hold within your heart the faith that you hold in knowing us and knowing that this Universe is not operated by chance nor simply what many of the people on Planet Earth call 'Nature'.May we ask you to remove the doubt that you have with in you? Do you understand?

ANDREW: Yes, I understand, and I think it's a very pointed lesson.

TOM: Can you see God?

ANDREW: I cannot, no.

TOM: Do you believe there is a God?

JOHN: Yes. I absolutely believe that.

TOM: Then if you can believe that, why can you not believe that you have the ability, the energy, and the power and that this energy, ability and power is, of all things, the most important: remember that you have a genuine desire to help, which is different from a desire that controls.

ANDREW: Is there something about the nature of doubt itself, which we need to know?

TOM: It creates a difficulty. If you had within you a giant cable, with millions of minute copper wires, and a few of those wires were weakened, it would not break the cable but it would not be complete. Is this not so?

ANDREW: Yes, it would interfere with communications along the cable.

TOM: That is the essence we speak about. May we say that you have a doubt because in your explanation to yourself and to each other, you cannot comprehend the nature of who you are.

JOHN: I think one of my difficulties is my acute awareness of my inadequacies on a physical level...

TOM: You are not as inadequate as you would like to believe. To believe that you are inadequate may be used at times as an excuse. When there is a difficulty before you, place the situation with us and it will be resolved. Give us those things which you call inadequate, and believe in yourself and that we will help. There are no inadequacies between us. Know that in your heart. Yes.

ANDREW: You see, we have no perspective, that's one of our difficulties in our actions: we do something here on Planet Earth, and we don't see the carry-back from it. Is it possible for you to explain how in any given situation, our doubt has prevented something important from occurring?

TOM: If the cable had a million minute wires and there were those on the peripheral that had a weakness and were broken, this did not make the cable break, but it weakened it and it needed to be shored up. Yes. Now you asked about the results of your meditations, in which we asked you certain things, which you did, but in your mind you are not sure that you have accomplished those things.

ANDREW: Yes. The best example of that is the day we went out to the nuclear reactor centre and we did our meditation, and it was absolutely overwhelming to us. And then when we'd finished we got lost in the dark, and on another day we then had a puncture, within a half-mile of that very spot. And we know that was not just chance, but we still don't know what happened within that complex.

TOM: You prevented an explosion that would otherwise have taken place. If it had taken place you would be not in your physical – you would be returned to us. We cannot prove that to you. But if you have upon your automobile a bubble upon your tyre, and you have within your household a dear person that is loved by you, would you then say to that person it is all right to drive your automobile with a bubble?

ANDREW: *I get the point. I understand what you are saying.*

TOM: Must we have an explosion to prove to you what we say?

ANDREW: *Hmmm...*

TOM: We peer at you and we say at times "They have forgotten who they are, and they are trapped in the thinking of the physical, because in the physical it is necessary to see an object, or to hold an object". But you should know that what you have accomplished in your years was not to be seen before. You have made a difference. We have begun a new time in your land and your Universe, and it is a time for you to remove the string that attaches you to the past time in the physical and to doubt. We know that what we ask of you is much, and we know that it is difficult with those that surround you – we speak of those people that are also in a sense involved with the work – it is difficult to prove to them what you say. They have difficulty believing you. The proof will come in time. Has not proof come to you of the coded knowledge that you have held within you in years past There have been parts that now have been proven in this physical world. Yes?

ANDREW: *Yes, that has come about.*

TOM: Then need we say any more? What do you desire? Do you desire that there would be a phenomenon to prove what we say? May we ask what you desire?

ANDREW: *Well, I speak for myself, but the only thing I desire is to accomplish this mission that we have committed ourselves to. I would like to have the main goal accomplished, which is to let your message be known, and for it to be understood and taken in the best possible way. This is what I desire, and nothing else.*

JOHN: *Well, I feel your question was asking, what did we desire in order to convince ourselves? Most of the time I feel I have that kind of faith and acceptance, but there are periods of doubt when I do feel a desire for some kind of tangible evidence, and then there are other times when that need goes away.*

TOM: When that need comes to you it is because of the physical. May we say that your mission will be accomplished, because within you there is commitment, and there is a growing awareness of beings from outside Planet Earth. And it will not be long before people will begin to ask 'Who are these beings from other worlds?'

II

PLANET EARTH

7

Life on Earth

As Tom says, further on in this chapter "In your world things are very simple, but people make them very complicated". In this chapter Tom often repeats sentences, but with subtle differences interwoven into what, at a casual glance, seems to be a repetition. By the end of the chapter we have been given some brilliant concepts.....

TOM: May we explain to you that your planet Earth is the most beautiful that exists in the Universe. It has a physical variety that no other planet has. In all the Universe there is no planet in existence that has the physical characteristics of Earth. It is the rarest of beauties, and it does attract souls which, once they have come, would continually like to come back again. It is of a different nature from any other planet. It has within it portions of all planets in the Universe, it is like a composite of the Universe, with all the good and all the evil and it is what attracts souls. It has with it a gravitational pull that is different from other planets, and because of this a soul begins to feel – in truth – a physical body – they become in their minds adapted to their physical bodies, and they forget the freedom and pleasures they have without it.

The Earth was created to be a paradise. When souls achieve harmony it will become a paradise again. But when we say a paradise we speak of a paradise of creativity, one that brings knowledge, one that brings joy and love; a paradise in which people may heal themselves or may even experience pain, if they wish. It is not a paradise where all challenge, all growth, or all pain will be removed.

It will be a paradise where people, through their own experience, may evolve their own understanding of their connection with the Universe, accept their own responsibility for themselves, for their fellows, for Earth, and therefore for the Universe, and may bring all of that, including themselves, into perfection. Humankind needs to understand the uniqueness and purpose of Earth, and the directness that it has in its evolution. Humankind needs to understand that it is not alone and there is no death.

What people must begin to understand is that there is no escaping, for in the future of their lives there must be payment. If they also knew that each of them has the quality of greatness in them, and that they have opportunity to be uplifted in joy, and that when there is acceptance of not being alone and of no death, then energies of fear may be released, and energies of joy may replace fear, then Earth may begin to fulfil its position in the Universe.

As well as Earth becoming the greatest of joy, we related before that Earth has the greatest of beauty.

When we say 'beauty' we mean that of the soul which then penetrates the external. Mankind has confused physical beauty as what is seen with the outer shell of the eye; not that of the inner soul of the planet or those that exist upon it. That is also what humanity must learn upon Earth.

JOHN: *Could you explain what the purpose of physical existence is, particularly on this planet?*

TOM: This your planet is a planet of balance, for you to learn to balance between the physical and spiritual worlds. Earth is the only one of its kind, the only planet of free choice in the entire Universe, the only planet created for the balancing of the spiritual with the physical, in other words, the creating of paradise.

Humanity has created corruption within, which came about because people became more involved in physicalness than in attempting to balance and understand. But now your planet is at a point where it may move out of balance quicker than at any other point. This time of history that you are in is the time of change. It is time for humanity to begin to understand this, to live on this planet of great beauty with a true balance of spiritual and physical, and to live in unity with the Creator, in manifestation of love, in connection with the Creator, in that which was created.

JOHN: *This has been the message of many of the world religions, and humanity has never really accepted this. Can you explain why we do not accept this positive message?*

TOM: People in their innermost know, or have a feeling, that they are from something other than just themselves but people upon Earth have gone into competition with the Creator. We understand this, for people understand that there is a nature within them that may do all things, but they neglect to identify and know the Creator. They alone wish to be the Creator. It cannot be. The problem we have had before is that many times we have been to Earth: we have come to help, and it was expected of us to do what we cannot do, what this planet must do for itself. You are a part of this planet because you chose it in order to help it.

JOHN: I really want to say, speaking for myself, that I do really accept the responsibility that we have to do things for ourselves.
It's just that we get a lot of complications and difficulties in living on Planet Earth.

TOM: In your world things are very simple, but people make them very complicated. If you approach things in a simple manner, many things can be overcome and accomplished with a great deal of acceleration, and with not too much use of energy. The worry and the concern burns up more energy than the activity of dealing with the problem.

ANDREW: So here we are on Earth, just a tiny speck of dust in this infinite, vast Universe. Could you tell us why you've taken any interest at all in this little speck of dust here called the Earth?

TOM: In order for the Universe to evolve, it is important for Earth to evolve. The souls that have come to this planet have become irresponsible in their physical bodies. It has become a planet of desire. The souls that are here behave as if they were in quicksand and were being gobbled up and swallowed in this desire. It is important for you to evolve, because without this planet being evolved, the other planets in the Universe are not able to go forward. It has stopped the growth of the Universe. It is important for the level of consciousness of this planet to be raised. It is the love from this planet that generates the energy that feeds God. And this planet has stopped the growth of part of the Universe, instead of evolving in the manner it should, to become one with the Divine. I will explain one step further: many of these souls that live here, when they die, are trapped in the atmosphere of the planet, and then they are reborn over and over on the same world, and they seem to be going nowhere. This planet originally was created to teach balance between the spiritual and the physical world. But in this physical world they got involved in materialism, and so these beings never evolve beyond the belt of this planet. Their desires are still in their minds and emotions, and their desires hold them to this planet, and so you have a multiplication that is going on until this planet will sink.

ANDREW: *Is that why we have so many souls piled up on this planet –
they just can't get beyond it?*

TOM: They cannot get beyond it because of desire, greed, hate, because of enjoying their physical pleasures. And we have no objections
about their physical activities on this planet: it is when this becomes
their primary concern, and they are no longer concerned with evolving
the planet, their fellow humans, or finding their divinity. You explained
this when we listened to you the other day when you called it a
'bottleneck'. We just consulted and decided that if we looked in a
bottle, and if there were a plug, and we could not get it out, that's
exactly what this planet is. Your description was correct.

ANDREW: *Thank you. Could you explain why it is so important that a
few humble beings like ourselves, who are all very simple creatures,
or others like us, can really help to unplug this bottleneck?*

TOM: The energy that surrounds you creates a vortex that then radiates out, and then can raise the consciousness of this planet. Even
though you feel it is an impossible task, it is not an impossible task.
You people chose this situation, you willingly gave yourselves to
come back unto this dense, heavy Earth. People like you have reincarnated on this planet many times, often not because it was necessary, but because you needed to understand and to get the feel of
this planet, in order to raise its level of consciousness. With this
energy, it creates a vortex of love and peace and harmony, and others
will gravitate towards you, so that you may explain to them to help
raise the level. Everything needs an energy base. We are energy, and
through people like you this planet will be saved. We work through
people.

That which was planned for the planet Earth did not come to pass.
While it was discovered that, of all the planets in the Universe, it has
more beauty, more diversification of changes than any other, it was
also discovered that those that lived upon Earth had a great physicalness that was not witnessed on the other planets.

JOHN: *I am a little confused as to where the physicalness came from.*

TOM: From the gravity and the heaviness and the density of the
Planet, and the senses through which you have the feeling of Earth.
These do not exist on other inhabited planets. Souls on Earth began
to feel that they had a substance they did not feel on other planets.

You understand your forms of breeding?

JOHN: *Sex, you mean?*

TOM: Sex in the beginning was a form for breeding, and also it was given sensations within the physical body to make it joyous. But it began to become a priority over the years, and the beginning of control of one human by another. That form of control does not exist on other planets. This heightened the intensity of desire within the subconscious and in the minds of souls that reincarnated on planet Earth. Desire of this kind is not in existence on other planets – it is therefore of great importance that Planet Earth moves into balance.

There is no objection in the Universe for this method of breeding, for that was a decision that this was the way that the planet Earth would re-populate itself. What was an objection is that it became the source of all priorities, and that it came to control all the souls. For if you look upon all those that exist upon Planet Earth, it is the one source that creates much of the difficulty, is it not?

JOHN: *I gather that this was the single planet in which you had this kind of difficulty?*

TOM: Yes. This is the only planet that has created a bottleneck. The souls that live on Planet Earth, in their soul-recycling and reincarnations, refuse to leave Planet Earth. Each of the planets upon which they exist or on which they have a birth is for some form of teaching of them, but they are so much in desire for this physical planet Earth that they do not further themselves. There is temptation, there is greed and there is desire.

JOHN: *How did this problem start in the first place, and how was it not checked earlier?*

TOM: It happened because we were not aware of the problems that the physical would create, and the feeling of heaviness and of pleasure. This is the only planet in the Universe that has the physical qualifications that create this problem. It does not have a sister planet, nor a brother planet.

JOHN: *It is the most dense of inhabited planets in the Universe?*

TOM: Yes.

ANDREW: *I would think if there was this desire and pleasure problem, it could all be traced to the role of say one atomic element, like sodium for example, or something like that. Have you traced it down to something like that?*

TOM: I will consult... I have been informed that the problem is created within the soul of the individual. Earth is a dense planet, and it in turn then gives a different feeling to the body – but it is actually within the soul of the individual.

ANDREW: So you are saying then that the dense material can really influence the soul that much? I didn't think it was possible.

TOM: It feels pain, it feels pleasure, it feels sorrow, it feels happiness. The physical body has a different feeling on Earth than in all of the other planets, and in all the other souls that exist. In other systems, in other galaxies, there are other physical beings that do not have the density of you on Earth. On your planet the soul begins to feel different from what it felt before, and it has the feel of pleasure and desire.

On another occasion, in reply to the same line of questioning, the Nine gave the following example:

ANDREW: Why do souls get stuck on Planet Earth?

TOM: The stuckness is brought about by gravity density and the illusion that the gravity density is reality. The stuckness is emotional: it derives from the inability to remove self from self in the gravitational density. When you remove self from self it creates an unblocking so the emotional gravitational density may be relieved, and the true reality may be viewed. This planet was created to be the paradise and in order for Earth to have all its variety it was necessary to make of it a gravitational density.

ANDREW: Are you saying that for our growth, for our evolution, that gravity is one of the things we must come to terms with, and hopefully conquer it?

TOM: What is important is to balance yourself. It is the merging of the physical with the spiritual that is the manifest purpose of humankind. But humankind has confused itself by remaining in its density and not correctly viewing the nature of its spiritual self.
  It is misinterpreted and misguided by some of the religious leaders of your world, who attempt to control humankind – and the religions that would wish to deny the physical are not in balance, as also are those people of the physical who wish to deny the spiritual. For some

souls, their choosing to be born in this time was not in the evolutionary process of growth for themselves, but in service to this Planet, to bring about the importance of understanding Earth's place in the Universe and of the human beings upon it. There are many who have come to Earth at this time, who chose to come here for the necessity of the Universe, to help, yes.

ANDREW: As we understand from our scientific point of view, is the relationship between gravity as a force and mind as a force where the balance is supposed to occur?

TOM: When you accept, understand in totality, with complete trust and faith in self, in your connections with the Universe, then you bring about the balance and are no longer in bondage. Through the mental process of mind. If you disconnect the mind from what it is holding on to, it will be free. This disconnecting can go by stages, so that you can develop trust and faith in your ability to maintain your inner connection with the Universe. Then you will be free. When the critical mass begins in humankind, when enough of your souls are becoming free, then the space vehicle of Earth moves into its evolutionary fulfilment.

ANDREW: How close are we to that kind of evolutionary time process?

TOM: Know this, that with acceleration due to each human's involvement, it will come quickly and will not be in devastation, as it would be if such acceleration came by itself, by force of circumstance, without your involvement.

ANDREW: That's beautiful.

TOM: You understand, when there is a change that is coming upon Earth, and when there is a loosening up of confinement, that which confines attempts desperately to confine even more?

JOHN: Yes.

TOM: Know this: you all have come to Earth to beautify it, to purify it, to love it and to be in joy with it. Know this: that in your time, through your and others' dedication, through the quality of your being upon Planet Earth, you may bring it to the fulfilment of its creation. That for us is a great joy and we thank you.

The cosmic aspect of this drama is to save Earth in which many souls are trapped. Without the saving of this planet neither we, nor you, know how many thousands or hundreds of thousands of your years, that this planet will then be in a stagnant state. We do not truly know the results of what will happen to the souls of those that are trapped. You understand a sickness, a disease, can spread if it not controlled?

ANDREW: *Yes.*

TOM: Do you understand that if this not controlled and is not handled properly, that this may then contaminate the rest of the Universe? Are you aware of that potential?

ANDREW: *Well, from what you tell us, yes. We don't know from our own experience of course.*

TOM: Do you also know that if the entire Universe was contaminated and if the contamination manifested – all that is good, all that is love would be destroyed – are you aware of this?

ANDREW: *No, we were not aware of this.*

TOM: Because if this contamination should spread from this small physical planet Earth to the rest of the Universe, then all the souls will live in fear and hate, with no hope, in darkness. And there may not be many of us then that can take care of the situation, if it develops to that point.

IRENE: *One of the questions that I wanted to ask had to do with this notion of human suffering, and how it came about. I understand that when humans first walked in innocence, there was probably no human suffering.*

How did it come about, what has its purpose been? Is its purpose tied to the fear that man has of evolving? Why does it exist?

TOM: First know this: Earth is the only planet in the entire Universe of choice. Humankind first walked with the gods, and you know the story of the temptation of the tree of life: they were tempted to experience the joy of unity with the oneness of creation. Then the Creator said 'That is forbidden to you.' Nevertheless permitted the choice to be made if humankind so chose. They did that choosing. From that day forward, it is not the Creator that has punished, but humankind has punished itself, for they touched in truth the knowledge of who they were, and it frightened them, for they knew that they were not in the state to comprehend completely.

It became necessary then to populate Earth, so that all the cells of the Creator could become individuals and free souls, in order for them to become one in unity and harmony by choice. Therefore also Earth is the only planet of conscience, and people chose to feel the emotion of sadness that they had destroyed that trust that was placed in them, and they began then to sacrifice self and their children. It is time to end this farce of sacrifice, for that is what it is, it keeps them in bondage. Release humankind!

IRENE: So some religious leaders then exploited this guilt?

TOM: Exactly. They exploited, for it was a means of holding people in bondage. Listen carefully: when there is one who understands the energies of all the created and how they may utilise those energies to make themselves a god, then they keep people in bondage.

IRENE: In the beginning, why did the Creator forbid man from the knowing?

TOM: What was important was for humans to begin without being forbidden to know, but with choice and trust.

IRENE: So the idea was not 'You can't have the knowledge', the idea was 'All right, here's the first example of choice, I'm saying you can't have it, now you have a choice whether to obey or to disobey'.

TOM: That is correct, and also understand that when you obey it is an exercise, then you no longer need to obey.

IRENE: The idea being that obedience doesn't sacrifice free will, it in fact promotes it because you don't give obedience that importance.

TOM: That is the great truth. Yes.

MIKI: Some people seem to carry much heavier burdens than others, suffer more than others. Is this only to give those souls an opportunity to learn a certain lesson, or teach others, or is it misfortune?

TOM: In your world each of those that you have mentioned are applicable. There are some, because of their surrounding environmental state of awareness, or the technology within your world, that have created great misfortune. None in this time-period in reality chooses to suffer: it is brought about by the wrong thinking of those in control of others. There is but a small minority that choose to suffer to teach others.

MIKI: I believe that the Creator knows everything in present and in future. How can humans then use their free will? Can you give me an understanding of this?

TOM: Yes. Just as the Creator is all-knowing, each soul is all-knowing, and there are different paths that each soul may take. At the time of coming to the planet Earth, they made their map, they limited themselves in their choice, but they did bring with them a map, so they would have a choice whether or not to follow that map. Because the Creator knows all does not mean that there is interference in the lives of humans.

If your children were in the privacy of their sleeping quarters, you would not think of entering indiscriminately upon them, for there may be private things that they do, and you would not choose to humiliate them, nor to invade their privacy deliberately, is that not so? You are a creator. You created your children. As the parent in the creation of those children you attempt to guide them. And at times you impose your will upon them for their protection.

The Creator simply jogs your mind, but does not impose upon you. The Creator probes you, to attempt to jog you to follow one of your directions that you once chose. If you choose a direction, and in your deliberations you choose to go in an opposite direction, there is no interference. But in reality, because your privacy is not invaded, the Creator does not choose to see what you will do. That knowledge is kept until the time of your doing it, and afterwards. If you imposed your will upon your children by insisting that the door of their quarters of sleep be open at all times, so you can view them, and if you chose to go in upon their privacy, then you know what your children would do, do you not? They would protect themselves against you. In the same way, the Creator chooses not to keep your door open or to invade it deliberately.

Sometimes, over the years, what the group were led to expect did not occur, and this has created questions, of which the next exchange is an example:

JOHN: I'd like to say that if you are who you say you are, then you can be anywhere in time, in past, present, and future. And how is it then, that you've told us that some things would happen, and they had not happened? If you can be in the future then you would also know that something would either happen or not. Could you explain this phenomenon to me so I can understand it more clearly?

TOM: We will attempt to explain it in this manner: we are sitting upon a mountain – visualise this within your mind. When we sit upon this mountain, we have a view of the entirety of Earth. Underneath us sit other mountains which you cannot see through with your eyes for you are in a physicalness. We could view what is behind us, that which you call the past, as complete. We can remember what it was like on the other side of the mountains in the past. In front of us, we can see other mountains, but we cannot see behind them, only over and between them. And when you come down from the mountain, to go into the future, you cannot see over the whole landscape. As you come around a mountain, you will find several roads or tracks, each leading into the future. If there are blockages in all but one of the paths, then there is only one path to take. But if you know how to remove a blockage, you may then take another path. And you will have greater choice.

There is never just one future. There are several choices of future. This is involving your will. If we know what is the future then that means that we in truth have become involved, and have manipulated your free will. It is not for us to be involved with your free will, or with manipulation. We see many futures. As an example, we will use your country (Britain). If before your World War [1939-45] your Churchill had not been in stable health or had been assassinated, then the future of your nation in the end may have been mostly accomplished, but not in the same manner. And it could have completely changed the future of your country. If it had not proceeded as it had, there could have been a big difference. We understand that this is not a satisfactory answer in an explanation but we know not a way to explain. We are not pre-ordaining your future.

JOHN: *Yes, I understand better. I think it was a product of my misunderstanding, that when you said such and such would happen, I assumed that this was a certainty, and I should have seen that as one of several possibilities.*

TOM: This was our error, not yours. If we had related to you a failure and error on our part, we had concern that you would not be able to sustain your involvement and efforts.

There is one situation we will guarantee to you from us: we will not permit the destruction of the Earth. It is not the civilisations of Twenty-four that will not permit it, for it is not possible for them to prohibit it. It is only possible for us to not permit it – for they also have limitations. But in using our power with theirs we would not permit the destruction of Earth. When we say this, we mean the total destruction of the Planet, yes.

8

Accelerating Earth's Evolution

The first part of this chapter addresses specific issues and then when Irene joins in the discussions take a philosophical turn, as she explores with Tom, various ideas and attitudes. The chapter lives up to its title, it feels as if it is speeding up....

JOHN: *I think the most important question to people on Earth at this time is, what can they as individuals do, and how can they as individuals make things different, so that our planet fulfils its destiny?*

TOM: First and foremost they must recognise that each of them contains the entire universe within themselves. Each of them contains all creation. Therefore when they understand that, then hopefully they will understand that if they go against their own integrity, the integrity of the Universe may be affected. They must consult within themselves for their motive in all actions; they must learn to love themselves, and the only way they may love themselves is never to do what they will dislike themselves for. What is important is that each person upon this planet earth must understand that there is existence elsewhere. They must understand that they hold the key to the evolutionary process in the Universe. It is a time of awakening. It is a time to understand that within the self they hold the key for bringing Earth to its fulfilment and that free will is never interfered with; the destruction of Planet Earth is not necessary. This must be understood clearly, for the free will of humankind can bring fulfilment to Earth.

JOHN: *Many have talked of a coming transformation, and it seems we are approaching this time. Can you say anything about such a transformation and what that means?*

TOM: It is true that Earth is on the threshold of transformation. It is on the threshold of releasing souls and beings from bondage, so they may continue to elevate, and purify Earth so the Universe may continue its path. It is a glorious time right now to live on your planet in physical form. Know always that this energy of individuals will remain individual, but what will be understood is the power of thought, the energy of love, the power that humans hold within themselves to make your world a representation of the Universe. Your world is a glorious place for all portions of the Universe to exist, and to fulfil, and to be at one with creation, in great joy.

JOHN: *If you had one message that you wished to pass to all of mankind, what would that message be?*

TOM: Know fully that you hold the key within yourself, each of you humans, to bring about change. It is your responsibility, your free will, your choice.

JOHN: *Now there are at this time many confusing messages coming from different psychic and prophetic sources. What are the criteria that people should use to discern between these different sources?*

TOM: First and foremost we explain in this manner: as there are corporation heads, one of which knows all, and different divisions underneath which know the area of expertise of their department, it is the same in the realm of communication from those who exist in other realms. A few sources know all of the picture, and many know parts of it. But be careful when they make you glorious: always challenge, look for consistency, and never accept that that goes against your natural inclination or your higher intuitive self. Be careful they do not feed your ego in order to manipulate you, for there are also those who would wish the destruction of Planet Earth. Do not fall into the trap that Planet Earth will be destroyed.

In your world there are many that speak, many that bring forth information: we bring forth to you information that has not been brought forth in time past, and it is the next step of forward evolutionary movement. It is important for the peoples upon Planet Earth to understand they are not alone, and that they carry within them the coding that can evolve Planet Earth to achieve its proper purpose.

Remember this: those who seek to control are in high profile in the front of society and lead people in a direction that helps them evade their own responsibility. But bear in mind that acceleration is now absolutely important. We have come to the beginning of acceleration of evolutionary forwardness of Planet Earth.

There is a great necessity to accelerate, for the oceans of Planet

Earth, the trees and forests, the skies and atmospheres, the very essence of breathing, the life-force, have reached a level of contamination bringing the downward destruction of Earth. We call upon your energies and commitment for alerting the peoples of this planet, the governments of Earth and the communities of Earth. The innermost core of humankind is beginning to grow and to glow. The essence and understanding of their beginnings is awakening, to bring about change. You are part of that change. You are children of that change, you are responsible for that change. Without your commitment to acceleration, if the change were to come in its own time, without your input, then the planet would be in a situation in which most of humankind could not exist. Accept your ability to create the pattern that brings about understanding and the truth of who you are.

Earth was created to be the paradise of all paradise in its perfection. It is time for forgiveness, forgiveness of self: for humankind to understand that to maintain fear and dissension is to maintain annihilation. Humankind has begun the process of annihilation. Yet there is a great future for the fulfilment of the destiny of Earth.

Accept that you have a part to play in bringing it to fulfilment. You have no limitation. Your limits and boundaries are created only by your fears. This does not mean that you should climb a thousand-meter mountain and then plunge off it. It means that you must have practical application of understanding of yourself, in truth. It means that you must begin to extend yourself in the capacities of your mind and thoughts.

Your physical bodies have limitations upon this physical planet, but your minds and thoughts can expand and grow, touch all corners of the Universe. And when it understands the truth of self, it can relieve the burdens of this physical world that have held it in bondage. You humans are a kaleidoscope, and will appear at times confused – yet with one turn you can become elements of beauty and purity, and with that you may travel the spheres of the Universe.

JOHN: *Now, if we were to imagine for a moment that everything remained in a static state, humanity did not improve its consciousness, understanding of the environment, and responsibility, it would be valuable for us to understand how long it would be before we would actually totally destroy our environment..?*

TOM: With regards to the atmosphere surrounding the planet Earth, you have no longer than 20 to 25 of your years of existence. Without oxygen there cannot exist life upon your planet Earth. If the peoples upon your planet Earth do not come into sensibleness, they will eliminate   themselves.

The above reply was given in 1978. The following exchange took place in 1989:

ANDREW: You used an interesting phrase earlier, that "time is accelerating". What's the real meaning of the acceleration of time?

TOM: If this planet were to pursue its course in the way it is doing, without acceleration, then you know that that would bring destruction?

ANDREW: Yes.

TOM: What is now accelerating, due to the meditations humans have done on this planet Earth, is the beginning of the acceleration of time, which then creates the situation that Earth becomes a light-space vehicle, and humankind will become suddenly aware. It will be similar to the 'hundredth monkey effect' beginning. So if you now begin to understand the power of meditations in small groups such as yours, you can change the world.

and in 1989 this question was asked, concerning famine:

ANDREW: One of the things I observe is that there is more and more hunger on this planet, and riots because of the shortage of food and high prices. What can little people like us do in that particular area?

TOM: It is not necessary for anyone upon this planet to die from lack of nourishment. It is only because of ignorance, or because of the governments of the world attempting to control others. We will not permit the extinction of any groups of humans. You understand? But you must now incorporate it in your meditations – through meditation you may prevent the destruction.

IAN: How are the chances of evolution on this planet? How are the chances of survival?

TOM: There has never been a time in the past as there is now to bring forth the evolution of your planet. All things are possible, and change may come with rapidity. We will give you an example: one year ago

[1987] in the nation of Israel, at the time of Passover, the people of Israel were devastating the nation with litter. It was a sight that brought great sadness. And in one year, what has evolved in the nation of Israel is what is called a miracle upon Earth, for during this time it was cleaned up, no debris, and people found greater respect for themselves and others. If this can happen in the nation of Israel, which is largely stubborn, then whatever you choose to do can be done! The movement for change is in motion – those who know may stop the malignancy of hunger upon Earth, and can also stop catastrophe brought about by man, and can make your planet what it was created for.

IAN: How much are you supporting and influencing evolution, and the people who want to help evolution?

TOM: When anyone asks the question 'What can we do?' we are there. You see, we cannot do an iota of movement until a person asks. We may not, cannot, and will not, interfere in free will. But when a human asks – and at times they only ask in joviality, they do not mean it from the depths of their soul – then we may help them to evolve. It is important for people to be aware they are not alone in the Universe, and also that they must take responsibility, for they cannot escape responsibility.

JOHN: Could you give a word of advice to individuals, because many people say 'Well, what can I personally do?'. Is there some small thing that individuals can contribute?

TOM: It is very simple: behave only in a manner that you may love yourself for; behave only in a manner in which you would wish another to do toward you; do no movement, thought, or thing that you in your soul, in your consciousness, cannot have self-respect for. When that begins, then all will change. All will change also when people accept that also those that live elsewhere in the Universe are available to give to you love and understanding. All will change when people understand the energies within.

We have been working very hard – though that is not the proper word because we do not really work, but in your world there is no word, so I will use that one. We have been working to prevent the crisis, and we have not at this point [1974] been successful. Many things have been set into motion many thousands of years ago. But we wish you also to realise that there are things which were not part of the planning, and which are human things, that come about by greed and vanity and desire. We speak of the governments that control the world, that create the crisis. It was not part of the plan, do you understand?

ANDREW: Yes, we do, and we appreciate this discussion.

TOM: The time has come for the people of the Earth to demand from their governments, to demand from their religious leaders, to demand from their teachers, knowledge and understanding of what is truly happening. It is now the time of the people.

Beforehand your governments and your religions and society kept your masses in ignorance and kept humankind tied down. Acceleration will cause those in your world to demand answers from their scientific community, and their authorities. But the way to reach people, we have finally decided, is through their own physical body and the healing of their physical body. Many people will be healed and many people will become open to healing. It is through healing that the consciousness of the wider Universe will be raised. It is important for humankind to know that it must begin to take responsibility for Earth, and that science must begin to understand that it does not hold within it the power to dictate to the rest of humankind, but it is only a portion of humankind. In its elitism, science has discarded the other echelons of humankind. Science has become the religion that manipulates and controls, and those who lead science must now begin to accept their responsibility.

It is a sad time for the world because, as in past times and in emotional times, the physical beings of this planet blame all others except themselves for their problems – which are in truth caused by themselves. It is as if in order to exonerate themselves they would cause a blemish upon another, and they would throw them into a pit of snakes. They will in fact be ashamed at another time , but that has been the history of Earth. We cannot have that in the future, nor at this time. It is a time for each individual, each nation, to stop and to respond, and to realise that it is within them that the blame lies, not with others. How can the nations exist in peace when the people do not exist in peace within themselves?

ANDREW: Yes, that is the big question: how can every person find peace in his or her own heart?

TOM: Can you find the peace within your own heart?

ANDREW: No, I have great difficulty, but I think I am possibly in better shape than many people.

TOM: Are you sure?

ANDREW: For myself I say so, yes.

TOM: Then you have made a great step, and we would say yes, you have found peace.

JOHN: It would be enormously helpful to us if we could get from you some kind of picture of the ideal Earth, say 50 or 100 years from now. What kind of things in a material and physical sense would we expect to see on such a planet?

TOM: It would be a planet of balance that would have the eye-views of beauty and peace and gentleness of colour. There would be gentleness and peace among the species upon this planet Earth in the care of humankind but most importantly would be the challenge to humankind in its peaceful, joyful existence to create a quality of existence that will bring forth the information and knowledge of the great joy of oneness in the Universe. When humankind thinks of love and joy and peace and music and colour and balance, things will be very different. People have become so adapted to believing that they need strife, conflict and arrogance, that they have fear of boredom. We promise you, it will not be. There will be no time for boredom, for the challenges that will exist upon this planet Earth as the exemplary paradise, and expansion of the Universe will continue for eternity. Therefore there is always new knowledge, new colour, new sound: there is an ecstasy in the perfection of Earth that is not induced by other means. However, it is not and will not be, a place of continuous holiday, we tell that to you.

JOHN: Can I ask two practical questions: in some way I believe the environment will change, and it will become richer and more lush in terms of plant life, is that..?

TOM: That is correct. For negative energies negate life.

JOHN: And in some sense that will be used to overwhelm the ugly structures of today, which will be...

TOM: That is correct. They will have a portion remaining to remind of antiquity times...

JOHN: And one other thing is the question of transport. There is massive amount of physical movement around the planet, of people and things, and that contributes a great deal to the destruction of our environment. Will there be less physical movement because of alter-

native means of communication?

Tom: Not less movement, for there will be the custom of knowing different areas upon Earth and travel to them. But transport will take a form that will not congest, pollute or destroy. Know this: Earth will not look the same in each place, therefore it will be necessary still to have travel, yes... it will be possible to travel.

JOHN: It seems to me that there will probably be a deterioration and breakdown of institutions, economics, political and social balance, and so on, and I feel that this process will probably begin fairly soon: is this a general indication?

Tom: But do you have the knowledge of why?

JOHN: Well, I feel that this is something that has to happen before we can build anew. Is that so?

Tom: This is a partial possibility. But let us explain to you, that the difficulties in your economic systems, with pollution in your air and streams and earth, with pollution within the spirit world surrounding the Earth, and with the desire within souls for the things taken within them to give them an untrue sense of who they are [drugs] — these manifestations are also the beginning of the breakdown.

JOHN: What about the future of schools and education?

Tom: Here there can be breakdown. There are reasons for there not to be an ongoing education. The human mind is rebelling because of poisons, but also it cannot absorb the knowledge in public education, which has not truth. This has been a process: if you will review your systems of education, through the last twenty to thirty years [up to 1975], there has not been improvement but only deterioration. For it had not the benefit of the soul.

Council says I have not answered your question, your assumption that some kind of breakdown is necessary before reconstruction: the answer is affirmative. At this time balance must be accomplished because the Earth that you exist on cannot continue many more of your years. Within two hundred of your years there will be an ice age on this planet if something is not done, and then the souls, who have been bottled and trapped on this planet, will for ever be trapped. This is because of the negativity they are involved with and the selling of their souls. They will not be able to evolve and to understand, because they will be constantly involved with the desires and sufferings of the physical. Beside the challenges that are coming in your immediate future with your many world problems, with your pollution, the problems of your food, and the problems of your governments, remember this which we tell you: within two hundred years of your life this planet will be frozen. The reason that we come, and the reason for the work you do, is to make people aware, so we then can save the souls on the planet, and stop the problem that has been created for the Universe. This is now a dangerous time that we are in [1975], and the negative energy is building.

Back to technological aspects of our evolution:

With our technology we will be able to help rid the Earth of the problems that your pollution and your technology have created.

ANDREW: Can you give us a thumbnail sketch as to how this knowledge will be transferred from your world to our world?

TOM: It will be necessary for us to become visible and physical on your planet. There is not enough time to give this data, and for you to work out the technology, and the years that it will take. As you know, this planet will not be able to sustain itself. Its waters will be polluted, its earth will not produce the food necessary. And the Earth will be crowded with beings and the souls that keep reincarnating on it, because they remember their physical desires of eating, of breeding, of their touches – this is really the reason that they are trapped within the ether of this planet.

ANDREW: If somebody came to me tomorrow in all good faith and all willingness, and said "Yes, I accept what you say as true, that these things are happening as you say they are happening, and what can I as a single individual do in a practical way to help reverse this trend?" what would your advice be?

TOM: If this individual believes it and then tells another, and that one tells another, and that one tells yet another, then things can change. Remember there will be many that will be coming to people like you and asking questions. This will be a time for the masses: this will not be a time for the governments, nor the religions, nor the societies to control the masses. The masses will be told – they will be told on your radio, your TV, and your publications. And they will hear, and they will listen, because the evidence will be about them.

ANDREW: So, it is a matter of believing that you exist and acting thereon. Is that the essence of the message?

TOM: This is true. Because without acknowledging our existence then we cannot help you. And the preparation will be to bring to people the knowledge that we will help, and that we can help, and that we do not create a problem, that we only come to help, in love and peace. And there will be many of the masses that will not understand the life-form of which we speak. They will not be able to understand the cosmos and the bottleneck that this planet has created. But remember: this is not always necessary. The fact that we do exist, and the fact that they accept this, and the fact that they will see that we come with no harm, that we come with love, is what matters. And when we help this planet in technology, we can also spread truth and love, so the souls of this planet can then evolve and can prevent the problems, which are turning the Universe inside out.

ANDREW: If the knowledge of all this is to spread through TV and publications, and the like, how will peoples living simple lives, without access to mass communications, such as in many parts of Africa and Asia, get to know about this?

TOM: They will not need to know because they already know. When you speak of Africa or Asia, they are not aware of exactly what, but they know there is something happening. Also the religious leaders of India are very much aware that something is happening. It is the advanced countries, the so-called developed countries, that create the problem.

If Planet Earth can be saved – and it will be saved – the entire Universe will be raised to a level in which all souls will have gained the nature of what they have searched for from the beginning of time. And remember that when the souls of the Universe have calmness and joy and peace within their hearts, and generate this love, it overtakes even those souls that are negative and dark, and brings life and love to them.

Can you imagine that when you accomplish what you have come to this planet to do, the entire Universe will be glowing with a light that will seem to be blinding, because it will be a light of pure love. All will become one, and that is what all have striven for. We ask only that you never, even in your darkest moments, even when you are disturbed with each other, even when you are disturbed with nations and with peoples, that you never lose sight of what we have related to you. When we look over the planet now, we see only a small glow here and there, and there are many dark areas, but we know that what you have come to Earth to do, when it is accomplished, will be a releasing of pure love in the entire Universe.

IRENE: *We were talking earlier about rules. I would like to go further with you, and this is all from instinct. I believe that there are no rules any longer. Now there may be rules as you understand them, but rules as we understand them no longer exist because of the level that we're moving toward. I also believe that this isn't the first time that all of us humans have experienced this, though you have a clearer memory of it, let's say, than we do, will you accept that?*

TOM: But we all have memories.

IRENE: *Okay, well we move along. Yes, we were all here before.*

TOM: That is correct, and your memory is correct that you were here in times before when there were no game-rules, you are in absolute correctness for there are no – what you term – ground-rules.

IRENE: *Exactly. And it is our humanness that will allow us to make the evolutionary leap (once we understand completely) that we weren't able to make the last time.*

TOM: That is correct. What is operating from your inner self is your trust, your faith, your inner knowledge and the beginning within of the comprehension of existence in times past, and the accountability that will evolve of necessity.

IRENE: *All right. What is happening, as I believe it, is that we have evolved within our own humanness to a point where it is now necessary to integrate the spiritual with the humanness.*

TOM: That is correct, this is what Earth is for.

IRENE: *That this alchemy, if properly put together, will bring about the transformation.*

TOM: That is correct. Until Earth becomes a light-space vehicle. That is immortality for ever.

IRENE: *Once humankind accepts their joy and that they no longer have to suffer to survive, they don't have to worry about being bored when paradise is regained. You dropped a realisation into my head, which is that when one looks at the history of humankind, one realises from the earliest days they have set up problems, wars, disagreements, fighting, death, killing etc., just so that they could overcome it, then they can have a moment of peace, and then it's disrupted again. What can we do to break this pattern? How do we begin? Now I know it also has to do with the integration of phys-icality, spirituality, etc. But what else is going on there?*

TOM: You see: what is necessary is to take inbuilt human courage that became arrogance, and return it to courage again. The courage to be who you truly are, without the arrogance that was felt to be necessary because people believed they were special. Yes. Now, include that in your meditation, for when people begin to understand, then you humans will accelerate. Do you now understand?

IRENE: Yes. So courage becomes one of the cornerstones of the human foundation for the elevation?

TOM: And charity.

IRENE: And?

TOM: Compassion.

IRENE: And?

TOM: Kindness.

IRENE: So those are the foundations. And it's upon those that we are to build our structure. It is from that that we can connect to other-worldliness.

TOM: You see, what that creates is what people term 'a high'....

IRENE: At the same time that we're discussing this, there is something else that is also existing, in another time and place?

TOM: Correct.

IRENE: We and you, together, can make that connection.

TOM: Correct.

IRENE: I can only get this far! There is something about the connec-tion that has to do with reality outside the one that we know. What you're talking about is a foundation to build a human structure, but at the same time we must have a corollary in another space and time...

TOM: This is correct.

JOHN: What can you tell us about that other reality?

TOM: It is the mirror. Do you understand that the film, when it is removed from you...

IRENE: *Wait a minute, wait. So what you're talking about is that in that other space and time — so ridiculous words become — there will come a time when we'll just be able to communicate with thoughts, right?*

TOM: Exactness.

IRENE: *Yeah, but we're not there yet.*

TOM: That is correct. And then you will go on for ever and ever and ever and there is not an end to eternity. When you look in two mirrors together what do you see? You see yourself forever.

IRENE: *Right.*

TOM: Know also, energy builds, creates, it also encourages and it enforces... You need to remove the film from yourselves which is the film-image of Earth which holds you in bondage. From the beginning, which is guilt — you understand the serpent, in the Garden of Eden?

IRENE: *The 'One', prior to creation had a knowing. Out of this knowing came many things, among them the desire to create, or perhaps recreate, Earth. I'm skipping steps: Adam and Eve in the garden. The lessons of obedience, the understanding of free will and the exercise of free will in the choice of disobedience.*

TOM: The importance also is the exercise of free will in obedience. You see the opposites?

IRENE: *Absolutely.*

TOM: Yes. What you must understand is that you yourself must uncover this revelation. As each of you must be revealed.

JOHN: *I don't understand what you mean by 'be revealed.'*

TOM: When you understand that, then you understand what we had said.

JOHN: *(Sighs)*

TOM: This is not an exercise in gaming. It is an exercise in developing your mental process of thinking for yourself.

JOHN: *Right now my brain is like a scrambled egg!*

TOM: When you understand who you are, then all that we are, the knowledge within us then may be transferred completely to you.

IAN: *Isn't it true that parts of us will be revealed in the process of structuring?*

TOM: That is correct.

IAN: That we don't need to bother about these hypothetical things?

TOM: That is exactness. When you begin this, then there is revelation in many. For this your world, this Universe also, had to be structured. Now is the beginning of days of great importance for you, but most important for us. You will heal yourselves and Earth. The beginning of the healing lies with those that have been through self and removed themselves from blocking. Understand our great love for you, our great joy in you, and remember and understand, we wish Earth to know of our love and of our existence. We give to you love, we bring to you peace and we are in gratefulness that you are with us. We leave you now.

9

Crossroads

This is about our choices, and the way our behaviour reflects throughout our planet. It is about our attitudes to materialism, ecology. And while the first of Tom's speeches appears to be a repetition from a previous chapter, once again, there is an addition....

Tom: Earth, with the human existence upon it, is a giant bottleneck in the Universe. The physical planet Earth is the the most physical in the universe and it is the most beautiful because it has such diversity. Those that exist upon Earth that have existed upon other planets – when their birth is brought to this planet, those souls must develop balance between the physical and spiritual.

But on Earth souls become, because of the density, more physical, and when their physical bodies disintegrate into the Earth, the spirit of them has no desire to leave the planet – it has caused a 'recycling'. And each of the recyclings causes them to have more desire and enjoyment of more pleasures.

We have no objection to this, if in this method there would in truth evolve a balance with the nature of the Planet and its purpose would be taught and assimilated. When this recycling began, there were those from other planets that had the need to come to Earth and so you have had population explosions of entities coming in. As well as in physicalness on the planet they exist in the chakras of the planet and in the spirits surrounding the planet. And they have within them, the desire for recycling.

Miki: I'm involved in a campaign aiming to end all starvation by the end of the century, and I would like to know about our primary goal. Is it to feed all the people on Earth, no question about the number, or is it rather to limit the number of people?

Tom: When your planet has brought itself into balance through service, of yourselves and others, when it is then evolved to a higher

115

vibration, then the population explosion will also diminish, for negative energies will not then be in a form where they may then overpower a normal balance of positive and negative energies.

When all are peaceful within themselves with regards to fulfilment of bodily needs, that also will be a stabilising factor in the nonproliferation of people being born. Then of the greatest majority will be evolved souls, to form your planet Earth in the true paradise that it is meant to be. Yes.

JOHN: *I know you have some difficulty with our number system, but there are five billion people on this planet at the moment: what is the level that the planet could comfortably sustain, with reference to what you've just said?*

TOM: It could be, without difficulty, if the greatest majority were in a state of evolution, with regard to all supplying [of food, materials and resources], nine billion. You understand the primary importance in relieving hunger? It is an energy in a thought-form. When the concept of ending hunger begins to be understood, and it should be spoken of, if enough believe in it, then it becomes a reality. It is important that the power of that kind of thinking be understood. When that is understood, all things are possible.

MIKI: *Yes. So the true purpose of our project, is creating the consciousness that starvation can be ended, is this the main work to be done to finally end starvation?*

TOM: Yes. It is of great importance. In order to keep people with that focal point within, it is important that there be some form of publication to assure them that they have meaning and that it will be accomplished. The fact that there are now committees of cabinets in government examining this question is a by-product, and is needed in order for the world to believe that there is motion. The most important matter is for each individual upon your planet, no matter which division they are in, to understand that they are part of a whole, and they also make a difference, for if you take a drop of water and make enough drops of water you soon have a collection of a pond. That pond then can breed life when it is in togetherness, you understand   that?

MIKI: *Very well, yes. Thank you.*

ANDREW: *Concerning catastrophe: is cataclysm more or less ordained and in the works? Is what you are speaking about just mitigating the effects that will be felt, or is it a fundamental solution?*

TOM: Each of you has free will. Each of you of your civilised world can work with the energy of positive belief. An example: if you have approximately one hundred people, those hundred people can turn the tide of one million. Do you understand?

ANDREW: Yes. We understand that such a ratio works when you have the proper light and purity to dissolve the darkness.

TOM: Yes. So therefore that does not mean there has to be catastrophe.

ANDREW: It's not inevitable?

TOM: It is a time of transformation upon this planet. It is not ordained.

ANDREW: Yes. Well, right now we're having unusual weather phenomena. We're having floods, droughts, we're having many little things, but they hit particular parts of the planet very hard. For example, there have been more volcanoes go off than previous records show. There is a cloud circling the globe which is supposed to contain tons of sulphuric acid − well, this is devastating. Where do these phenomena come from? Is that just part of the Earth process, or man process, or external influences..?

TOM: That is not natural, it was brought about by man interfering in atmospheres.

ANDREW: I see, it's our misuse of the planet that's bringing all this about?

TOM: Yes. And you have grass-roots movements within your country, and other countries, of small, micro-peoples that are fighting to dissipate the power of those organisations which bring pollution. They will succeed if they continue with that thought.

If humankind does not revert to utilising all that exists upon Earth in a manner of non-destructiveness, it is not you that will be in bleakness but your youngest ones. Humankind has a responsibility not only for this planet Earth, but for the Universe, as Earth is of the greatest necessity for the survival of the Universe. We wish you to understand the great importance of your human destructive element in removing oxygen from this planet, in destroying dolphins through hunting and in the contamination of the waters on your Earth.

There are those nations that lack the source of life: water. Envision this happening to all of Earth through the destruction of oxygen provided by your plant life. Then take that a step further and understand that the pollution-destruction of your oceans then eliminates all possibility for rebuilding Planet Earth. For there exists different means of removing salinity to rebuild those nations that do not have the source of life [water], but if your oceans are in contamination and poisonous with your chemicals, then how can you rebuild?

You have two thresholds and you have the choice as to which you pass through. You are Planet Earth. And the peoples of Earth must begin to take responsibility. It is your youth's future.

As you know, on your planet, there are upheavals in humankind, and also upheavals in the physical aspect of Earth, with its eruptions and its corruptions: the entity of Earth is attempting to purify and cleanse itself. And there is the burning of the Planet by your sun, brought about by the corruption of your ozone layer protection. Therefore you must understand the power of your mental and emotional capability to change things for the better. As you have power to create a situation to protect the Earth, there are those who have power to attempt to negate Planet Earth, in ignorance, not often deliberately through pollution and error. Therefore it is now the time to bring people together in meditation to re-weave the canopy that surrounds Earth, so this planet will not be burned, or bring about destruction or illness.

JOHN: What you're indicating here is that the ozone layer is the most serious immediate problem facing Earth right now?

TOM: That is correct. You can all create a weaving with waves, and your scientists will see the effect of it.

JOHN: Are CFCs the principal negative factor, as described by environmentalists, or are there other factors affecting the atmosphere that we do not understand?

TOM: Your planet Earth, in itself, creates gases that create a problem for your atmosphere, but then humankind compounds it, by raising so many meat-fodders – animals create gas emissions, and humankind creates gas. Therefore, it may seem inconsequential to you, but the forests that chose to come as forests are removed, and then animals are placed on the land, so you have a doubly dangerous situation. Therefore, is it not good for each of you to incorporate every means possible to remedy this, to create less movement, to create fewer emissions of gas, to correlate your space and time so as not to use unnecessary gas-making equipment, or to create processes that do not emit gas?

Put a small shift in the mind, and you humans will also understand that you can release yourselves completely from all this bondage to what you believe are necessities – for when you understand who you are, you will fly with your own wings. We use an analogy, to explain that you each have the power to make a complete difference upon Earth in creating a shift. However, if people do not want the responsibility of it, then they say it is not possible. Then there is more of a problem.

GUEST: *So does this also imply a major change in the diet of people on Planet Earth?*

TOM: A complete change cannot happen upon Planet Earth at this time, for those of humankind of certain natures cannot exist without the proteins of animal. What is necessary is an educational process, for people to understand that they have enough protein of animal, and that all must be balanced. There is ingestion of so much protein of animal that is not in balance, therefore the raising of animals is out of proportion to the need. It will take many generations until the time has evolved where people no longer need to eat animals. There are those people and cultures that do not need it – they have evolved to that point – but to others this would bring about sickness.

However, the gas substances, like those made when you make noises, can be used in conversion into energy of the gases from animals: it is the waste from animals and people that releases this gas.

JOHN: *Rotting vegetation from plants and forests also produces this..?*

TOM: That is correct, and when you do the clearing of the land you release more gases.

Do you know you can bring about correction through world unification, for bringing Planet Earth into balance and order? It is of great importance to mend the holes in the ionosphere, through the effort of all nations. It is of great importance to understand those nations that must have the balance brought back, for when these nations have gone out of balance internally, it is then shown externally. Insidious diseases begin to bring the downfall of humankind. For humankind is not in balance, and microbes of destructiveness do not permit humankind to live to the fulfilment of its destiny, in bringing this planet Earth to its rightful position. If you want to really concentrate on bringing a change in your countries in this arena, change the heads of the medical profession, and bury them like the ostriches, but do not permit them to surface.

ANDREW: *They're tough old birds. (Laughs)*

TOM: You must take responsibility for stopping the devastation, beginning with yourself, extending it to your family, and including your community, to stop the disruption of those resources which exist for the benefit of humankind and its paradise.

JOHN: *There is discussion about the extent to which the weather pattern changes are caused by environmental degradation, or whether part of it at least is caused by longterm cycles of weather patterns. Are these changes man-made or cyclic?*

TOM: A combination of the two. But it is in total out of balance. Rather than a subtle smooth change, it is a disruptive change.

ANDREW: *Yes, we have all lived through terrible storms. Very, very destructive in terms of vegetation, trees and so on...*

TOM: You know, when you are winning, the obstructing forces attempt to destroy your existence.

JOHN: *I would like to know what can I do personally to stop the growth of the holes in the Earth's ozone layer?*

TOM: Do not use any product that can contaminate – this includes products that affect other things and do not dissolve properly. There are natural elements upon Earth that release emissions that you cannot control. But you can control those emissions in your own arena. You can also inform those surrounding you about it, and also you can give your energy in meditation for mending it.

There is not time to say 'I will start tomorrow', for it was necessary to start yesterday. If your governments do not take responsibility for stopping giving permission to manufacture products of contamination, then the mothers must organise, for it is their children's world. As you have blockaded other things, then blockade contaminating products. Those who manufacture will hear, we promise you.

Do not use paper products that have colour. Be careful also of paper products that have bleaching that you ingest in your system, for when the toxins are in your system, and when they are released, it also helps contaminate. A smallness here, and a smallness there, and a lot of little smallnesses make a big effect for prevention of human annihilation.

Elevate yourself in information, and when you have found information pass it to others and organise for publication. It is your planet, it is your children's world, and your grand-children's. It is a beautiful planet, which must continue to exist, and you wish in the future to come to it again, but in its wholeness, as it was meant to be. Know this: you are not alone upon Earth. You are not alone in the Universe, be joyful among yourselves.

JOHN: *I have a feeling that as long that as there is greed on the planet, there will be need. And many conscious people seem not to understand this concept, and I feel very alone with this, and I wonder if my strong feelings about this are in fact correct?*

TOM: You have brought forth a great understanding. What you speak of is important, but this is the understanding of myth. We will explain in this way: it is important to be relieved of the problems of barter; it is important that the disadvantaged be in peace and harmony; there is a place for all humans within the matrix regardless of their form of understanding; there needs to be warmth and love, and order above all else, for if there is not order then the mind is chaotic. And if there be mechanical or electronic objects that relieve the burden of the individual, we have no objection to that.

The difficulty is that when these things become the most important, when the appearance, or the price is the most important, when the owning is the most important, and when growing bigger and bigger with more possessions is the most important, when it is thought that presentation of possession means success – that is a shell that has insecurity, do you understand? Like a lobster: a lobster has firm flesh, and there are times when it is soft and is not edible. Mushy. We now speak of a humankind which presents itself like a beautiful lobster but is mush inside. It is bitter to taste, not edible, and it can actually poison you.

JOHN: *Yes, I understand that very well. Now, the expression that Jesus used, 'that it is harder for a rich man to enter into the kingdom of heaven than for a camel to pass through the eye of a needle' turns out to be true. Although there is no harm in wealth itself – it's harmful by virtue of the way almost all people inevitably treat it.*

TOM: That is correct, you have complete understanding. Another understanding is this: business is a way you can give, do you understand that?

JOHN: Okay, yes, thank you. There's one question that concerns me, about poverty. Why is it that the great suffering that we've seen has been amongst peoples who are already suffering? I speak of the starvation that exists [1985] in Sudan and Ethiopia, and the floods in Bangladesh: it seems to me that these things are hitting poor and humble people who are the least to deserve this. I do not understand that process.

TOM: Those who speak of the laws of karma would say 'it is their karma'. We wish to express to you that this is not so. It is a karma of the world that has created this, it is a situation, as the Nazarene said, of the money-lenders in the temple. It is a situation of greed, of political motivation. All of that brings down the flood-waters which wash the foods away [in Bangladesh]. Those that are suffering do not deserve that suffering: it is the world's karmic situation. Those who turn their head, those who believe the suffering is necessary for elimination of population, in order for the planet to have a more definite place, those who are callous, we would not wish to be in their situation in a future time. As with the six million Jews, who brought forth the nation of Israel, these souls are also sacrificing to attempt to elevate the Earth to the position that it should be in – a planet of love that has attained complete balance between the physical and the spiritual, the negative and the positive.

JOHN: It still seems to me to be a strange lesson that greedy people and greedy nations have to learn in a way that is once-removed from them. It's harder to learn that way than if they learned it by direct experience for themselves?

TOM: It is the people within each nation that must make the movement to bring change. A nation has a head of government according to its deserving. Therefore it is important for the peoples within your worlds of sophistication to bring about those changes.

There needs to be an arousal within those peoples to understand that they must take a hold, and move in forwardness to stop their governments from doing what they have permitted them to do in the past. It is a time that people must now take control.

III

NEW LIGHT ON EARTH'S ANCIENT HISTORY

10

The Seeding of Humanity and the Aksu Culture

In the early forties, twenty-five stone disks were found in caves in the Bayan-Kara-Ula mountains on the borders of Tibet and Western China by a Chinese archaeologist. These strange disks belonged to the tribesmen who still live in these caves. From the Ham and Dropa tribes, they seem unrelated to any other ethnic group, being of frail build and about four foot high. Some twenty-five years after their discovery the disks were eventually deciphered. The hieroglyphics on one of them read: "The Dropas came down from the sky in their gliders. Our men, women and children hid in the caves ten times before sunrise. When at last they understood the sign language of the Dropas, they realised that the newcomers had peaceful intentions."

The Chinese archaeologist speculated that these disks and the present occupants of the caves corresponded to ancient Chinese legends relating stories of men who came down from the clouds..........

Tom has said, in reply to questions of origin "All beings on this planet have lived on other planets, but there are those that are a mixture. Physical beings may be reborn on another planet. A species is a mixture of two or more planets at the time of its physical existence. It has a strong ego and it has free will."

MIKI: When did humans start to have souls, to be real human beings?

TOM: When the dawning of reason began to come to the more evolved members of the species; when the natives upon Planet Earth began to evolve in body; when reasoning began with the assembling of tools and with the forming of a method of communication: that was when soul first came to this planet.

JOHN: We have spoken of 32,000 years ago but not of the time before that. Is it true that there were evolved civilisations on this planet millions of years ago? There have been artefacts found, metal and so on, which are very, very old, and which would indicate previous intelligent   civilisation.

TOM: I will ask for permission..... we may say this to you: Yes, approximately 20 million years ago there were beings with soul on this planet.

JOHN: Were they evolved technologically to the extent that they were on Altea or as much as we are?

TOM: No. Not greatly. Some of them were on Planet Earth for the preparation of the planet, in terms of plants and animals and understanding. Also, some of them were the Others.

GUEST: Are you able to say whether the mission of those preparing Planet Earth was accomplished?

TOM: Is not Planet Earth beautiful?

GUEST: It certainly is, yes. I was wondering whether everything they set out to do was accomplished at that time?

TOM: Do you not view it?

GUEST: Yes, certainly.

TOM: Did you now answer yourself?

GUEST: Yes, I seemingly did answer myself! I was wondering also, what specific kinds of preparations were they making at that time, 20 million years ago?

TOM: Arranging the etherics and chakras – what you term 'chakra' – around Earth, in the other spheres also, for those who would come to Earth to pass through, for their learning process, and the preparation of your fauna and flora energy-fields. Yes.

GUEST: And when you speak of the chakras of the planet, are you referring to what we might call power centres in the landscape at different points on Planet Earth?

TOM: What you call ley-lines, yes.

GUEST: I was wondering also what the Others were up to at this time?

TOM: Trying to cut the ley-lines.

GUEST: Did they actually have any success in making things difficult?

TOM: They succeeded with the Serpent did they not? Therefore humankind was entrapped.

In 1975 the following discussion took place:

GENE: *Have the civilisations represented by The Nine visited Earth in humanity's distant historical past?*

TOM: Yes, many times.

GENE: *And is it also true that some of them remained on Planet Earth interbreeding with the humans here?*

TOM: There were civilisations that colonised the planet Earth. The original beings that evolved on the planet Earth were what you would call the black race.

GENE: *Do I then understand that the races other than the black are result of interbreeding between the black and the people of the civilisations?*

TOM: No. The orientals, the whites and reds have been colonised, have been of other civilisations.

GENE: *Are they the results of breeding on Earth or were they brought to Earth?*

TOM: They are the result of breeding upon Planet Earth.

GENE: *Since the whites and reds and yellows represent breeding of advanced civilisations, does that mean that the black is inferior to other races, or are they merely different? Can you explain what the difference is?*

TOM: The black is an equal race upon the planet Earth. Those that colonised from other civilisations to the planet Earth (and the Hawk's civilisation had a portion of involvement) attempted.... How can we explain? Before the time of 32,000 BC, seeds were placed upon the planet Earth. Then by 32,000 BC the seed had evolved into a human being. Then at that time those of the other civilisations came to this planet with a being we could call the Hawk to interbreed the seeded peoples with beings from other civilisations. The blacks evolved from the planet. It was an experience: to see in which manner the originals, that were not seeded, would evolve in comparison with those that colonised. Those that colonised, after a period of time, because they came from other civilisations that had perhaps more intelligent technology, began to feel that they were superior to the black. They contrived to dominate the blacks. What was planned for the planet Earth did not come to pass. After the seeding, it was discovered by the civilisations that, of all the planets in the Universe, it is the only planet that has such beauty, such diversity of changes, and such density – more than any other planet in the Universe. It was also discovered that those that existed upon Planet Earth had great phys-icalness and sexuality, not witnessed on the other planets, and the colonists began to live in desire for physicalness, and began repeat-edly reincarnating on Planet Earth. As they recycled, they began to hold the originals of the planet Earth in bondage.

More discussions on this subject with other sitters:

STEVE: *I'd like to ask about the historical information we've been given about civilisations on Earth before 32,000 BC. I understand that the black races were the only people on Earth at this time, is this so?*

TOM: It was those that evolved on Earth. It was the original on the Earth.

STEVE: *They were not in just one location in Africa, were they? Because I understand that there have been finds in Siberia and China.*

TOM: They evolved on all the landmasses of the Earth.

STEVE: *Yet people of China, Siberia and South America are not negroid.*

TOM: When you speak of others, the red, the yellow, and the white, they were descended from colonisations from other civilisations many thousands of years ago. This is not the same as the colonisation from the higher civilisations of 32,400 BC. The originals were the blacks.

JOHN: *And so, is it true to say that blacks are the only race that went through a complete evolution from here?*

TOM: Yes. Those that are the nature of black were the indigenous of this the Earth. They may, if they have the wish, go as souls to other worlds for evolution, or evolve in different situations within this planet. It is their choice.

JOHN: *We speak often [this is 1981] of the East-West conflict, but I think more and more of us are becoming aware that the real im-balance on Earth is the North-South conflict, in the sense of the relative prosperity of the North and the poverty of the South. It's hard for me to understand why that imbalance exists: can you com-ment on this?*

TOM: This planet has been evolving for thousands upon thousands of years. We have explained about the colonisation of your planet Earth from other civilisations: those that are, as you identify it, of the South, came largely from Earth. They did not have an input of other civilisations to assist their evolutionary process.

JOHN: Yes, but is there a sort of an energy that brought the colonisers to the North rather than spread them evenly around the planet?

TOM: You mean of grid-lines?

ANDREW & JOHN: Yes.

JOHN: I mean, that was a long time ago and yet it is still the north that seems to have the 'strength'.

TOM: That was the settlement area, yes.

JOHN: Do you perceive that as a serious imbalance, as we do – in one sense there is a more longterm problem..?

TOM: The tragedy is that by this colonisation, those beings and species considered themselves superior. It was not meant to be that way: that is the imbalance. There should have been a putting of their hands in the hands of others. The seed of Abraham should have spread through and completely around the Earth – then this situation would not have arisen. But because it was not done in that manner, because there were others who greatly distrusted the colonisers, were jealous of their situation, the colonisers remained in a combination of tightness for survival and protection. In that respect, yes, there is imbalance.

JOHN: When the Hawk came down to Earth, at what stage were the Earth people? They had not had any previous contact in any form at all with the civilisations. Were they what we would call 'Barbaric' or – ?

TOM: You might call them simple structured societies.

JOHN: Yes, and then there was a mixing of genes with them..?

TOM: Yes. That was the beginning of more advanced culture on Planet Earth.

ANDREW: What kind of a race was found there with whom to begin doing the bioengineering? Were they blacks, whites or yellows..?

TOM: The civilisations have never mingled with the original race, of Earth, which is the black race. But other beings had been set upon Earth by other civilisations – civilisations that you would find of superior intelligence to you, but not working in direct cooperation with the Twenty-Four – who transported groups of beings that were outcasts. These in turn evolved as human. It was this race which was mixed and intermingled by those who landed in 32,400 BC. They were placed. We cannot use the word seeded because it is not the appropriate word.

JOHN: Thank you. One question which leads out of this is that about 34,000 years ago Neanderthal Man didn't suddenly aquire a large brain – as far as we understand it – and then suddenly die and be replaced by Cro-Magnon Man. Can you explain that particular point please?

TOM: The Neanderthals were not the beginning of humankind.

JOHN: And they died out – so what were the origins of Cro-Magnon man then? It was always thought that one led to the other but now it seems they have a different strain.

TOM: How could one lead to the other when they came from another civilisation, not upon this planet? You are trying to set it within the realms of what your scientific anthropologists attempt to reconstruct, eliminating the seeding. [Refer Appendix Notes]

JOHN: So the first appearance of Cro-Magnon man as we know it, in a scientific sense, would have been in the Tarim Basin in Aksu?

TOM: That is correct.

In 1974 Andrew and Tom had a discussion which links to the preceeding subject:

ANDREW: How was the first colonisation carried out?

TOM: A small number of beings arrived on Earth, and they founded the first civilisation – and when I say the first civilisation that is not truly so, but they were the first arrival of people of ours – and that was over 32,000 years BC.

ANDREW: And where would that have been?

TOM: At Akisu, near what you call the Tarim Basin. [written Aksu, pronounced Akisu by Tom, Aksu is in Xinjiang province, China at 41.01N & 80.20E]

ANDREW: I see. I gather that that civilisation eventually did not suc-

ceed, and things did not go well.

TOM: It was not the fault of those who landed.

ANDREW: I just wonder what was the failure then, was it premature?

TOM: It was too soon. The minds and the souls of the spirits were too dense. It was a high civilisation, not properly adapted to Earth.

ANDREW: Are there any remains of that civilisation?

TOM: I will check, will you wait? They tell me yes, but not that can be seen. It is under the surface.

ANDREW: What kind of elements of civilisation did the visitors try to give at that time? What were they concerned with? Was it agriculture or medicine or writing or astronomy or what?

TOM: It was language. In order to raise the beings of the planet from a near animal level. It was a form of communication.

ANDREW: Do you have any examples of this language? For example, what was the name of this gentleman, the Hawk?

TOM: I will give it to you in your alphabet but it did not have that alphabet. The alphabet had no vowels, but it had vowels when spoken.

ANDREW: Yes, the sound had a vowel but no written representation.

TOM: It would be a T, R, H, K, R, H, K. The difficulty is that our Being does not have the tones available for us to refer to, in her mind.

ANDREW: Yes, thank you, we'll figure out how that's pronounced.

TOM: When the civilisation was lost – and in every civilisation that has been lost – there were small groups that were not lost but travelled a long distance to remove themselves from the area.

ANDREW: Yes, and where did some of these people go? I mean, in what culture would we know them now, if at all?

TOM: They do not exist. But they moved to three areas. It was a large civilisation, and outside the Aksu civilisation there was another subsidiary civilisation. The Hawk also attempted to bring the principle of one leader.

ANDREW: What was that one leader called in that language, what was the word?

Tom: It would be a Y and a K, but it had a vowel sound.

Andrew: Something like Akh?

Tom: Yes, but not quite.

Andrew: How long was the Hawk on Earth for that particular mission?

Tom: One thousand, six hundred of your years.

Andrew: That's incredible! Did he have any offspring?

Tom: All of the world.

Andrew: You mean he was the sole source of the seed, so to speak?

Tom: No. The seed was from a civilisation and this was the beginning of the true understanding.

Andrew: Did he just live as an ordinary human being, as far as everybody else was concerned at that time?

Tom: He attempted to, but was not permitted. He was called the Hawk by them, as he also was later called the Hawk by the Egyptians because he came from us.

Andrew: Did these early people see him appear from the sky?

Tom: Yes.

Andrew: In a craft or something?

Tom: Yes.

Andrew: I see. They associated that with a hawk?

Tom: Yes.

Andrew: Did he appear on Earth looking like everybody else, or did he look different?

Tom: Realising the close-to-animal stage of these beings, his costume was made to resemble a bird. In order for them to be able to understand.

Andrew: During the sixteen hundred years that the Hawk worked, was there success in bringing about some elements of civilisation?

Tom: It was slightly more but that is close. He brought civilisation. He brought language so the people could communicate. And enlightenment. He brought the knowledge and technology of how to build strongly, how to protect, how to grow, how to cultivate in order to grow strong, and how to heal within themselves.

ANDREW: *Was all this done by natural healing and natural selection of seeds and so on? Was there any science or knowledge that we would identify with physics, chemistry, mathematics or astronomy, that was given at that time, or was it too early?*

TOM: It was all done, in a way that they were able to understand.

ANDREW: *How long did the average person live on Earth at that time? What was the average life span?*

TOM: Twenty years. The colonists were able to raise the life-expectancy to one hundred and twenty, to one hundred and fifty, and many lived longer.

ANDREW: *So they must have been quite impressed by the fact that the Hawk was around for well over thousand years.*

TOM: Yes, he was regarded as a god.

ANDREW: *And that's how the whole mistake arose, how the notion of gods arose amongst men? I see. When did the Hawk make another appearance on Earth after that first venture 32,400 years ago?*

TOM: In the time span between the first coming, before the Hawk passed into your world again, another being continued the thread.

ANDREW: *This was at Aksu?*

TOM: That is correct.

ANDREW: *How long was that for?*

TOM: The new one was with that civilisation for 2,020 years of its time. He came as the son of the Hawk.

ANDREW: *Did he indeed appear to be an earthly son, even though he came from your place?*

TOM: The people knew the difference.

JOHN: *What was the name?*

TOM: I will try. You do not have the sounds to reproduce it. It had a sound of a vowel but it had no written vowel. It was R, T, T, H, R. But remember it began with a sound that was not written.

ANDREW: *Yes, with an unstopped vowel. It would sound something like 'Arthur' — something like that?*

TOM: Yes.

JOHN: How much longer did that civilisation last after this person's existence, if at all?

TOM: It existed for but a brief six hundred years longer.

JOHN: Could you say what happened at the end?

TOM: It was natural.

JOHN: Was this one of the periodic natural disturbances that they sometimes call a polar shift, or something?

TOM: Yes. Both of these beings returned to Earth in the time of 6,000-5,000 BC. It was at that time that more beings came with them.

ANDREW: And in what lands did they then appear?

TOM: It was what you call Egypt..

ANDREW: Were they also in Sumer or Ur?

TOM: Before. Then in Egypt.

ANDREW: Did they come from the sky at that time..?

TOM: Yes.

JOHN: You said that the Hawk arrived in a craft?

ANDREW: They saw it as the form of a bird.

TOM: Yes, and those with him mingled with those here, and created a new species.

JOHN: They had what we call physical intercourse, to produce children, is that correct?

TOM: It was more evolved, higher.

ANDREW: A method of upgrading the local species on Earth, right?

TOM: Strengthening.

ANDREW: And they used their own means and knowledge to do that, right?

TOM: Yes.

ANDREW: And when they appeared on Earth, they found certain beings that they thought would help to strengthen the species, so they mingled with them and developed a hybrid. And then they watched, to see what would happen with that hybrid.

TOM: That is in essence the truth. The problem with the beings that existed was that they worshipped the visitors, this was handed down through the species. And the species then worshipped.

GUEST: Is it possible for you to give more images of the Aksu culture, and about any phases it went through, or any other characteristics which would be useful to know?

TOM: Akisu was a seeded colony, arranged for the evolution of your planet Earth, and for teaching the process of progress, for a leap forward of humankind. There had been a realisation that if we waited for humankind to evolve of its own accord, it would still be in its own state of six toes, you understand?

When there is one group accelerating, the acceleration creates a spin-off, then that touches others for their acceleration also. Therefore implemental devices were brought forward, organisation for the colony, for communal development. Also there were forward offshoots of some who went to what you now identify as China – a great communital country now. And out to other domains, more gradually. That was the beginning of what you term the "Giants merging with the daughters of men" you understand? Also, at times there were species created from merging together, that were brought forth: one civilisation connecting genetically with another civilisation, created a species. That was in the beginning.

JOHN: Can you say when language began? Did they have any language at all before the time of Aksu?

TOM: When you ask about language, do you mean verbalising? Writing?

JOHN: Yes. Verbalising.

TOM: Do you call grunts and gungs [sic] verbalising?

JOHN: I'm talking about language with some kind of grammatical structure.

TOM: Not totally.

JOHN: So the leaders, the giants who came down, added to that and built on the language?

TOM: Helped the creation of the understanding of the clicks and clacks, you understand? From that evolved development of sound wave and together with implementation, the development of music, the attempt to imitate the sound of reed-plant, rubbing together, imitation of wind through trees?

JOHN: This is what you once described as a tonal language?

TOM: That is correct. That is the tonal language of the Universe. However, in the dissension, then the babble came. Everyone was babbling like non-humans. That culture moved across plains, and pockets, segments of groups, moved forward. It was again necessary for re-seeding. You understand that when there is separation of people there is also loss of knowledge? If there is not a group to repeat the knowledge, it is lost. When not utilised, it is not forthcoming in the brain. Therefore it was necessary for re-genetics, yes.

GUEST: Was this done with new people who came to Planet Earth?

TOM: From the same civilisations. Before Abraham there was one who taught the people, said to be from the sea?

JOHN: Ioannes?

TOM: Yes. Except he was not from the sea.

JOHN: Who was he in terms of the civilisations?

TOM: He was from the civilisation of Altea.

JOHN: I thought so. Just on that point, the leader of Altea was the mythological character Atlas, that is correct?

TOM: That is so.

JOHN: At one time, I think you said Atlas and Zeus were one and the same person.

TOM: You understand how mythology has confusion? For you see, they say that Zeus made mating with a swan. The swan came from the heavens.... Do you understand the complexity?

GUEST: Yes.

TOM: Primitive man had assumptions. Council has said I have not answered. That that holds up the world was Altea, yes.

JOHN: But I asked if that was the same as Zeus.

TOM: Humans created that mythical godhead. They gave characters to civilisations to make them gods, when they were not. Zeus with the swan was…. the swan was a ship. When Zeus went into the ship, they called him a god, for it was their mountain, you understand?

JOHN: *I don't know what you mean by their mountain.*

TOM: The ship came to their mountain.

GUEST: *Mount Olympus.*

TOM: The corruption is Zeus. Atlas became Zeus. But Altea was the one.

GUEST: *May I go back to Aksu? Was it a large number of beings who came to Earth to found the Aksu culture, or just a small number?*

TOM: In the beginning it was a small number, and then it was understood that more were necessary for seeding.

GUEST: *Did it take a long time before the dissension started, and how did it begin? What sort of issues were involved?*

TOM: There were not connections as they moved into outlying areas, and confusion reigned, and they became involved in what you would call 'local developments', and at times merged with the peoples of those areas. Therefore there was loss of memory and reverting back to a more basic state. Therefore it was necessary to re-enhance the genetics. Is that sense?

GUEST: *Yes. Did it take a long time between the first arrival and the separation, the dissension?*

TOM: Migration would be a better term. Humankind and particularly those humankind of genetic 'exploration' had curiosity, and always there is one that is curious in humankind, is that not so? So within one century there was moving out, and the necessity of re-enhancing was within five hundred of your centuries. We speak not of those who remained. We speak of those who spread around in other places, yes.

JOHN: *As I understand it, you talked about the Hawk being there for about 1,000 years, and the others who followed him for about 4,000 years…*

TOM: That is correct. Were they not geneticists? There were the people moving outward.

JOHN: *Now, Phyllis had a dream the other day, and she felt that she* was in Aksu, and she saw a sort of celebration and three different groups going in different directions. This dispersing, was it in about 32,000BC?

TOM: Yes.

JOHN: Now, I made an assumption that a civilisation took responsibility for each of those groups. Is that so?

TOM: Yes, it is, as you would say, sound.

JOHN: Well, I imagine this was Ashan, Altea and Hoova. Is that correct?

TOM: That is absolutely correct.

JOHN: Yes. Now I'm trying to determine which ones went in which direction. The ones that went to China, were they of Hoova?

TOM: They were of Ashan in combination with Hoova.

JOHN: I see, they mixed before they went..?

TOM: There were those that were mixed, and those that were colonists from other planets. In Aksu, there were those that were of pure strain; those who were a mixture of one civilisation with people of Earth; and there were those who were mixed strain, mixed again with those of another civilisation. Do you understand this? How may we explain? We will use your solar system as an example: If there was from another planet, we will say – how may we explain? Suppose that you had a colonization of, say from your planet Venus to your planet earth, then it was mixed with that of Ashan that would be one strain, then if that of Ashan that was mixed with Venus then mingled with Hoova, that would be of a second strain, is that not so?

JOHN: Yes. So they also travelled overland, when they split up from Aksu, is that correct?

TOM: Yes.

JOHN: Could we place the three occasions of the seeding? As I understand it, the first time was many, many thousands of years ago. The second time was at the time of the Garden – the time of the Tarim Basin – and then the third time was at the time of Abraham. Is that correct?

TOM: That is correct.

JOHN: Yes, so the first seeding came with the arrival of the Hawk?

TOM: That is also correct. A second one arrived after a millennium.

JOHN: A thousand years after the Hawk?

TOM: Approximately.

JOHN: O.K. Now, in relation to that, the groups of beings who were in the Tarim Basin – were they purely evolved or had they mixed with some of the other seedings that had also taken place?

TOM: That is correct. They were of Hoova.

JOHN: They were purely of the Hoovid, so they hadn't nomadically met with any of the other groups that were also seeded – as I understand it?

TOM: That is correct.

JOHN: And Altea was one of the other civilisations that had seeded, is that correct?

TOM: That is correct.

JOHN: You once mentioned the 'small people' and I never understood what that meant. Was that referring to the people who were seeded by Hoova, were they smaller?

TOM: We speak that humankind, when they landed, were smaller. Those who came were giants compared to those that existed on Planet Earth.

ANDREW: Going back to those early periods of mingling and hybridisation, we understand from our science on Earth that a major phase of the ice ages ended around the time of the original landing of 32,400. What can you tell us about that? Was it actually ending or was it still in existence?

TOM: It was already over.

ANDREW: Was Aksu at that time a fertile green area, not desert..?

TOM: It had not become sprung, but it was warming.

ANDREW: The area was still cool, relatively?

TOM: That is truth. It was not lush, but browns and reds.

JOHN: I'd like to ask about what we know as the Adam and Eve story. We discussed this and came to a consensus, that first a space being called the Hawk came to prepare, then another came with a man-

date, not to engage in physical intercourse with the females here, until the time was right. The temptation then came, is this correct?

Tom: The first being came to give knowledge to the natives that existed upon Earth, about plants and animals. Then the second space being came, and he had great sadness for he saw the mating of the natives and the animals of Planet Earth. His sadness was not for the mating but for not having a companion to communicate with. So then one was given to him to communicate with.

At that time it was asked that he not become involved in the ways of the planet Earth, for at the level to which he was evolved, it would have been disastrous for him to become involved in physical mating without adapting, without his body adjusting to a new equilibrium. So he was asked to refrain from this, to adapt him to pressures within his body, and for him to understand the functions that would come within his body – and also, as an example to those that existed, so that mating would be utilised only for the highest purpose.

Then the One that Fell came upon him and his woman companion, and placed within him a sense of the true knowledge which gave him the desire to be equal to God. The tragedy of this is that he came originally came from the Creator and forgot this. So there was no need to attempt to be equal to God. But while on Earth he found the need for this.

John: I would just like to understand about the One that Fell in this context...

Tom: It was the Archangel of whom you know... we wish not to use the name. In your Adam and Eve story he was the serpent. You see it was never meant to be of two sides. It was all meant to be in equality.

John: Do you mean the male and female or negative and positive?

Tom: Negative and positive.

Irene: When Adam and Eve chose not to understand the definition of obedience, which was part of the dialogue in paradise between you and them, and when they saw the truth of what obedience meant, and turned away from the responsibility of that, then humankind was set forth on a path where we had to define good and evil for ourselves in the context of bondage?

Tom: That is correct.

Irene: And the time before the Fall is where the purity lies within humanity. It is on that purity that the transformation of the modern world will take place..?

Tom: That is correct. This modern world is the result of that contamination, and therefore transformation would be the result of non-contamination.

Irene: Yes. And that's why reality is changing in our modern times, and the process now is the piercing of that veil — because all reality does is continue to mirror where we were since the Fall..?

Tom: That is correct. It is the illusion that you humans are equal or superior to the Creator and creation, and the reality you take to be real is illusion.

Irene: So, what is necessary now is the establishing of a philosophical construct of Eden, so that everything else will have its proper order.

Tom: So it becomes a waterfall of purity.

Irene: Well, that's great.

Israel: Let's go do it.

Tom: It will be. It is now in motion, but there are also those who will seek to disturb this. Know who you are, trust yourself, trust us, and know it will be done, and continuously view your motive in order to keep yourself in alignment with your highest purpose. And that is what is necessary upon Planet Earth, for you know of the contamination on Planet Earth, and the way that people may then attempt to misconstrue this forwardness and dawning of paradise.

Irene: Are you willing to say anything about the identity of Eve or her symbolic identity?

Tom: We will not at this point. As you know, Eve became identified with the notion of original sin. And Eve, the feminine, was buried, and the male aspect consumed Earth. Because it was out of balance in its consumption, and because it wished for the punishment of the female, the male aspect felt that the female had brought disaster upon the Earth, when in truth the male never accepted responsibility for its own choosing. Now it is time for that responsibility to be taken. In those times, Adam and Eve had complete harmony and balance with nature. They had understanding of the rites of nature and of each issue within nature, and the communication with not only animals and flora, but also with rocks, soil, water and wind, and the moon and the sun and all. In the present day, the time of the female, the essence of Eve is coming to the fore, and what must be done is the complete merging of male and female. Not for the male to attempt to bind the female, and not for the female to attempt to suppress the male, but to work in complete joy, in harmony and unity, as two pillars that are holding up the world, separate but together. Yes.

STEVE: *Considering the question of balance of the positive and negative in Earth history, has there ever been a time when an excess of the positive has been the problem?*

TOM: Yes. I should relate to you the time. There was such a state of positivity, when all the birds sang, and all the animals loved, and all the flowers bloomed, and that was during the period of Adam and Eve, the period of Aksu. That was a time of paradise, but also a time when the nature of the positive was out of balance: it was our error.

STEVE: *So there had to be an introduction of the negative in order to promote further evolution?*

TOM: In a form of speaking, yes. We had not anticipated the results of desire. When humanity has no challenge for growth then they can dissipate energy.

STEVE: *How did the mythology of paradise and the Garden of Eden arise?*

TOM: Earth is the most beautiful of all that exist in the Universe. It has variety that no other planet has. It has a varied climate that no other planet has. In truth, if the souls on Earth were of the highest evolution it would be considered a paradise. This planet Earth may be a paradise when the density is removed. But when we say that, we speak of a paradise of creativity, a paradise that brings knowledge, a paradise that brings joy and love. A paradise in which humans may heal themselves or may experience, if they so wish, pain. But it is not a paradise where all challenge will be removed, all growth will be removed, all pain will be removed. It will be a paradise that humans can create, through their own evolution, their own understanding of their connection with the Universe, and their accepting of responsibility for themselves, for their fellows, for Planet Earth. All will be brought into perfection .

11

The Altean Venture: Atlantis

Many of our ideas about Atlantis might be changed by the transmissions that follow. As noted before, a few hundred years here or there does not make a lot of difference to the Nine. All the dates are as they appeared in the original transmissions and BC has been used where it was said.

Within this chapter the term Altima is used (as it was in the early transmissions). When asked about 'Altima' by Andrew in the early 1970s Tom had replied that it was the name of a unit working in co-operation with them. The term Altima later became Altea.

Atlantis would seem to be deeply buried in our psyche to such an extent that people become quite heated and emotional when discussing it. There have been more books written about it than most other subjects in the world, and with the approach of the millennium no doubt the list will be added to. Among other things, perhaps Atlantis can provide us with clear reflection?

ANDREW: The next myths that we hear about are those about the Atlantean civilisation. Did it exist and how long did it last? We have a beginning presumably just after the Aksu period.

TOM: We were waiting for when you would ask. I may explain – but briefly: Atlantis ended 11,000 years ago of your time and it began 32,000 years ago. What is called Atlantis was a colony which developed and with which we made contact. (When I say we, I do not mean The Nine but other civilisations.) These civilisations translated technology. From there other colonies went out, taking the knowledge and technology with them. At that time, because of the gravitational pull, not all the technology was refined enough in order for it to be functional on this planet Earth. The time has now come when all this technology may be utilised.

ANDREW: Yes, what did they call it themselves? I'd like to get the true name.

TOM: They were in truth Alteans. They were of the civilisation of Altima.

ANDREW: Oh, they were Altimans. So that's why they are called Alteans and this somehow became corrupted to Atlanteans. I see, thank you.

JOHN: Was this about the time of what we call 'The Flood'?

TOM: It was before .

JOHN: Was Atlantis in the area that we would now talk of as the area around the Bermuda Triangle?

TOM: It went from Greece to what you now call United States.

JOHN: Oh, it was very large.

ANDREW: So there were multiple cities of this civilisation?

TOM: Yes. The Mayan culture was one which was left over – it was a colony that lost contact and reverted.

JOHN: Now, relating to that, there was a culture we call Mu or Lemuria in what we now call the Pacific Ocean – was that before or after Atlantis?

TOM: They were one and the same. As you had an Egyptian culture and one in Ur, which were one and the same.

ANDREW: What was the principal means of transport that the Atlanteans used to get around the face of the planet? Did they just move around by sailboat and ship or did they have aircraft?

TOM: They had aircraft. They also could move in their body.

ANDREW: Of great interest to me is the relationship between the remnants of the Atlantean culture – the High Culture and the beginnings of the Egyptian ......

TOM: [interrupts] Egypt was a colony that was very...we will use the term 'hard core'.

STEVE: So Atlantis was originally a Hoovid colony, an extension of Aksu, and yet it became Altean in influence..?

TOM: Originally, in the seeding upon Planet Earth in Aksu, one colony went to what became Atlantis, and another was developed by Hoova, through Abraham, in Ur and Canaan.

STEVE: *There's a problem of dating the Atlantis period: the date of the end was, I gather, about 9,000 BC? We have a beginning presumably after the start of the Aksu period, 32,000 BC.*

TOM: That was not the beginning of the civilisation of Atlantis. The civilisation of Atlantis was a seeding, similar to the genetic seeding involving Hoova, Aksu and Abraham. The civilisation of Atlantis was seeded by Altea over a time period. It was in existence in phases, for approximately 12-17,000 years, but not consistently.

GUEST: *That is a very long time in human history. I wonder if there were any important phases in the development of Atlantis that are important to know about?*

TOM: The land of Atlantis was developed by Altea, one of the major civilisations of the Twenty-Four, which was technologically advanced in many areas. Those of Altea upgraded again and merged with those who had already been geneticised. As Atlantis expanded over an enormous land mass, and colonised on far reaches of Planet Earth — for they had the technological ability to do this — difficulties developed. This was because of Planet Earth with its beauty, variety and sense of feeling, because of their love and their technological expansion, and because they were attempting to bring Planet Earth to its true fulfilment of paradise. They became involved in the emotional feeling-state of physicalness, and became very involved in the creation of larger and more prominent mating organs. They also attempted, through their scientific knowledge and understanding, to genetically exchange creatures with soul-beings on Planet Earth — through transplanting. Do you know what we mean?

GUEST: *No, not quite....*

TOM:You are a soul are you not? So if we then placed your head on a cow, would that not be an exchange of a soul for a non-human soul-body?

GUEST: *Yes, I see.*

TOM:They were, because of their brilliance and knowledge, attempting to not merge with the thinking on Planet Earth, but they thought that by creating these creatures they would perhaps have the strength of the creature, or the creature could be serving them, or they could develop a means for more physical pleasure. And that was not the order of the day, as you would say. They also had realisation that they had gone beyond the limits of their agreement.

ANDREW: *What caused the disappearance of this Atlantean culture which spread from Greece across to the Americas? Was it disease? Was it....?*

TOM: It was brought about a great destruction. It was not Armageddon. It was not. It was the spreading of the colonies and the weakening of the civilisations and it was a natural phenomenon.

ANDREW: *It was what we would call the decay of a culture.*

TOM: Yes.

ANDREW: *And some of the remnants of that, I presume, were present in South America, North America and so on?*

TOM: All over.

JOHN: *This is a hypothetical question: If they had made better use of their resources then the physical destruction of that culture might not have taken place, is that so?*

TOM: You would like to believe that. What we are explaining to you is that the loss of it was due to a natural phenomenon: your oceans, your earthquakes. Remember that you live on a physical planet. Do you understand?

JOHN: *Well, we understand that there are repetitions of tremendous upheavals on the physical planet and I imagine that was one of them.*

TOM: But your religions of the world would like to relate these upheavals to the gods.

JOHN: *Yes.*

ANDREW: *They speak of the floods, anyway.*

JOHN: *So, 11,000 years ago the religious story of the creation could be related to the flood of that period?*

TOM: Yes.

GUEST: *Are the teachings of the Kahuna in Hawaii a leftover of the Altean knowledge?*

TOM: They are a mixture – and they are of the tribe of Cohen.

GUEST: *Hmmm. The Altean period lasted 12-17,000 years: when did the Altean's unusual technological development become problematic?*

TOM: In the last of its thousand years..

GUEST: So before that time this was quite a healthy civilisation?

TOM: It was not stagnant. It also took in what is termed today the colony of Mu.

GUEST: And the colony of Mu, where did these people originate from?

TOM: Ashan.

GUEST: Centred in what we now know as the Pacific Ocean?

TOM: That is correct.

JOHN: During this period, I assume they had open contact with Altea..?

TOM: Availability of craft in the sky. All was lost. Humanness started again, then out of that came Ioannes.

GUEST: When did the culture of Mu begin?

TOM: It was approximately the same time as Atlantis, after the settlement of Atlantis and the developing of colonies in the treks outwards. You know that the peoples of the Philippines are descendants of Mu, as those who live on islands in music-skirts...

JOHN: Polynesia?

GUEST: Bali?

TOM: Yes.

GUEST: And they eventually joined forces with the people of Altea and merged with them?

TOM: They were from Altea, originally, seeded then by Ashan. Some of those in Atlantis were from Ashan. There were three seedings. Yes.

ANDREW: Did the Hawk have anything to do with Atlantis?

TOM: In what you would call 11,000 BC there was a return, and the Hawk and his people stayed all the time, and were different beings in the minds of the Earth people.

JOHN: *During this time, did the people of this Altean civilisation have what we would regard as a normal birth? And go through a normal life-cycle?*

TOM: No. Most cases of normal births are the beginning of lives where the person has come to learn. The births we are referring to were births of souls who came to serve. These are beings that know themselves and have a different intent within their core. When beings like this were recognised as a founder or as a god, as in the case of Horus in Egypt or Ea [Ioannes] in Ur, they were not birthed. Birth is for learning. When you are not birthed, you do not have the same emotions as physical people.

JOHN: *Could you describe the function of the Hawk and his group in Atlantis?*

TOM: They were teachers, but they also mingled with the physicals.

ANDREW: *Where were they centred on Earth, at that time?*

TOM: The Hawk lived in what you now call Crete. The other was in a different place, but they were in communication as they had vehicles with which to communicate, because they were leaders.

JOHN: *They were not considered gods then?*

TOM: Yes, they were. Another leader was centred close to where you now have Florida and Bahamas. That is a part that is no longer there. And the one who had succeeded the Hawk in Akisu was a leader in a place off the coast of your South America. There are some islands there, but not islands of consequence. It was a very large land mass, and there were seas that lay between these lands.

ANDREW: *What was the Hawk known as in this Cretan period of 11,000 BC? And when did he leave?*

TOM: I cannot find the name in our Being's brain, but it would be like 'Heronimus'. He did not leave. He continued until he became Horus, in Egypt, after the end of the Altean civilisation.

ANDREW: *I see. And that culture, I take it, disappeared when the so-called Atlantean culture disappeared?*

TOM: It was swallowed. There are remains, and there are remains of peoples who have forgotten, but who in fact worship in the same way as before. Do you understand why it was swallowed?

ANDREW: *No, we do not understand why.*

Tom: Would you like to know?

Andrew: Yes, very much so.

Tom: As the leaders mingled, there were those who opposed that mingling. The Hawk and other leaders felt that they were powerful enough, such that if they did mingle, they could overcome this opposition. But what they did not know was that those that opposed had more powerful desire. Then the three leaders came together, and from that period they were in a weeping state, because of the great loss. Then they decided, in conjunction with us, to go and be the founders of Egypt. One of them went and founded Ur, and then later they came together again.

Andrew: I see. The submergence or disappearance of the Atlantean culture, spread out as it was – was this an 'Act of God' or was it...?

Tom: We were angry.

Andrew: You were angry? Were you angry with the leaders for their role in mismanaging the situation?

Tom: No. It was our ignorance in not understanding the density of the planet Earth. It was more despair, really, than anger. We are more compassionate now.

Andrew: Could you give us a small glimpse of the level of civilisation attained by Atlanteans?

Tom: You in the civilisation in which you live now have achieved but a part of what the Atlanteans developed.

Andrew: I see, so we're very primitive! What was their outstanding achievement, as far as you know, in Atlantean civilisation?

Tom: In the field of medicine, of a far superior nature than your medicine. You are primitive in electronics, and they had all the knowledge of using the mind to move objects and themselves. If it had not been that below their waist they were always in trouble, then it would have been a fine civilisation.

Andrew: I see. And their medicine was not able to help them with that part of their problem?

Tom: They enjoyed it. We have no objections to enjoyment – it is when it becomes all-consuming. And it became... would you really like to know the truth? We know not whether those upon your planet may handle it.

JOHN: *Well, we can decide whether we should pass that on.*

TOM: Rather than using of the knowledge of medicine which they had, to improve their mentalities or their physicals, they used their knowledge to improve their sex organs.

ANDREW: *I see. Are there any remnants of this species or breed on Earth, or are they all..?*

TOM: They became a being but are no longer in existence as a being.

JOHN: *One thing about China: the system of medicine that they have there, acupuncture, is that a system of medicine that came from the Atlantean time?*

TOM: It is primitive compared to the knowledge of Altima, but it is more advanced than the knowledge of America. In Atlantean medicine it was possible to replace even the true heart and the true brain. However, in your medicine you can, for example, replace an arm — except that it does not have a 'true heart' in it. [vital spark] At their time, all the vital organs could be replaced with no difficulty and without severe problems for the physical body. Also the organs that were transplanted were far superior to those that they were replacing.

ANDREW: *That's incredible. If they had all this ability as you say, then they must have had a fairly long life. I mean they could extend life considerably, couldn't they?*

TOM: That is, in effect, what their project was at that time.

ANDREW: *What would be the life-expectancy of somebody who had good medical care in the days of Altea?*

TOM: It could in truth go into a few thousands of your years.

ANDREW: *And yet with that long life they did not somehow gain an overall wisdom?*

TOM: They were involved in transplanting.

ANDREW: *Yes, I see. Well, I guess all that knowledge can be regained someday...*

TOM: It is within the mind of the dolphin. The dolphin has the answer. Yes.

This we say to you: it is important for humankind to understand the devastation brought about in times past when Alteans existed upon planet Earth and also why a great many people of that time have chosen to be in the form of a porpoise or a dolphin. And some, now upon this planet Earth are here to inform humankind that they chose that form so that they cannot recreate those scientific experiments which have engendered the mythology that is known throughout humankind today. They have not eradicated their mating desire, do you understand? We do not wish it to be eradicated but we wish it to be understood properly.

At the time of the great anger and despair concerning what had been done in Atlantis, and concerning those that used the know-ledge only for their own benefit, there were, at that time, colonies that were not of a destructive nature: those in truth were not de-stroyed. But also, in the Atlantean culture, there were people that were not of the destructive nature of the majority, who were never-theless in the particular areas where the land mass was destroyed, taking with it many people. They understood the necessity for the act however. There are some of those people who now exist on Planet Earth, who have chosen to be on this Planet Earth and they are of a species that have chosen to appear in a manner that does not con-form to the physical of their previous existence.

We were not sure that this choice of physical body would be of benefit to their future soul growth but it was their wish and in their intellect and understanding of their physical nature during their past experience, they felt that perhaps they could then be of service in a proper way. And so they now exist upon your planet in a different form than they had before. They are not acknowledged as a species of a human nature – yet let me tell you – they are more humane than any human on your planet. They are the species of dolphin.

ANDREW: I see, what about making contact with them?

Tom: They are very sensitive to all consciousness work, but they are also guardians of the seas, and many that oppose the transformation of Planet Earth live in the seas too. They observe and guard, and they also, when necessary, monitor other civilisations of the Universe that approach Planet Earth with questionable intent, and they attempt, because of their great strength of mind, to remove them. They are guardians. They are in service in a similar way that many of you humans are in service, and while their language is difficult for you, it is much better for us. The communication that we have is more in their normal range.

ANDREW: *So, if we researched the language of dolphins, we would move closer to learning your own manner of communication?*

TOM: Yes. And do you understand that those that live as dolphins chose that form because they would not be tempted with the physical?

ANDREW: *Well, I think they are very clever and very intelligent to choose that form and way of life. Because they have less problems and complications than any humans on Earth, and probably more joy in living. And, as you say, they are in service.*

TOM: But it is difficult for them, because of their form and their thinking, to perform a true service without the link with humans.

ANDREW: *Well perhaps we can provide that link...*

TOM: Understanding the link between Atlantis, the dolphins and humans will release the knowing within humans of how they brought about their destruction in past times. Know this: at this current time, humans that existed in the time of Altea have come back to exist in this time also. Some who lived the life of the dolphin have now returned in uprightness without water: this will release that internal knowing and knowledge. This is of great importance, for when that connection is made and the truth rings out, an understanding illuminates, yes.

STEVE: *In one communication we were given to believe that the end was a natural cataclysm, and that it is foolish to attribute it to the gods. On another occasion we are given to understand that the end was as a result of 'Our anger', and was in retribution. I can 't reconcile these two.*

TOM: The Council has said to relate it in this manner: the Atlantean culture was created by the Alteans for us. There was error in the way it was created. Altea created difficulty for the souls in Atlantis, in their experimentations, and also created difficulty with their knowledge in hydrogen technology. Had we intervened and done something to contain this danger, we could have saved the situation, but in our distress with Altea, we created the destruction. Do you understand this?

STEVE: *Was it then a natural cataclysm? Are we saying that natural cataclysm was the means?*

TOM: It was brought about by experimentations in hydrogen. Is not hydrogen within your oceans?

STEVE: I see, the experimentation was done by the Alteans? Is that correct?

TOM: Yes.

GUEST: You mentioned that the Atlanteans used a hydrogen technology. Was this a weapons technology, or some other technology which became harmful?

TOM: You understand that means water? It was not for destruction of others, but it was not totally understood, and was a dangerous means that then could have created a chain-reaction, because all oceans and atmosphere and lands contain water.

GUEST: Is this connected with what nowadays we call 'heavy water'?

TOM: Yes.

GUEST: And were they seeking to generate energy or...?

TOM: It was curiosity about elements on Planet Earth, attempting to understand, being fearless without sense. Therefore the porpoises are souls, and the big [Humpback] whales that nurse their youth, were citizens of Atlantis. Also there are now returning many citizens of Atlantis and Mu for helping Planet Earth at this time, to fulfill what it was created for and to be in service. Many have memory. Those in the sea are those who were not sure that they could live in an upright position and not contaminate. Therefore they knew that by choosing the sea they could do no harm, and they enjoy mating joyfully.

GUEST: Now there is some confusion about the end of Atlantis, because you said once that it ended by natural processes, which I assume are the rising of the ocean levels at the end of the ice age, but also you have talked about 'your anger' and the sudden...

TOM: The end of the ice age came about because of our disturbance. You understand that if you are in anger, and you are from us, that your energy has power? Also that if you are not from us, your energy also has power? And as I have said it was not so much anger as it was despair. It was a chain reaction. The Atlanteans caused storms on the planet that they did not understand. They created their own demise, for interfering in the nature of evolutionary development.

JOHN: Some of these problematical characteristics are reappearing now, both in terms of destruction of the planet and our tampering with genetic engineering...

Tom: That is exactness, yes.

Guest: Was Altea himself present through the period of the Atlantean culture?

Tom: That was not possible. He is the head of Altea. It was an exercise for those civilisations to understand what humanness had to endure. You understand? I say 'understand' too often!

John: I'm wondering if we could have an exact date of the final submergence of Atlantis, and did this happen in a very short period of time or..?

Tom: It happened overnight... You must understand that when we speak of that time we are distressed. You humans have no recollection – and we do – if there could be a thing that would disturb the Council of Nine, it is that. There were those that, you would say, came in sheep's clothing but were wolves. It was our oversight. We perhaps underestimated the influence of those who would like our position, who were never in a position to have it, do you understand?

Guest: You have mentioned how at the end of Atlantis, people went to Egypt and to Ur, carrying with them much that they knew. I also wish to ask about other parts, including Central America, the Olmecs, Mayans and Aztecs, and also the ancient megalithic cultures of North West Europe, including Britain.

Tom: That is correct. Including those you identify as the Hellenes. From Troy.

Guest: The Hellenistic peoples of Greece and the Mediterranean?

Tom: That is correct. You know that in the dispersion and the traumaticness, when Atlantis had fallen, there were civilisations building in 8000 BC in Crete... There are those also in the regions of Middle Asia in the arena that is Israel, Jordan, also in the regions of the Saddam ... ?

Guest: Iraq?

Tom: Yes.

Guest: What about Central Asia?

Tom: Also in portions of China, of India, in regions of Tibet.

GUEST: And the Americas?

TOM: They were colonised also from regions of Israel. Did you not have Phoenicians, and they merged with aboriginals?

GUEST: In the Americas? With regards to that, do you have any other information about ancient visitors to the Americas?

TOM: It was colonised by the Phoenicians.

GUEST: I see. Could we just review the sequence of events in the history of Atlantis, then..?

TOM: You are attempting to arrange a chronologicalness. Is it not perhaps more useful to bring out the purpose?

JOHN: What you're saying here is that different civilisations, when they have these seedings, they were bringing different qualities, appropriate and necessary for human beings..?

TOM: And for Planet Earth. There cannot be derived a full picture, for portions of the mosaic would not be understood, yes.

12

Ancient Egypt

Egypt, from the Nine's perspective, would appear to have been born out of the demise of the Altean venture. For humankind, Egypt, together with Sumer, remain fascinating examples of high civilisations which suddenly appeared in the region around the middle of the fourth millennium BC. It is speculation that such a body of knowledge that both Egypt and Sumer possessed was taught to them, rather than developed by them. This chapter is full of astonishing, sometimes controversial information. Reading with care and patience would be beneficial – there is more than meets the eye in many of the sentences.

ANDREW: Is it true, according to Platonic legend, that some of the Atlanteans then brought the desirable elements of the Atlantean civilisation to Egypt? For example, I am very curious about the legend of Horus and the winged disc, in which he would appear in what was called a flying disc.

TOM: He arrived in a spacecraft. Remember that he was not birthed. In that time he went all over in what you would call a space craft. The Alteans were masters of that. And then they went beyond spacecraft, and in their mind they learned how to travel without a craft. Horus, Tehuti, Isis and other leaders taught them.

ANDREW: What were the arrangements whereby Tehuti and Isis and Horus came together in Egypt to start a new civilisation?

TOM: They all came simultaneously. Do you understand that they were able to be in different places at one time? Horus came to Egypt and Isis went to Ur, and others were in other places, but they also could be simultaneously together in each place.

ANDREW: I see. They were interchangeable, how very interesting. Now, many historians have noted the similarity of the cultures of Ur and Egypt. Other people have noticed that there was a similarity also with the Chinese culture...

Tom: That is correct. They were founded by the same people.

ANDREW: And who was involved in China?

Tom: The one who had been in the place near South America. Each of them was able to be simultaneously in any place.

ANDREW: I see, and what other places on Earth were simultaneously being developed at that time?

Tom: It was only the three places, and it was from these three that advanced culture then spread all around the globe.

JOHN: I'm very interested in the Great Pyramid and its meaning.

Tom: It was the Sphinx that had more to do with the beginning of Egypt. When the day arrives when there is understanding upon the planet, and when the arrival of other civilisations happens, to help the planet, then that will be the day when the full secrets of what you ask will be given.

In 1976 Andrew had asked several questions about the pyramids which Tom did answer:

ANDREW: We have some questions about the Great Pyramid. Could you tell us who first built it?

Tom: It was in conjunction: Hoova, Ashan, Altea, and also the civilisation of Myrex. It was four civilisations that raised it. When you ask who built it, you are speaking of the Twenty-Four civilisations.

ANDREW: Does that mean that humans did not have any part in the building?

Tom: They had a great part in the building. The engineering, the programming was done by the four civilisations. The attempting to transfer and transmit the knowledge came from the civilisations. Stonehenge also came from the civilisations. Yes.

ANDREW: And could you give us the dates when the Great Pyramid was started and when it was completed?

Tom: The Great Pyramid, and there were others that were of similar nature, was begun in a time before the destruction of Altea. It was begun approximately 150 years before the destruction of Altea,

13,000 of your years ago, in the colony in which it had been begun. Then, approximately 7,000 years ago additions were made and then it was completed.

ANDREW: *Was it originally of a flat top structure, and then completed as a pyramid or was it designed originally as a pyramid?*

TOM: It was originally designed to be a triangle. It was not completed though for a great length of time. It took — from the beginning until completion, because of destruction and changes — 6,000 years.

ANDREW: *I see. I climbed into a very secret part of the Great Pyramid, the chambers above the King's Chambers, and found and photographed the signature of the Pharaoh Khufu [Cheops]. Was he the one who completed that particular part of the structure?*

TOM: It was completed before. The understanding came to him.

ANDREW: *You mean the understanding of what the pyramid is about?*

TOM: Yes. Khufu was the reincarnation of the Hawk.

ANDREW: *And when did he live, what was the year?*

TOM: Altea has said it was 6,257 years before the Nazarene .

ANDREW: *Yes, thank you. And could you tell us, in whatever way you wish, what the purpose was for building the pyramid, and what is its inner secret that people are so concerned about?*

TOM: Partly, it is regeneration of cells. It channels the energy from the civilisations. The Great Pyramid, and other pyramids, spiral an energy upward. But also the civilisations bring energy into Planet Earth through the pyramids. In the chambers of the pyramids, there are areas which are, what you would call rejuvenation chambers: they do preservation of cells. There is more to them, but of this we cannot speak at this time.

JOHN: *Yes. The other two pyramids beside the Great Pyramid, they are from much later? From what date are they?*

TOM: They came approximately 1500 to 2000 years after the completion.

ANDREW: *When was the legendary Tower of Babel?*

TOM: That was in Ur. After the destruction of Atlantis: Ur was a colony from Atlantis. Its existence was within 200 years of the existence of Pharaoh Khufu. Its destruction was 3,000 years later. Yes.

In 1991 Tom answered some more questions about the Pyramid:

MIKI: *Some years ago I asked you when would be the time that you would reveal the secret of the Pyramids. So today I ask again whether you can reveal the secret of the Pyramids?*

TOM: The answer comes at this time, your circulations...

JOHN: *Crop circles, do you mean..?*

TOM: Yes. Upon this planet Earth in relationship to you... in arrangement for your planet Earth, in the maintenance of rotation. The pyramid energy was purposeful in emitting energy for what was circulating about your Planet Earth.
    Once the pyramid contained upon it elements of crystal that emanated an energy outward. The crystal was removed by humankind in their non-thinking mode of operation. In that removal they created a difficulty for the generation of necessary energy for its purpose. Is that clear?

DAVID: *When you said about the energy of circulation of the Earth, what does that mean?*

TOM: Have not there visited upon Planet Earth, now in recent time, those   rings?

DAVID: *Yes. Crop circles.*

JOHN: *There are further questions about how the pyramids were built, and were they built principally by people from other civilisations with the help of people from Planet Earth, or was it done entirely by other civilisations?*

TOM: Peoples of Planet Earth were of marginal importance in understanding the formula for creating this structure. When humankind.....(is there a word 'debased'?)

JOHN: *Yes, when humankind debased...*

TOM: ....through non-understanding the purpose of its interreactions, much of the memory was closeted.

JOHN: *Yes. One other subject, relating to that: the pyramids in Mexico, were they built for the same purpose and in the same way, or were they human attempts to copy?*

Tom: There were some created for the observation of those they call gods, to help them come to create an energy-field that released sound and colour waves upon Planet Earth, and there were... how you say? I know not how. There is in your native beings the desire to bring blessings from the heavens, and so the people then create what they believe will bring it down.

Guest: A number of people I know of are going to the Great Pyramid to see if they can contribute to opening up its energy. Is this the correct time to do that?

Tom: They may open the door a portion, but if it were opened more it would amount to a flooding of energy, and humankind would not comprehend   completely.

Guest: I understand. Also, I would like some clarification on how the great blocks of stone were placed in the Great Pyramid. It is my feeling that it was through the use of crystals that the stones were able to be placed on the pyramid.

Tom: It was with the benefit of crystal, with the benefit of vocal sound tuned to crystal, with the sound of 'OM'. Do you understand?

Guest: Yes. I had a vision of a being sort of on top of the stone, and under someone's command and direction the stone was lifted and placed into place by this system. Is this correct?

Tom: Yes, however there were many voices.

On March 22nd 1993 researchers announced the discovery of a narrow shaft, so small that they had to use a remote controlled camera to explore it. The shaft was closed off by a secret door.

Andrew: How much of the knowledge from Atlantis was given to the early Egyptians?

Tom: It was given to the early Egyptians, including the knowledge of medicine, with the exception of the knowledge of what could be done with the sex organs. Also you must understand that the primitive people with whom they worked in the land of Egypt were a very fearful people, because of their simplicity and their unconscious recollection of the destruction, and so they built upon their belief-structure a great system of worship. Also they worshipped those that were not of such a good nature: they chose not to mention this, and made them look good, out of fear of being harmed.

ANDREW: So, for example, Isis was, as I understand it, seen as the consort of Ra, who was one of those not-so-good ones of whom we are talking.

TOM: This is true.

ANDREW: And Horus was seen as the son of Ra and Isis. So, my question is, where does the Hathor goddess figure come in? Because she seems so much like Isis to us in many ways.

TOM: The goddess Hathor was a goddess of the night, what you would call a lady of the night. She was a lady that was a consort of all the gods. She was a lady of the evening. You have ladies of the evening in this nation in which you exist. It is the same.

ANDREW: Then how did she become identified in literature as being the wife of Horus?

TOM: She was the wife, but of all the gods: she was given a position by the people because she was powerful and because she could control the gods, and there was fear that if they did not worship, there would then be destruction.

ANDREW: And then there was Sekhmet [a fire goddess], how did Sekhmet, as another feline, relate to Isis and Hathor? These functions are very hard for us.

TOM: They were actually sisters.

ANDREW: I see. And Nephthys [housekeeper to Osiris and friend of the dead], was she in the same category?

TOM: It was only the goddess Hathor that controlled the rest, or attempted to. When people did not listen, then she controlled the gods. It is difficult to explain because you do not understand what was brought from the Altean age.

ANDREW: Yes, I was going to ask whether Hathor came from the Altean age, or whether she came from Altima or Hoova or where? What's her origin?

TOM: She was not from Altima, but her knowledge was. It was her knowledge of the physical control of others. She came from a species that has been a species for most of existence, because it was a mingling of all of the civilisations of the Universe: they have the strongest desires for goodness, but also the strongest of physical desires in all the Universe.

ANDREW: *Well, is she a member of the opposition or... we don't quite understand these things.*

TOM: She had all the goodness and all the desires. It is two beings.

JOHN: *It's a total mixture of both.*

TOM: It may be used by the others, as it may be used by us. It is a sacrifice. It is temptation, do you understand?

ANDREW: *That became kind of law in the Universe?*

TOM: How else could we weed out the physical desires of people and beings and species? If you be trapped in desire, and it sucks you dry, then you are lost, is that not true? We speak here to those that exist on this planet.

ANDREW: *Now I understand, yes, okay. And that is her function?*

TOM: Of the goddess Hathor? It has been always, all the days.

ANDREW: *There is an Indian goddess who is perhaps more appropriate, who is called Shiva...*

TOM: It is always one and the same.

ANDREW: *But Shiva is more clearly spelled out in our literature. Hathor is a mysterious figure.*

TOM: Do you understand why? Because in Egypt, they wanted to placate Hathor, in their minds, so they could believe she would only help them. Thus they made her the wife of the gods.

ANDREW: *Thank you for all these things...*

JOHN: *I would like to run through the sequence of transference of civilisation after the downfall of Atlantis. You told us, I believe, that the Sumerian was the first civilisation thereafter, but I'm trying to arrange in order the Greek, the Chinese, the Egyptian, and the Sumerian civilisations and their periods after Atlantis.*

TOM: At the time of the destruction of Atlantis, there were colonies. There was first Sumer, there was secondly China – there were meetings at times between the two, do you understand? There was also Egypt, at that time. The Greek culture came last, after the Egyptian. It was not simultaneous with Ur and Egypt.

JOHN: Yes. The Greeks retained the Atlantean legends more than the others, it appears. Is that correct?

TOM: It is truth. Because of the channelling through Plato. Plato was given impressions which prodded his mind, to ring bells in the head.

JOHN: Yes. When you say the channelling of Plato, I have heard that Socrates was the channel and Plato was the one who recorded it, is that correct?

TOM: It was Socrates, but it was the interpretation of Plato which was important. If the full information were given in detail, it would lead to confusion and misunderstanding. But by giving pieces, through assimilation of these pieces, and further research and discussion, the knowledge is gained.

JOHN: And the man-animal figures of both Greek and Egyptian cosmology?

TOM: They came from Atlantis.

JOHN: That is the experimentation?

TOM: Yes.

JOHN: In the time of the first Greek civilisation, were there any visits at all by the higher civilisations?

TOM: Yes. The gods.

JOHN: Well, I understood that the Greek mythology that we have was from an earlier time.

TOM: From Egypt – and from Atlantis. But do you understand that Greece also had the visitations from Altea?

JOHN: I didn't know that. What form did that take? Was that in space vehicles?

TOM: If people had the knowledge of a flame, it came as a flame.

STEVE: I'd like to know about mythological characters such as Mercury, Apollo, Diana and such: were these actually physically existent beings on the Earth at some time, or are they, as Jung says, archetypes of the unconscious?

TOM: They were physical beings. But archetypal.

STEVE: *In my investigations of correspondences with your communications I have come upon the Gnostic philosophers, a group of thinkers in the early Christian period. And it seems that many of their ideas correspond to ideas in the communications, particularly the name 'Aeons' which I understand has been used for reference to the Nine. Are these correspondances correct?*

TOM: Yes.

STEVE: *The name 'Aeons' refers to the Nine?*

TOM: That I am the spokesman for, yes.

STEVE: *And so, these revelations, when they appear in the Gnostic literature, are previously-channelled ....*

TOM: (interrupts)....Yes.

STEVE: *......communications, and are correct.*

TOM: Yes. The knowledge was given to a few, as the knowledge of this time is given to a few. In that time it was for only a few but now the exception being that in this time it must be given to the masses. It is a point of reference for validation.

STEVE: *Yes, I found these correspondances very impressive.*

TOM: Much truth was destroyed to keep the masses in control.

STEVE: *You're speaking presumably of the religions, the churches suppressing the Gnostic revelation.*

TOM: People and organisations of government and religion do not suppress anything unless it is a threat to them or it is a truth. Is that not so?

And then later, referring to the demise of civilisations, Tom said:

There was the collapse of the first arrival in Aksu, and then there was the collapse of what you call Atlantis, and then the collapse of Egypt, and then if you continue there was the collapse of many of Earth's civilisations. Have you now discovered why they have all collapsed?

ANDREW: *Well, presumably it has been when desire has overcome the higher evolutionary movement of the soul, is that not so?*

TOM: That is part of the truth, but also around 11,000 BC, going back to the time of Atlantis, the other group of beings that were colonised were then mingled with those of Hoova. That was the beginning of what you call the Hebrew culture.

ANDREW: Oh, that far back, I see. And would that have started not in Atlantis but in Ur? Or am I wrong in that assumption — did they start before the period of Ur?

TOM: They were before the period of Ur.

ANDREW: And who was the leader of this Hebrew colony?

TOM: It was of four generations of Abraham.

JOHN: So the beginnings of the Hebrew culture were a mixture of Hoovids and these other beings, and this accounts for the characteristics of the Jewish People?

TOM: Yes.

JOHN: I thought that there were no survivors of Atlantis?

TOM: No. There were colonies that were not destroyed.

ANDREW: I thought they went on to be dolphins.

TOM: Those that were destroyed, that were not in error, became dolphins.

ANDREW: That's beautiful.

JOHN: And those that were in error, were their souls annihilated at that time? What happened?

TOM: How can you annihilate a soul? You can only pray and hope for it.

IV

VITAL LINKS IN THE CHAIN

13

Hoovid Branchings, Hebrew Roots and the Crescent

Exploring the connections between the Hoovids and the Ishmaels and the Middle East in relation to these matters, this chapter is of vital importance to our understanding of the planet and our contribution to the Universe.

While reading, it would be well to remember Tom's observation "That before you criticise the Hoovids, reflect that you might well have Hoovid genes yourself."

IRENE: Please tell us of the sons of heaven marrying the daughters of Earth.

TOM: You know that in the Word-Book [the Bible] utilised upon Planet Earth, there is an essence of truth, and a great deal of human corruption, for keeping humankind in bondage? You know also that the Hoovids and other civilisations came to this planet Earth for colonisation. And for the preparation of Planet Earth.

Also, upon this planet Earth there were those beings that existed and emerged from the essence of the Earth. Then those of the Hoovid and other civilisations – what on the Earth they call 'gods' or 'sons of the gods' merged with the daughters of humanity. This is why all humankind looks to the heavens as the source of their beginning. For they were derived from the heavens, and also there were some civilisations or sub-civilisations that were able to come for the impregnation of women of humankind, and to set their stream. And in the time of Aksu the 'Hawk' came, and then the Hoovids were chosen for the implantation of individuality and determination, and perhaps an ingredient of tenacity. And over time we saw those elements become stronger, at times to the point of corrupting the beneficial qualities of tenacity, determination and individuality.

Then came the Nazarene, who is the head of Hoova, in order to soften that individualism. It was a great necessity, but we do not remove individualism or free will. But we needed to expand compassion, for in the need for survival, compassion was not developed. Compassion is now an element of development.

IRENE: But this question of compassion goes back to before Abraham, it goes back to the Garden, to Aksu?

TOM: That is correct, they were Hoovids. You see the problem there was: knowing full well who they were, where they came from, and knowing of the temptation of the opposition, it was a matter of obedience. The Hoovids did not obey, and have not obeyed since, in spite of all the rituals, and continuous asking for the Almighty to intervene, and all the prayers being directed to the Almighty.

Higher elements within the Hoovids understand this is pointless, for the Hebrews must take responsibility. But those higher elements, those of the Kabbalah, are not accepted by those who stay in the ritual. Ritual serves a purpose, but not to the exclusion of all other things. There is an error. They believe that they must study the word to the exclusion of all other things, for they feel that will be their connection, and some might not have understanding or compassion for others. They set themselves up on a pinnacle and they do not comprehend that, by doing that, they are putting themselves up there as a target for slaughter, Do you understand?

IRENE: Yes.

TOM: Most of the civilised world contains these elements, for they have spread and multiplied across Planet Earth. Within the nation of Israel they are intensified but you need to be aware that this has come about through human life, for in the centre they are the purest and gentlest. Are we now confusing you?

IRENE: No, not at all. One of my questions has been: why is there so much focus on the Jewish people throughout the world, and what is going on beneath the surface..?

TOM: They are the saviours of this planet, they must fulfil their choosing. The Hoovids have come here three times to break through the barriers of those of the inbreeding, to help bring elevation to Earth. The concentration of Hoovids is in the nation of Israel, for it is a representative microcosm of the entire planet Earth. And thus Israel is important, for Earth is unique, and no other planet exists like it in the Universe. All these years the Others have bound it.

IRENE: So, once the Hoovids are released to their true selves, the other twenty-three civilisations will then be able to do their work more fully on Planet Earth?

Tom: That is correct. For they are bound and hindered by this element of obstinacy in the Hoovids. We know of the essence of the Hoovids, the abilities, the genetic code, the DNA of the Hoovids, the life-force... when that is released, the Universe is released. A very large order! Yes.

John: So the Hoovids came three times. Are you talking about the first time being Adam and Eve, the second time Abraham, and the third time Jesus?

Tom: You may put it like that but in truth they came as the eve of Adam, then the implantation was before Abraham and the development was the nation of Abraham... you see?

Irene: When did the competition with the Creator begin, and why? And was that also a testing of obedience?

Tom: It was a testing of obedience, and it began when they left Ur – before that they listened and viewed. You see, Abraham began the testing, for he knew that he contained within him the essence of all creation. He also knew that he contained within him all knowledge, and he also had this strong connection with creation, and therefore, when asked for the sacrifice of his son, he knew innately that he could do that, for in the acceptance and the doing, it would not be necessary. This was the first lesson. Humankind has forgotten: we have constantly reiterated the importance of acceptance – for then you no longer need to accept. But the descendants of Abraham lost the internal knowledge: they only kept the knowledge of who they were. In their need for survival, they did not accept total obedience. They were always making deals. Where one group would be in awe of creation, the Hoovids would look at the creation as something to be utilised.

Irene: That's how they survived.

Tom: That is correct. And in the surviving they lost certain elements of awe and obedience, yes.

Andrew: Tom, could you explain why you chose the Israelites many years ago for the Yehovah leader, what the plan was, and how it is working out in terms of the religious, historical beliefs that they live under?

TOM: Yes. They are a nation of people with strength. They came from an area of a planet of strength.

ANDREW: You mean that they are seed that came from another planet than Earth?

TOM: Yes. They came from Hoova. They had strength within their character, and also because the planet from which they came was a warrior-like planet. In their seeding here, they were asked only to be at peace.

ANDREW: And historically, how was it planned for them to act as catalysts and leaders amongst the peoples of the Earth, as they seem to have done...

TOM: We asked them to work according to plan. The only problem was at the time of the man called the Nazarene. In their minds, in their culture they knew and in the seed of their soul ....if you understood their origins you would then understand the factors of doubt and questioning. Part of the reason for their existence on this planet was to overcome that factor.

ANDREW: That I can understand. Have they been successful or not?

TOM: They were not successful at the time of the man you call Jesus.

ANDREW: Was Jesus truly in the model of their expectations of the Messiah?

TOM: Yes. But because of their nature, they mostly did not recognise him and throughout the generations, within them lives the know-ledge that they have made an error. But because of pride, they will not acknowledge this. Do you understand?

ANDREW: Yes.

TOM: So from this aspect we arrive at a nation that is fierce with pride, and from this grew the desire to help their own nation, so in effect our plan was turned around. Yet this is really their salvation because it shows the nations of Earth that they are a nation that will not be conquered – in spite of the fact that they made an error – every nation has made an error.

ANDREW: Yes. Is there any possibility of rectifying that error and still saving their pride?

TOM: They will come to acceptance.

ANDREW: There is this small matter of names: the difference between he whom we call Yehovah and he whom we call Jesus or Yeshua.

TOM: They are one and the same.

JOHN: Could you tell us about the nation on Earth related to Altea?

TOM: The primary concern for this planet is the Hoovas. Altea is here to help in the situation. As brother would help another brother.

ANDREW: Yes. But the relationship between what you planned in Egypt as a civilisation, and what Moses learned from that, and what he carried into his relationship with Hoova and then what was carried by that tradition into the later period, all these things are of great interest. It seems to be a continuous thread, even though much of it has been lost – am I saying the right things?

TOM: You are correct.

ANDREW: So it was most necessary that Moses learn all the deepest secrets of the Egyptian tradition in order to know who he was and what his role was?

TOM: Yes.

ANDREW: Which of course he never revealed. I suppose it was forbidden at that time, was it not?

TOM: Yes.

GUEST: In the early days of Israel there was much bloodshed and violence, particularly when Joshua and the Jewish people moved into Israel, after their forty years in Sinai. Can you elucidate why Jews sought to see non-Jewish people as the 'enemies of God' to the extent that they killed so many people when they returned to Israel?

TOM: Why did the Christians see so many people as the enemies of God when they found non-Christians?

GUEST: Was this not a precedent started by the Jews, perhaps?

TOM: That is not so. This is the reasoning why: Hoova announced to Moses that the land they were taken out of belonged to them. What you have not considered is that when the Israelites were given something or it was their place, they were uprooted and enslaved. As they were told by Hoova of the understanding of one God, and that Israel was their place; and then others did not wish them to enter.

Do you understand those that are now [this was early 1992] Serbians and Croatians? Their war is tribal, is it not? Is tribalism not a basic animal instinct? Look at it this way. Is it not tribal with Ishmael? Therefore why is it permitted for one group to be tribal, but not for another? Is it not true you still have tribal conflict upon this planet even in this time of free thinking?

Think of an animal such as a dog. You bring this animal into your home, then you bring another also. In the beginning, when you give them their food, the natural instinct in them will be to snarl and to attack, is that not true? Now take a human. In those days, and even these days, if they have been beaten and subjected to inadequate life-conditions, they are like a dog. It is only when that dog is repeatedly treated well, and understands that it will always have food, that it will stop attacking and taking from another. There is one difference with humans. They have that instinct of the dog, and they also have the emotions which dogs do not: therefore that basic instinct also fires up the emotion, then reason does not come in.

You still find this in primitive tribes who believe in their one God also, and they say they have been told 'this and that'. So why do you then single out the Hoovids from others? What you should look upon for the Hoovids is this: a small group of people that have survived at all odds, a small group who have continued to educate and forward all of their peoples – this does not say there is perfection or the development of utter graciousness of personality. It is one group or nation that does not hold its own in bondage or as downtrodden. We ask you, why should not the Hoovids have their way?

GUEST: *Yes. May I explain? As far as I understand, when Abraham arrived in Israel he bought a plot of land, and that seems to have been a sensible thing to do politically. There was also Moses, who had taught the Jewish people, in the Ten Commandments, about not killing and not stealing. Can you say something about that?*

TOM: There were only two commandments for the nation of Hoova. Those two are: 'Thou shalt not worship false Gods', and 'Thou shalt do unto others as you want others to do unto you'. Those are the only two commandments given to the nation of Hoova. There are many rules. The other eight commandments were given to all the nations. So what has kept the nation of Hoova all of these millennia is those two commandments? So then we ask you, do you now understand?

They are the only nation upon Planet Earth that daily challenges their God. The only nation that has the impetus to fight with their

God. They are not subservient. They challenge as you are now challenging. They challenge their God, their Hoova and they will continue to do so, for they know and feel they are one with him, therefore they have the right to challenge, where all other belief-systems do not believe they have the right. It can be a burr in your bottom, can it not?

GUEST: Yes. Now in the history of Israel the people of the north (the lost tribes of Israel) were taken away and dispersed by invaders. Were these people eliminated, or did they mix with the peoples of other countries?

TOM: They are all over the world, and as examples, some are in Afghanistan, some in Ethiopia, some in North America – in the native White Spirit people – in Phoenicians, in the people of the musical language written of by Caesar and in the Orientals. There is now the beginning of an understanding of the dispersal and the in-gathering.

GUEST: So this dispersal – could you say it was an unconscious fulfilment of the task that the Jews came to Earth to fulfil?

TOM: Are you attempting to establish that it was acceptable for them to be dispersed, because they then fulfilled what they did not fulfil originally?

GUEST: Not exactly, but I am aware that it has been said that the Hoovids came in order to mix with the people of Planet Earth.

TOM: That is a truism, but they that stayed together did so because the others had been dispersed. If I would have a word of my own to say, would you like to hear?

GUEST: Yes.

TOM: I will ask the Council if I may say it. They said I may say, but you may not be pleased with it. It is this:

We would have one warning to people who are working with higher consciousness, to be very cautious about your attitudes toward the Hoovids: for it may very well be that you are a Hoovid also, yes. What we are attempting to say is that the majority of people that are involved in spiritual elevation contain the genes of Hoovids – so look upon what I say, and how you then place yourselves in that.

Council has said I must convey that we also have great frustration, for perhaps in many of your aeons we have not explained clearly the situation of the Hoovids. What continues to persist is the negating of

Hoovids on Planet Earth. Look at all the world, in every nation, and see which negative characteristics developed that made that nation feel different from others.

Your nation [England] believed you were superior to other nations, and your righteousness was the very essence of righteousness. When you have the in-gathering of many and the clapping goes all around the world — then all will be free of the bondage of their bringing forth from their civilisations what was of the best.

ANDREW: There is one terrible burning question which every Israelite in the world wants to know: why was it permitted for 6,000,000 Jews to be killed during World War II?

TOM: Did you not know of others that have been killed?

ANDREW: Yes, I know of many others, but these are the 'Chosen people' and there must be a reason. It was not blind or accidental....

TOM: It was the final bringing together of the Jews.

ANDREW: That's a difficult thing to tell to Jewish people...

TOM: If you tell the truth, even in all sincerity, you will infuriate the nation of Israel, as they are always infuriated with such things. Perhaps it is better to try to make the world aware of the greatness of the nation of Israel?

ANDREW: Still, this is a very delicate matter...

TOM: Explain that there is not a death in the world that has no consequence.

ANDREW: What happened to those 6,000,000 souls who were sacrificed in this way?

TOM: They are not stockpiled.

ANDREW: They have been freed?

TOM: They are in essence and in truth have returned to the civilisation Hoova.

ANDREW: That's most important, most important to know.

TOM: The greatest portion of those six million came at that time to sacrifice self, to make your planet Earth aware that there were those that would attempt to rule and control humanity.

And remember this too: as a result of the six million the nation of

Israel came into being.

There is anger in Israel against the six million for their method of going, without questioning, by being led like sheep to the slaughter house, but in them they knew that this was their choosing. This was why there was no combat amongst the majority of them. On the one hand this created disgust amongst the Germans but on the other hand it also created awe that they could go in quietness. But within their souls they knew that they had chosen this, to bring forth the nation of Israel, and to make Planet Earth aware that there are negative forces that could attempt to destroy all and to feed on the power of others. When the nation of Israel can accept within themselves that there was a majority that chose, then there will be understanding. The method of extermination they did not choose: that is the karma of the nation of Germany, yes.

STEVE: *As the aim is presumably to heighten consciousness on this planet, to unite the people of this planet, I find it very difficult to deal with the notion that the Israeli people are the 'chosen people' for this work. In this time the idea of a chosen people is a very difficult and rather retrograde concept.*

TOM: Do you have the understanding that within the nation of Israel is represented all the nations of your planet Earth? Do you understand when we use the term 'chosen' it is not necessary to associate that term to them: what we are trying to say is that if they had followed their program, which they had chosen, there would be no need for the world situation you now have, for all the nations upon the planet Earth would be 'chosen'. Do you understand that within the nation of Israel is a representative of each of the nations and races upon Earth? If you reach the nation of Israel, the energy would generate then to all the planet Earth. What should have taken place thousands of years ago will then come into being. It is not that they are specially chosen, for what they have chosen is similar to service: you do not buy service, you pay for service. They are paying for service. Being a chosen people is not necessarily like being an elite, for being chosen brings great difficulty.

STEVE: *Yes. It seems to me that perhaps they're one of the most difficult groups of people to bring round to higher consciousness. What appears to be happening is that higher consciousness has been generated among a large number of people scattered throughout the world.*

TOM: We have knowledge of what you are referring to, but consider this: if you imagine the Universe as a wholeness, and you see a black spot in the Universe which is the planet Earth, which has bottlenecked the evolving of the Universe and is stopping the growth of souls that should by this time have evolved further... and if you then look upon the Earth and see the nation of Israel as a black spot on Planet Earth, it is important to reach the nation that is all nations within one nation, to raise the level of all the nations. Yes.

STEVE: *Yes. What we have seen in the Western world in recent years [1976] has been a conspicuous heightening of consciousness among younger people, due to a merging of Eastern and Western traditions. A flow of ideas, methods of consciousness training and suchlike from East to West. Is this not a valuable thing?*

TOM: If they may take it and bring it into balance. We have explained that the East is not in true balance, nor is the West. It is important for you to understand that both need to be brought into balance: that is vitally important for Planet Earth. The nation of Israel is a blend of both.

STEVE: *Yes, that's true. Only ....*

TOM: What you are asking, concerning Israel, is a question that will be asked by many.

STEVE: *Well, yes, that's why I'm asking it.*

TOM: The people of Planet Earth tend to reject the nation of Israel, but they are yet to recognise within them that the greatest portion of humankind also contains a portion of the nation of Israel within themselves, and thus also has the same tendencies that they feel are attributable to the nation of Israel.

GUEST: *In what way are the Jewish people any different? Is there something special about their relationship to the land of Israel?*

TOM: Those of the nation of Israel came to Planet Earth many thousands of your years ago. They came to evolve your planet Earth, and in their genetics they know their choosing, and they relate closely to the Creator, for the memory is coming from their innermost. But what this in actuality means is that they have a great responsibility, for they have an ability to elevate Planet Earth into a collective consciousness that may bring all people into their proper places, so that Planet Earth may then fulfil unity in the Universe. They are a people that have great energies, that have great ability in their genetics. The people of Israel also have the ability to bring into existence with their minds all that they desire, but also all that they fear. Israel is a microcosm of Earth, and as the nation of Israel is affected so is the planet .

GUEST: How can Jews elevate the planet? I didn't quite understand.

TOM: The nation of Israel has within it powers that can release in humankind all that is buried, all that may be brought forth into light. As they hold this code they also reject this code, for they are the greatest of sceptics upon your Earth. They reject it, for inwardly they have the knowledge that it brings forth great responsibility.

The minds of the people of Israel have an energy such that what they fear they create for themselves, and what they project in positivity they bring into reality. Everyone on Planet Earth, in their creation of thought can bring it to fruition but in the nation of Israel this is magnified and can thus create – if the thoughts are emotional or lacking clarity – imbalance within your Planet Earth. Yes.

JOHN: What would you recommend to the people of Israel, what could help in their job, both for themselves and for others?

TOM: The most important aspect is to understand that the Universe is with them, by their thinking they do not permit it to flow into them. When there is dissension within, it creates greater dissension without. It is time for all to come together in understanding each other, and when we say this we mean all the tribes within the nation of Israel. When Israeli people fear, creating a situation in which they feel all the world against them, then they bring that into their reality.

The error of the nation of Israel is that they accept their specialness without taking responsibility. People who are not Hebrew are in a difficult situation to tell them they are not special, and to get them off their backsides. They need to understand the overcoming of apathy. They need the information and knowledge that no one will do it for them, even Yehovah, and that they must do it themselves – particularly because they have the ability to do it. They are conditioned to believe that they are entitled to do what they themselves feel is best. This needs to be communicated gently.

DAVID: So this is a question of self-empowerment..?

TOM: That is the key. It takes only one person to begin the process. The nation of Israel is in serious difficulty and in great troubles at this time [1976]. Israel, in its state of consciousness, of uneasiness, of aggressiveness within itself, is radiating an energy. It has become a nationalist of thoughts. There is much anger among all, and they cannot do anything to bring themselves out. They do not understand that they are creating the difficulty. The nations surrounding it also create difficulty, and this radiates out into the world. In relationship to catastrophes, we will not permit catastrophes to completely remove and to deprive Earth souls. What we are trying to say is: those that communicate in negativity are in a realm that is using their emotion, their trauma and is not of the purest.

[And then in 1980] We are attempting to prepare Israel for understanding. There are more great intellects within the nation of Israel than in many lands, but there is in truth more emotionalism of minds that are not in control – minds that emotions control, rather than minds controlling emotion. Because of this energy of the nation of Israel, those that exist upon planet Earth cannot move forward. Those who oppose keep the nation of Israel in unbalance and imbalance, for they affect things through emotion.

The ego of those that exist in the nation of Israel is not in balance, their emotion controls their mind. It is with great sadness that we say this, for if they attempt to learn and do control their mind, then they may move the nation of Israel into the highest realm. Hoovids must learn to cultivate detachment from their emotions, so those of the opposition cannot use them. For the opposition are parasites of mind that would like to control, disrupt, destroy. They have done that to the nation of Israel. The people of Israel are controlled by their emotions. Their emotions are controlled by those that oppose, for they live on that energy. This nation of intellectual genius has given that genius away.

In this time, [1988] the importance of creating a direction of transformation, to bring about true transformation upon Planet Earth, must begin in Israel. The nation of Israel, being a microcosm of the whole world, contains within it the energies of all. In truthfulness, knowing that the Israelis are from Hoova, we also know that the change will have some difficulty. We underestimated the intensity of the effect of density on the peoples of Planet Earth, and of the fears of those upon it, brought about by the Others. Therefore there has been the greatest of delay. We also had the hope that the Hoovids would understand their purpose within their core, and would begin Earth's transformation. Again, however, we had underestimated the individualism of the creative being. Now it is of the greatest importance that this transformation begins, for your planet Earth is on a threshold. And in attaining and reaching the energies of this nation of Israel (which is a representation of Earth) the unbottlenecking of the bottleneck begins.

ISRAEL: How does Yehovah look at the situation at this point?

TOM: With the greatest of tears, for his nation, the nation of Israel in their... may we explain a situation? The nation of Israel makes judgement on what is important or not important for their self-image in the world. That is a form of lack of communication, and this creates difficulty in the rest of the world, for the Hoovids feel that in their mind they know, and that is enough. It must be understood that the time has passed when they may keep only to themselves. It is important that communication not be judgmental of what is important and not, for all peoples are different, and all peoples have a need to understand other peoples. This is the biggest difficulty, for because of the lack of communication, those outside Israel then think that the Israeli nation considers them to be inferior. The peoples of the world have only one way of understanding each other, and that is through communication. As the nations of the continent of Europe are unifying, so then know in truth that the nations of other continents may also unify.

[*And to a group of meditators in 1990*] Focus your attention for the unification of other arenas also, and keep foremost in your mind the understanding that the nation of Israel is a microcosm for Planet Earth. What is important is energy for the integration of wholeness and completion. To bring peace between the children of Abraham, for Ishmael is from Abraham also.

JOHN: You implied once that it might be important for the Jewish people to come to a recognition of who Jesus was.

TOM: There are many among the Hebrews who understand and accept that the Nazarene was a teacher. What is difficult is for them to understand is the affiliation of Yehovah with the civilisation of Hoova. As you know the 'God of the Hebrews' was maintained to be a jealous god. They misunderstood that totally, completely. And they also do not understand that these beings to whom they have given the term 'god' not just the Hoovids but gods of all the major religions and their spin-offs, were of physicalness made into gods by humans on Earth. That is now at a stage of revolution-evolution. It is those who come from Ishmael who are currently [October 1990] in the greatest difficulty, for their zeal has no respect for life, where the

Hoovids had and have respect, do you understand the difference? Those from Ishmael do not permit others to fulfil their physical life upon Planet Earth for its full evolutionary cycle.

GUEST: There seems to be a lot of focus on the Jewish people and their position in the world and I wonder if you could provide a little more information concerning the Islamic people, which might help balance things a bit?

TOM: What you are asking we have explained often and you say that we have approached positively to those of Hoova and not to those of Ishmael?

GUEST: Not exactly, but it can appear that way – that a lot of attention has been on the Jewish people.

TOM: That has been of necessity. We ask you this: Are not the Buddha, the Hindu, those of the great White Spirit mentioned? May we ask why you must speak in ofteness of Ishmael?

GUEST: For me, it has been mainly a desire to balance things up a little.

TOM: How can you balance what is not balanced? You need to hear what we have said. You have not understood the purpose of the nation of Israel.

GUEST: I was wondering what were the positive contributions of the Arabic peoples to the world as a whole? For example, the Secretary General of the United Nations [1992] is a man from Egypt, a Christian married to a Jew, and this seems to me to be a significant thing...

TOM: All Arabic people do not have Islam, there is a difference. Arabic peoples have contributed in greatness to Earth in times of past, in literature, colours, science... what has stopped that growth is the conformity of some religious sections in Islam. We do not place all in a pot, as we do not place all of the Hoovids in a pot. Closer to reality are those that follow Jethro and the daughter Fatima.

GUEST: Could you explain more about the influence of Jethro?

TOM: It is similar to those that call themselves Followers of Christ- the Followers of Jehovah, which is in truth, a sect. Fatima and Jethro are a sect of Islam, of the one they identify as the Prophet.

GUEST: What is the positive contribution Arabs can make to the world, and what do they need to learn in order to make this contribu-

tion?

TOM: If you tell them they need to learn they will be greatly anguished at you.

GUEST: Yes. However, we all need to learn things.

TOM: You know that, many individuals in the mass understand that, but when a mass is totally controlled by religious leaders, it cannot accept learning from others. What is of necessity is the allowance for others to live also. What is necessary also is the allowance of complete education for their mothers, for keeping their mothers in ignorance then breeds ignorance again. We speak now of leaderships of a nation that believe a woman has less value, then the corruption... it was once the same in your own states also, but with education and non-ignorance it moved forward – for in controlling women nations stop their own growth. They have convinced those mothers that it is beneficial for them to be less than they are. It is the will of their civilisation.

JOHN: Was that part of the influence of the Fallen One?

TOM: Yes.

JOHN: Because it kept them in bondage?

TOM: Kept. That nation was not dispersed.

JOHN: Do you have anything to say about Jerusalem, and its current history of being divided, and then unhappily reunited?

TOM: Jerusalem is the primary area of discontent. It must be unified, in truth. For it does not belong to Islam, it does not belong to Christianity, and it does not belong to the nation of Israel: if it belongs to anyone, it belongs to us. We are saddened that it is not unified. But we must say: the nation of Israel has protected it better than all others. We would wish that the peoples in that area begin to understand that they walk upon hallowed earth. And when it is unified, the world is unified.

GUEST: Not long ago I woke up with the idea that Jerusalem needs to become an international city...

TOM: That is not only yours. That has been thought of in the minds of many. Know that neither the forces of Ishmael nor those of Israel would agree with this at this time. The Ishmaels believe that by their possessing it, the God of the Jews cannot return. Therefore they then can remove the Jews. The nation of Israel will not agree with it, for when the Ishmaels had possession of it, they permitted all peoples except Jews to enter their own holy sites, and they destroyed the holy sites of the Jews and desecrated their holy places with faecal matter. When the nation of Israel is in charge, all peoples including Arabs may enter. You understand the difference? Until that painful memory of the desecration is removed from consciousness, Jerusalem cannot be at peace. And that will come soon, but until that time there is that blocked energy around.

GUEST: *One of the daring thoughts I had is that the UN is likely to look for a new centre for itself, and I was wondering – is it a correct possibility that Jerusalem could become a centre for the United Nations?*

TOM: The United Nations would devastate Jerusalem, for those who enter from most nations are not respectful to others. A central uni-fied city that all may enter would be acceptable, but Jerusalem may not be ruled by.. you understand the United Nations is not united? And you also understand that the United Nations, in moving, would wish to build monstrous edifices?

*   *   *

TOM: We wish you to know this: as it is here, it is also above. Therefore we now link with you in meditation: To bring about peace, balance, harmony, and removal of fear and hatred. For the Hoovids to accept their true purpose. For Hoovids not to have fear of loving again in joy and trust. And to remove the hatred from the Ishmaels. For the Ishmaels to forgive their journey in the desert, to forgive the Hoovids, to forgive Sarah and Abraham. That the Hoovids and Ish-maels may be true brothers.

14

The Covenant

At the time of the Covenant, the thought that God would come into a personal relationship with humankind was a new idea. God offered friendship and asked for trust in return. And that trust was to be expressed by living in his Way.

The transmission starts off with some observations by Tom about the balance between the peoples of the Middle East.

JOHN: Now one thing I've never quite understood: when you say, for example, that Moses is a mixture of Altea and Ashan, does this mean that the soul originally evolved on Altea? The original evolution of the soul?

TOM: It was in Ashan, then with the mixture of Altea – then Moses became a being upon Earth. There are special kinds of beings upon Earth that have the purification of two civilisations.

JOHN: Yes, but the origin of Moses...

TOM: The origin was from Ashan.

JOHN: And we are talking about the soul?

TOM: Yes. Now we will explain to you about the Bedouin. The Bedouin are of great importance, for the Jewish nation also comes from them. The mate of Moses was a Bedouin. But also the descendants of Rachel and of Leah came from a land that had the Bedouin living in it. Remember this: those Bedouin that have been instilled into the nation of Israel are also those that have the understanding of the natural laws that come from the Creator of the Universe. They are also more highly evolved in their awareness of their Creator. They are not the same as the Arab – they have a different thinking. They are between the Israeli and the Arab in that respect.

The text continues with the exploration of identities....

JOHN: *Are you saying that those of Hoova do not know exactly who Yehovah is then, is that correct?*

TOM: That is in truth correct.

ANDREW: *It is a very delicate point but are you speaking of Hoova now, or the Israelis?*

TOM: Hoova.

JOHN: *Now I have a delicate question, is it all right to ask?*

TOM:Yes.

JOHN: *I'm assuming then that Yehovah is in fact part of the Nine but the Hoovids do not know that?*

TOM: He is a composite of all of us.

JOHN: *I thought that you meant that Jesus has a piece of...*

TOM: Yes, but he is of all of us.

ANDREW: *So in fact when the ancient Hebrew biblical belief states that Yehovah is indeed God, they are correct then?*

TOM: Yes.

ANDREW: *So it is possible that a person, a being, a god, whatever the word is, someone like Yehovah, is indeed a personalisation of all of you?*

TOM: Yes.

ANDREW: *That is a different concept from a composite.*

TOM: Yes.

ANDREW: *What you have been telling us seems to indicate that Yehovah is the head of a civilisation, Hoova. It seems as if we are bringing the Jewish God down to a lower level — how can we deal with this most sensitive issue?*

TOM: Council has said that it is a perplexing problem for those of the nation of Israel, but if it could be explained in the intellect, not in the emotions, who the Hebrews are, why they have that sense of duty within, and why they have failed, and that the civilisations are attempting to help them, then the Hebrews will come to understand.

ANDREW: *Yes. I have a suggestion to make: somewhere I've read in a*

Talmud text, that in ancient times the rabbis did know that there was a God above Yehovah, and that Yehovah was indeed something of what we now understand him to be.

TOM: Yes.

ANDREW: I would like to ask about the Ark of the Covenant. Is it well preserved and in perfect condition? Have you seen to that over the thousands of years?

TOM: It has not been placed in vain. There are those on Earth who believe that it never existed.

JOHN: I'm interested in knowing more about the god of the Arabs, Allah. You've never really explained who he is.

TOM: There is but one that heads the Universe. It is a composite, yes. But when you speak of the god of the Arabs, do you have the understanding that our Abraham was the father of two nations?

JOHN: Yes.

TOM: Then you also understand that Allah is what those of Israel call Yehovah.

The nation of Israel has forgotten its heritage, its choosing and its Covenant. Abraham was told to go and spread his seed through all the planet Earth. Abraham attempted to spread his seed into the Universe not into planet Earth. Abraham in his beginning was not willing to give up control completely. Abraham was told to populate and to go forth, and the Covenant was not truly kept. If this nation had gone forth and populated as it was, then this the planet Earth would not be in such a serious state as it is at this time.

Holding on to tradition has been made by man, not from us or from the civilisations. It has been a way in which man has controlled other men. The people of the nations of Ishmael are brothers with the nation of Israel. It is important that brothers not fight brothers, but in your world it seems to be your system. It is important for this message to be given to the nation of Israel, for they need to understand that the powers of their mind can create that which they fear.

Your mind brings to you not what you want, it brings to you what you are. The nation of Israel must look closely at what they are. They want peace, but may we ask why they do not have peace? For what are their fears? It is what is in the hearts of the men and women of the nation of Israel that is most important. And when the nation of Israel begins to fear less, then also it will begin to change and then perhaps the nations of its father, the Patriarch Abraham, may also begin to change. For each feeds the other. Yes.

It is very difficult to get humankind to obey. When you view this planet Earth, and all the groups that exist. For many civilisations it is difficult to see, in truth, which are willing to obey. The Hoovids are the least willing.

IRENE: *And who are the most willing?*

TOM: The Zeneels.

IRENE: *And that's because they understand the greater profundity?*

TOM: Yes.

IRENE: *Why, of all the civilisations, are the Hoovids the least intuitive and perceptive? They have the greatest gift and great ability, yet they are the ones who are busy denying it the most.*

TOM: They are the most intuitive. But they chose to armour themselves because they are the most in competition with us. In their inner soul they know this and also who they are. However they became confused upon planet Earth, and those of the opposition are able to manipulate them.

IRENE: *So when you came and gave part of yourselves to establish humankind, the Hoovids were originally the captains of the captains?*

TOM: Correct. They came to Planet Earth three times. They are the 'sons of gods that came and mingled with the daughters of man.' They were twice again given the opportunity, for it was seen what was needed to bring Planet Earth to its fulfilment. But we made an error also, for the civilisation of Hoova, which is the civilisation of the Nazarene, which is love, upon its coming to Planet Earth, became the one of least love. The Others knew of its strength and corrupted it, yes.

IRENE: *What are the relationships of the other twenty-three civilisations to the Hoovids?*

TOM: They will be the colonisation of other worlds. They are in equality but the Hoovids were the ones with the tenacity to persevere upon Planet Earth. And in the beginning we did not truly know which of the civilisations would be the persevering ones.

IRENE: *So that when you created humankind, you gave yourselves time, you basically waited to see......?*

TOM: That is correct, we observed to see what we would do.

IRENE: And to see who would recognise what I believe was the most important gift you gave: which was free will.

TOM: That is correct.

TOM: And whereas the other civilisations found strength in being collectives..........

TOM: Collective: exactness.

IRENE: The Hoovids...

TOM: Were individuals. Correct.

IRENE: But there is a relationship here, is there not, between individualism and free will, free will is a double-edged sword, isn't it?

TOM: That is correct. You believe you are in control but you are always controlled. You believe that you have free will — and the truth is that you do, but when you understand you have free will, totally and completely, then you give up that free will. Do you understand?

IRENE: Yes, because the knowledge of what you truly possess becomes the very thing that allows you to dispossess it.

TOM: That is correct, like obedience.

IRENE: Now the Others knew that if they can control the Hoovids, the rest of the civilisations wasn't as important.

TOM: Yes. We would pray the Hoovids would understand that.

IRENE: Which also goes back to what you were saying before, which is the testing of yourselves, isn't it?

TOM: That is correct.

IRENE: Because you exist in an arena where collective consciousness and free will don't have meaning?

TOM: That is correct.

IRENE: And so for you to better understand free will, you needed to watch how your creation understood it.

TOM: We needed a lens, yes.

IRENE: And you also knew that there was going to be a battle with the Others.

TOM: We would have been naive not to, yes. But you understand, we did not know the outcome, for it is not our way.

IRENE: *The outcome in terms of your battle with them?*

TOM: That is correct.

IRENE: *I believe that. But what happened is that you knew that in some sphere, in some universe, that this battle was going to play itself out. You knew that you couldn't directly confront them because of the nature of what you are and the nature of what they are. Correct?*

TOM: Correct.

IRENE: *So you chose paradise with which to carry on this battle?*

TOM: Correct.

IRENE: *And you gave the Hoovids what you believed was the greatest weapon and gift that you could give them?*

TOM: Free will, yes.

IRENE: *Knowing full well that that could be their greatest strength as well as their greatest weakness.*

TOM: That is correct, as we had said in the beginning: the Others meddle with your weaknesses as well as your strengths.

IRENE: *And so once the Hoovids understood the gift of free will then they could begin to understand the joy of the other twenty-three civilisations?*

TOM: That is correct.

The following questions concern a visit to Megiddo in 1974 by some of the group. Megiddo is a mound of fairly modest proportions with a view over the fertile plains of Israel. These plains are allegedly the physical site of the battlefield of Armageddon, on the other side rises the symmetrical Mount Tabor and then beyond that, the rugged hills of Galilee. A stillness pervades the atmosphere around Megiddo. Archaeologists have cut through the mound in several places and in one of the deepest of these excavations is a circular platform of rough stone. This was the old Canaanite altar. Hawks nested in the rock face to the side of it and Andrew felt particularly drawn to that spot.

ANDREW: *We went recently to the old city of Megiddo, which accord-*

ing to our historians goes back about 6,000 years. Do you have anything to say about the little city of Megiddo?

Tom: It is a settlement of a longer duration – it was founded in 9,228 BC, by a small group which had migrated from a different area, at the time of the destruction. It was a stronghold for those that maintained a contact and communication with us, and it was a stronghold of truth. Those that opposed in their thinking or in their reverie had decided that by destroying truth, they would be able to control Planet Earth. It is an area where the 'Hawk' and others, and all of us have visited your planet, at one time or another. It is a meeting place.

Andrew: Is that the only place on our planet that has been visited by all twelve, the nine of you and three humans in a triangle.

Tom: Yes. It is a representation.

Andrew: What is the strange? .....there must be some power generator or something there that is not apparent on the surface?

Tom: You cannot feel?

Andrew: Well, I couldn't but the Being did...

Tom: Did you not notice that there was no movement in that particular area?

Andrew: Yes, that's true.

Tom: It is because it is the meeting place and has been the meeting place as each of us has descended at one time or another.

Andrew: When you descended, did you meet in the city itself, on the surface, or somewhere that we cannot see today?

Tom: It is not uncovered.

Andrew: I see, because while I was there I had a strange vision of beings who were there in yellow suits that looked like pressure suits. Was that at all a true vision?

Tom: Yes. As you know of the areas throughout your planet which are an energy core or a place of special feeling: at times these serve as a pipe line for different civilisations to come through on a beam of energy, which is an opening between the dimensions. Megiddo is the area where this process of setting up these energy cores started, and all the civilisations used it at one time or another. On Planet Earth, it was the place for what you call summit meetings, and all of us came there at one time or another, but not all at the same time. We came to communicate with the 'Hawk'. The beings in yellow which you saw were from the civilisation which was the guardian, yes. It is in truth, the underneath of what you would call the energy into which we may, as you would say, 'plug in'.

JOHN: *So was Megiddo part of Atlantis?*

TOM: No. We must clarify – you recall what we have talked of the destruction? Before that time, there were colonies of Atlantis. And those colonies moved to other colonies, or there were beings that moved to other colonies. That is the nature of things.

ANDREW: *That was 11,000 years ago. So this would add up. How did Megiddo ever come to be the symbol of – to be called Armageddon?*

TOM: Did we not explain? Perhaps it was not clear. Did we not explain that the colony, which was of the essence of truth, because of the energy of those that were good and those that were not so good – was obliged to enter into battle with those that opposed, and we speak now of those in the spheres. So this was always a battle area and has left that vibration in the physical and in the spheres.

ANDREW: *I suppose my question really is: how did this get into the literature, the Bible?*

TOM: Did we not just explain?

ANDREW: *Well, you explained it was a centre of struggle, but there's only one mention of it in the Bible, and it doesn't even mention battles.*

TOM: It was a battle on the physical that put it into your Bible. Remember your Bible is not always in truth, and there are parts of your Bible that are not in your Bible.

ANDREW: *Yes, you did tell us that. What's puzzling me is that here is the most important statement that could and should be in the Bible.*

TOM: We did not control what man put in your Bible.

ANDREW: *I see.*

The subject was then changed, to deal with more practical matters:

JOHN: *Why has so much importance been ascribed in the Bible to circumcision?*

Tom: It is truly a very simple explanation. There are no complications with us, it is only those that follow later what we have said that cause complexities.

If you recall the climate of Israel and the surrounding countries, they have great heat and sand and dryness. One of the greatest ills that afflicted those that lived in this area was the affliction of the genitals of the males. They knew that their genitalia gave them pleasure and also pain. They remembered the pleasure more and would not allow circumcision. The reason for the beginning of circumcision was to make the people strong, and to eliminate the cancer that was consuming women − if males in that climate are not circumcised, then it creates a cancer in women. It was done to make them strong, but it was also to ask them to have the faith in us. A grain of sand in a child creates much pain and much difficulty. It was that simple.

ANDREW: What about the religious aspect where it was a sign of the Covenant between Abraham and the Lord?

Tom: We thought we had just explained that to you. At that time, there was not a male that would do this. Does that give you the explanation?

ANDREW: Yes, that does for the beginning, now how about today? Is it still necessary?

Tom: In this time and this day there are many things that are different, but it is still better to be circumcised. You understand that in 1500 years from now there will not be a foreskin on a male. It is not necessary for you to be circumcised to have the understanding.

ANDREW: How about circumcision of women that's practised in some countries? Why is it not practised in the Jewish religion?

Tom: It was not what we asked. The reason why we asked for the males to be circumcised was their ego: the females did not have the same ego problem. We asked the males to make a practical sacrifice, and to believe that if they did this, their whole people would benefit. We asked them to believe in our knowledge and recommendation.

ANDREW: Is that the same reason you asked the sacrifice, if you did, of the first born?

Tom: That was not us.

ANDREW: It happened to be in the Bible, that is why I wondered how it got in there.

TOM: Many things that are in the Bible are not in truth.

ANDREW: Yes, we are trying to sift out which are true and which are not.

TOM: Circumcision came for two reasons: one to help and one to give faith. It is now carried beyond this, and people believe that it brings them closer to God. This was not the intention.

15

The Nazarene

It is when replying to a questioner who has used another term than 'The Nazarene' that Tom uses the term 'Christ' or 'Jesus'. The Nine call him the Nazarene. This chapter deals with the Nazarene as a person, his origins and mission and it needs no introduction, the transmissions speak for themselves....

GUEST: On Earth, there are many ideals for God: could you indicate which of these ideals most closely match the ideals of the Nine?

TOM: The ideal given by the man called Christ, as he was the last of us to visit Planet Earth.

GUEST: And of those descriptions of Christ given in the Bible, which is the most accurate?

TOM: There are many misinterpretations in your Bible. It is true that the man you call Christ lived a normal, human existence, but he was a man of discretion and he walked with discretion among the people.

GUEST: Was he one of the Nine?

TOM: No, but he emulated their thoughts and their understanding. He was all of us at once. He came with the perfect goodness that is in each of us. Within us, as within you, there are various elements, but he had from each of us the most perfect of the elements of us. There are many things that are not told about him, for what he did, he did in private and did not allow the world to see him in human frailties.

ANDREW: I want to follow up the statement you once made when you said that 2,000 years ago you almost succeeded in helping to raise the consciousness of this planet. Was this in the time of the man we call Jesus Christ?

TOM: This is correct.

ANDREW: How did you in fact work with this being called Jesus Christ? Could you please tell me? I think it would be most illuminating for all of us.

TOM: We do not call him Jesus Christ. We call him the Nazarene. His inspirational work and his healings were inspired by us, and his energy was supplied by us. He made the commitment, and when he made the commitment he knew what he must do. We had great hopes at that time. But what you call your civilisation and your societies created the problems. And then you made a god of him, as you have made a god of many.

This will not happen again. There will be not one, but a collection of beings that will raise the level of consciousness of this planet. It is very important that you do not deify us. It is very important that you understand that God is in each and every one of you, and that God is love, and is the love that creates the one God.

ANDREW: The mission of the Nazarene apparently almost succeeded but, as you say, there was failure because of the role of society and our so-called 'civilisation'. There are many on Earth today who fully expect the return of the Nazarene, and I gather from what you say that is not possible, since the single individual will not return to .....?

TOM: This is correct, a single individual will not return. There are many on this planet similar to the Nazarene. It will be a collection. Those that come and say they are the Nazarene or the Messiah, are not the true Messiah. As we have explained before, when they call themselves masters, they are not masters

ANDREW: On the one hand humankind needs to understand that you exist and that you come in peace, on the other hand they expect some single individual to return – by whatever means, clouds of glory etc; I have talked to people in some of our churches, and they say that only Jesus can return, and anybody else is a representative of the Devil. How does one cope with that kind of attitude amongst people?

TOM: You pray as we pray. This always has been a problem, but when we come, and when they see the good works, then they will know who we are. After all, the Nazarene said: "You shall know them by their works". When people see that we do not come in war because there is no war with us as there is on your planet, and when they see that we come with love and with technology to help this planet that is exterminating itself, how can they but know that we come from God?

GUEST: Jesus said that the two most important commandments that

we all had to be aware of are: that we should love God with all our heart, with all our soul and with all our might, and that we should love each other as we love ourselves. And that's what all the scriptures rested on, those two commandments. The way I perceive the first commandment is in the way the Jewish people used to love the Lord, their God, through rituals and prayer. I wonder how in our daily lives we could really do that, love God with all our heart every day?

TOM: As you know, in ritual it becomes redundant. Take time for self alone, in communion with creation. This would set the time for being with the Creator. It is important (but not compulsory) to find a method of meditation that would suit you. You can make that your ritual Also, if you take the second commandment: you know, on Earth there are many who do not love themselves. Through corruption many do not love themselves. We would extend it to say: utilise kindness to all and to yourself – you then fulfil that commandment.

DAVID: It's reported in the Bible that Jesus said "I am the way, the truth, and the life, and no man comes before the Father but by me" – and that seems inconsistent. Has that just been misinterpreted?

TOM: Is not man attempting to rule man?

DAVID: Yes, at times they are.

TOM: Then is it not so that it is man that placed it upon the parchment?

DAVID: Christians, who see the Nazarene as the most advanced example of how we should live, tend to point to the sentence that I quoted as being a very important statement.

TOM: Is that not dogma-ness? [sic]

DAVID: Oh, absolutely right.

TOM: Is that not an attempt to control the belief-system of religion? We ask you, do you not trust your own divine being?

DAVID: Evidently not! (Laughter)

TOM: Yes

ANDREW: In some people I have met and talked to while in Isarel, there is still the expectation of the arrival of a Messiah.

TOM: The Messiah [The Messenger] would be with the landing, should that happen. We speak of the man, the Nazarene.

ANDREW: *Would they recognise the Nazarene?*

TOM: Yes.

ANDREW: *Would the landing of the Nazarene be in the area of what is now called Israel?*

TOM: Yes, because the Nazarene is the leader of Hoova.

JOHN: *How is the danger of him being deified again going to be overcome? Will the Israelis understand this time?*

TOM: There would not be but one, there would be many Hoovids who arrive. They would explain, and they would bring the understanding that the Christ is within every individual.

HARRIET: *We were wondering about the Immaculate Conception, and whether you would tell us about that, and also if the Nazarene had offspring?*

TOM: You ask us to tell you our thoughts or our knowing?

HARRIET: *Your knowing.*

TOM: We understand not why humankind make complications out of simple information. The earth mother of the Nazarene was implanted by the Hoova, in what you term.. you do it in your planet without physicalness.

JOHN: *Yes, artificial insemination.*

TOM: Yes, Jesus was the first-born. He is Hoova, that the nation of Israel calls Yehovah. After his birth, then Mary and Joseph had seven other male and three female. The Nazarene's physical brother and sister siblings were not implanted. You asked if the Nazarene experienced the physical glory?

GUEST: *We were talking about the genetic influence of the Hoovids, and we identified the first two genetic implants of the Hoovids, and we wondered whether the Nazarene represented the third?*

TOM: He was like that but that does not mean he offspringed children.

DAVID: *So he had no offspring?*

TOM: You make your world complicated. He was a representative of

Hoova. In the genetic stream of Hoova, there existed beings of Hoova on Planet Earth. What the Nazarene did was to reawaken the coding of memory within. He was a man upon Planet Earth, and as with nearly all men upon Planet Earth, went through a sexual development, as do females, which comes from the source of soul within. For in the moment of sexual exchange, it is the one moment in your physical life when you attain the oneness of your Creator. It is that time and moment which is sought.

This is part of the difficulty upon Planet Earth, for humankind has misunderstood the purpose of sex, and in searching for the returning to the Creator, has debased it. And because the founders of religion knew the truth of this returning, and did not wish the masses to attain it also, they forbade it, and thereby made it dominant. Part of the difficulty of male humankind moving from one woman to another in endlessness stems from the misunderstanding and non-development of true exchange, and the purpose of this exchange.

It was necessary for the Nazarene to experience that with the Magdalene. In the exchange with the Magdalene he was able to maintain his true identity with the Creator. Is that understood?

When both partners whose motive is clean – we do not wish to preach – who understand who they are, and their oneness with their mate, and have attained the bringing of two together in unison and great glory, this then brings great joy. If you experience this, remember, do not let it pass, for it is catching a star, riding a star. Remember that, for it will always bring you back to the returning of your creation. Know also that you are part of the Creator, and that you also created the Creator.

HARRIET: *That's beautiful.*

JOHN: *So, what you're saying is that Mary Magdalene did not have a child?*

TOM: Not from the Nazarene.

GUEST: *Did Jesus, perhaps in connection with Joseph of Arimathaea, according to tradition, ever visit Glastonbury in England?*

TOM: The Nazarene circled Planet Earth, for it was of necessity for his energy to permeate the globalness.

DAVID: *Was that a specific 'Yes' to Glastonbury, one of the locations he passed through?*

TOM: Do you need a map to understand energies? What you term special or sacred or holy, from all beliefs, was touched. And in your Kingston in England also.

GUEST: *So the tradition which exists in Glastonbury that Jesus visited as a boy with Joseph of Arimathaea, is that a correct tradition?*

TOM: Yes, I just explained he travelled around the globe.

JOHN: *You are referring to the lost years of the Nazarene, between the age of twelve, when he was at the temple in Jerusalem, until his ministry began? Can you tell us about that?*

TOM: At the age of fourteen, and within a year of his manhood, he began a long journey. He went into the area of the Himalayas and he spent a great deal of time in Egypt, viewing the pyramids, learning about the energies and knowledge of the pyramids. He also spent a long time in the lands of the Himalayas. He had also spent much time with the Essenes. He took within him the triangle of knowledge of India, Egypt and the Essenes. He had the assimilation and the truths of all three. John the Baptist also spent time with him in Egypt.

JOHN: *Yes. Will any records of this be discovered?*

TOM: There are records in two of these areas: one in Egypt, and the other in what is now Israel. At the proper time there will be a correlation of finding these records within six months of each other. There will be fragments, and there will then emerge truths.

DAVID: *Is it true that the Nazarene travelled and learned in the Far East?*

TOM: There was a time of travel, including to the nation that you know of as the nation of the sun – Japan.

ISRAEL: *We know that the Nazarene, Yehovah, came three times. One of these was the Buddha. Could you explain to me the necessity of that incarnation and in that environment [India]? What was its purpose?*

TOM: Your nation did not go forth as they should, therefore it was of necessity for one to come who would cover a great portion of the Earth with the heart of understanding of the Universe. It is in alignment with the progress of the Universe. In actuality those of the Buddha's following have grasped truth into their soul and heart quicker than those who should have, the Hebrews. Do you understand?

ISRAEL: *Yes, if it doesn't work from the inside, try to make it work from the outside.*

TOM: That is correct, yes.

ANDREW: *What was the original language in which John wrote down the 'Book of Revelations'? You said that the original is the one to read and that the translations have problems.*

TOM: It was in Aramaic.

ANDREW: *Do you know if any such manuscript exists ?*

TOM: Yes, but not in an area or place where you may recover it. It will come in time − it is in the City of Jerusalem, and it will be found.

ANDREW: *I see, there is not a copy in any museum or anywhere where it is publicly viewable?*

TOM: You may go to your Vatican.

ANDREW: *Could you give us the story of how John received this message? Was it in a situation like we are sitting in here, or was he alone, or was it before the baptism of Jesus?*

TOM: It was before the Baptism: it was the Revelations that brought the understanding of who Jesus was.

ANDREW: *Was Jesus a witness to this revelation?*

TOM: Yes. He was young boy. It came as we speak to you, do you understand?

ANDREW: *Yes, I understand, right, that's remarkable.*

JOHN: *Can you say something about original sin and the act of baptism, and whether the importance of these continue today? Does the concept of original sin brings us into this world with guilt?*

TOM: In the beginning, when the Covenant was made with Hoova and it was broken, original sin followed the Hebrew seed. When Hoova came again as the Nazarene, it was released completely. For his sacrifice was complete release. But those that followed after the Nazarene perpetrated many things in his name, began a set of rituals, as previous to the time of Hoova. Do you understand?

JOHN: *Well, in the Christian service we consider that Christ in his death did forgive us our sins and presumed that inferred the original sin.*

TOM: He did not forgive you. The Universe relieved you.

JOHN: Yes, but symbolised by his act.

TOM: Yes. If there had been acceptance, the guilt of original sin would also have been relieved. It was the time.

JOHN: But the baptism today is still to relieve us of original sin..

TOM: It is not to relieve that. In each church is a different way, in a religion that was not begun by the Nazarene. Baptism is not to remove original sin, it is to indicate acceptance of the Nazarene. In the beginning it was Peter who started this, following the pattern of John the Baptist.

JOHN: There is a belief that the crucifixion of Christ took away the sins people committed since his death. In other words: Christ forgave sins afterwards. I feel this is an avoidance of responsibility, could you clarify this at all?

TOM: You are asking whether if they ask in his name, they are forgiven?

JOHN: People feel that by his crucifixion they have already been forgiven of their sins, in other words it seems to me a licence to sin, which doesn't seem right to me.

TOM: That is not the purpose. The crucifixion of the Nazarene was not to relieve people of the burden of their own responsibilities: it was to show everyone that for the love of God and for his commitment he would willingly die. Remember that the Nazarene did not attempt to communicate with the Gentiles, only to those of the Hebrew nation of Palestine. If he could have relieved them and made them aware he would have shown them, and in turn the rest of the Planet, the way to individual and global transformation.

Within the nations that you call 'Christian' and who worship him as a god, there are those that understand that he is of a trinity.

JOHN: Was Jesus the first person ever to be resurrected?

TOM: It is true that he was the first to be resurrected, but not in the sense that you understand. He was the first that was returned to his civilisation, Hoova, in the manner in which he was returned. There have been many who have been resurrected, but he has been returned to his civilisation. The people upon the planet Earth who saw his resurrection believed that it made him God.

ANDREW: So, with reference to people who came from one of the universal civilisations, and then went back, you mean to say that Jesus or Yehovah was the first who was brought here, and then returned physically intact, and this was not done earlier?

TOM: Yes. There were what you would call resurrections and returning to spheres but not returning to civilisations.

ANDREW: Is this really what we would call teleportation or bilocation or..

TOM: It would be bilocation. It was the first time it had been done.

JOHN: Is the one who took the body of Jesus, Joseph of Arimathaea, the same person as Joseph, the head of the civilisation Aragon?

TOM: It is two different ones..

ANDREW: We're really wondering whether Joseph of Aragon was with the Nazarene on Earth?

TOM: He was with the Hawk (Horus) in Egypt: he was the one that is called Imhotep. He was also a high priest in the time of the Nazarene called Annas.

JOHN: Was Joseph of Arimathaea also from Aragon by any chance?

TOM: I will consult....Joseph of Aragon has said no, that Joseph of Arimathaea was from Altea. It is only a similarity of names.

STEVE: We usually think of the Eastern methods of attaining enlightenment, the Hindu and Buddhist, as far more advanced than the Western methods. Is this so?

TOM: To be removed from the world is not the best. All may reach the highest of heights within themselves, but how would they react if they must reach the heights when there are those that need their service and their help? To escape the responsibility of involvement, it is true you may believe that you have become a master or a perfect being, for if you do not interact with others, then you will indeed think that you are perfect.

STEVE: Well, I'm thinking of the Eastern sacred books – the Upanishads and the Vedas, the Sutras and Tao – are these given from other civilisations?

TOM: It is so, as with others, yes. But it has not been used always for betterment. If the Eastern philosophers had the truth of their fellow men within their heart, their nations would be highly evolved. But they use it at times to make themselves masters, without uplifting the souls that need help. It is important that those who have understanding of suffering attempt to relieve suffering.

STEVE: *I would like to explain why I asked that question. It seems that all our communications are very much within the Western philosophical and religious tradition, and emanate from the same sources that Western civilisation and religion emanate from, and this is one thing that I have to struggle with. Because I have grown up to think that the Eastern methods and religions are more enlightened.*

TOM: How many millions of their people are suffering? Do you understand what we say? That also is a trap.

JOHN: *Yes, I think we see the faults in our own culture, and we look across the fence and think that they have the answer. But.. yes*

TOM: If you sit upon a mountain and look below you, and say "I am enlightened, for I sit and I pray, and those that are below me, it is important for them to suffer and I cannot do anything to help", then you have set yourself above them. We will use your term of 'karma'. It is not fully understood. In their thinking that suffering is their karma, they in truth have created suffering karma for themselves. To not be involved with your fellow men, to simply place a hand to help them, or a publication to ease their burden, they cannot be masters as they proclaim. To have mastered all the physical, the important thing is to master all of the physical with involvement, not detachment from those that suffer. Yes.

STEVE: *Well, just to repeat, do such books as I have mentioned in fact emanate from extraterrestrial sources, although they may not be fully developed and highly evolved?*

TOM: Yes. But also remember that people use that which benefits them, and they make their interpretation, in order to control others or to make themselves better than their fellow humans. Yes.

JOHN: *So you're saying they have as many distortions as the Bible..?*

TOM: As the Word Book. Yes. There is the most singular important thing that humankind has neglected, and we speak of nearly all humankind, and that is compassion.

When there is compassion for all living things, including those that are closest to you, then the shift in consciousness of the planet begins and will be accelerating. You see, in the nature of humankind you may have compassion for a child that falls that is yours, but not see the pain of another child that falls. You may have compassion when you see the slaughter of villagers if you are in affinity with them, but not of the slaughter of those that slaughter.

It's when there are those that you love, that do not agree with you when you have need of their agreement, that you lose compassion for them. It's when you may maintain that compassion, or gain it, or regenerate it, and feel the feeling that they feel without self involved, then you come out of the ashes and begin the growth. The building then is strong, and secure, and not fragile (but it could be burned again). Humankind has not had compassion for humankind. Even one of you, who might have compassion for a small child, has no compassion for an adult that does not agree with you. That also is changing.

JOHN: Yes, on that, it's interesting that we have difficulty having compassion for the nearest and dearest to us. We have compassion for those a little further away with whom we agree, and then we lose compassion again when we go further still, it's this middle ground.

TOM: Yes When you are able to remove self from self, and place yourself in the position of another, then begins the evolution of the planet. Then this planet begins being the paradise that it was planned to be, yes.

Express yourself in words of love and words of joy, and that makes the Universe in happiness, for when there is happiness, joy and laughter in the Universe it is a time of great celebration. This is what Planet Earth must do. Humankind must not take itself so seriously. It must begin to experience within itself the joy of its divinity, the joy of its oneness with the Universe. It must pull itself out of this bondage, it must stop living in a situation of victims. We have never asked for victims or sacrifice, but humankind in its guilt, creates its victimhood. For it knows that it has passed and has crossed that valley that it should not have, and now together with all we are bringing it back across the valley, for it to be one with the Universe.

This next transmission was concerned with other communications and their validity.

ANDREW: I want to ask about psychic communication: could you give us an idea as to who in the past, historically recognisable figures, were what you would call perfect communicators? As you say this Being is. Could you tell us of any that we can rely on?

Tom: I will consult for permission. There was the one you call Jesus of Nazareth, you knew that. There was the one that you call Socrates. There was the one that gave to you in code, Nostradamus. There was the one that was of one and the same as that of Jesus: the Buddha. Remember this: there was perfect communication and it was in translation that it became obscure. In all the translations.

ANDREW: In all of these cases, I see, right.

Tom: Then there was Elijah, and there was the one called Joseph.

ANDREW: Which Joseph was that? There are several in the Bible.

Tom: It would be the one that was in Egypt. And there was one whose name was Da Vinci. We speak to you only of those that have been recorded historically. There have been others.

ANDREW: A more recent figure like Helen Blavatsky, would she qualify?

Tom: I must consult........ yes, Blavatsky was true.

ANDREW: Are there any who have lived in the past 100 years who were scientists who recorded knowledge that is true?

Tom: That knowledge comes from a civilisation.

ANDREW: I see, you are talking about those directly speaking with you?

Tom: Yes.

JOHN: May I ask about the Theosophists? I assume that the person who spoke through Blavatsky and Alice Bailey was the same person, known to us as 'the Tibetan' – Dhjwal Khul.

Tom: That is not true.

JOHN: Could you tell us who 'the Tibetan' is then?

Tom: We are trying to find a way of explaining. If you have three people, who together create a triangle, and if the three merge in mind, you would have a oneness. The Tibetan is a triangle.

JOHN: Does he have a direct relationship to the Nine?

Tom: It is as if – we know not how to explain – it is incomprehensible in your language. It is not a physical being. The information comes from a triangle.

JOHN: *Is it of a high quality?*

TOM: Yes. It is taking from three, the perfect aspects of the three. Do you understand that?

JOHN:*Yes, I do.*

TOM: The Tibetan was different to Blavatsky.

ANDREW: *I've recently looked again at the writings of Michel de Nostradamus, and I've been very impressed how his predictions made 400 years ago are parallel to the ones that you have made about what is coming. Who was this Michel de Nostradamus that he was so prescient way back when, and were you behind his foreknowledge?*

TOM: When there was prediction people took it as a definite reason to be out of their responsibility. It was an error that we made also, for humans hold destiny in their hands. What was not understood by humankind was that prediction was made to have man change his way: if he did not change then the prediction would come into being. We cannot reiterate that point enough. We wish that to be impressed upon humankind's mind, for it is the beginning of human-kind's understanding that they hold the key, they are responsible, and they make the change.

You ask who he was? He was doing the same as you are doing at this time. We now wish for light to come forth, for the removal of darkness, for the removal of humanity's belief that darkness must take place. For there are two alternatives: the ones of darkness have existed too long it is time for those of light, and that is your choosing. Humankind does not need despair, hopelessness, or futility but hope, love, and the possibility of goodness.

Here is an exploration of 'principles' which can contribute another thread to the tapestry of our understanding...

JOHN: *Could you say whether in fact there are twelve principles that have come in, and if the final one is 'Balance' — is that correct?*

TOM: I will consult for permission.....It is affirmative but with reserva-tions.

JOHN: *Yes, well, could you mention some of the other principles and*

*the times at which they came? That might help me to understand
principles that came in at different times.*

Tom: In the time between the father of Abraham and Moses, and
spanning the time of Jacob, was the principle of law. When we speak
of law, we speak of the following of the law of the Nine. That does
not mean that the law that was given had the necessity of being
adhered to, from that point until what you would call eternity. But it
was important for that time. In the true sense, natural law does not
change, but law for order in the Universe in relationship to a singular
planet is adaptable to change. When we speak of law in that time, we
speak of a law that those that we had asked (as we had asked
Abraham, Jacob and Moses) do what we had asked, in faith. It was a
form of law.

*John: Yes, I feel that there is something important behind these
principles. I feel they're associated with the Twelve (i.e. the Nine
plus three) and the Nine. Are these periods regular in length, or do
they vary? Am I on the right track?*

Tom: We understand what you are getting at. Again we answer with
an affirmative but also with reservations, for there have been times
that are in closeness to other times of great distance.

John: I don't quite....

Tom: There are those times which have great expansions, and then
there are those times which are short periods.

*John: Yes. Has there been another one between the time of Christ
and now?*

Tom: That of Christ was the final before you today. The period at the
time of Altea was of wisdom. The principle of justice came at the time
of Ur. The time of Horus in Egypt was of knowledge, and knowledge
also became out of balance. Yes.

V

THE OTHER SIDE OF THE COIN

16

War and Peace in the 1990s

While, in 1994, it would seem a little out of date to leave these early transmissions concerning the imminent threat of nuclear catastrophe in this edition of the book, the replies given by Tom are still totally relevant, for they deal with the power of thought, the power of fear. The transmissions have been arranged in chronological order. The first discussions, during 1981, occurred at a time when there was a proliferation of nuclear warheads.....

GUEST: What about nuclear war? It seems that this present state of affairs [1981] is dangerous, and the risks are rising...

TOM: We have always said that we would not permit the destruction of this planet. We would not permit this planet to be destroyed in stupidity. But you understand that when destruction attempts are made, they create other forms that can then encourage more scattered energies. This is why meditation is important.

ANDREW: Yes, if I understand correctly then, let me paraphrase what I understand you've said on other occasions: you are not in principle against humanity learning a lesson from a small series of nuclear events, is that correct?

TOM: We did not mean it in that interpretation.

ANDREW: I'm sorry. Would you clarify?

TOM: We intended for you to understand that in the situation as it is going, if there were a small confrontation it would perhaps be a sufficient lesson in another world and another time; but in this time and space there is only foolishness – so that would not suffice. If a lesson could be learned without harming humankind... but that is not possible.

ANDREW: I see what you're saying. It's what we call 'A Mexican stand off' isn't it?

Tom: That means that each side is prepared, and each is afraid, through not knowing strength of the other?

ANDREW: Yes.

Tom: Yes. That is your situation. But if it is possible to overcome this, and for East and West to merge in understanding of peoples, to remove fear, then many things will come to pass.

ANDREW: Yes, we understand that, but isn't that a longterm process? We're talking about the transformation of very fixed minds.

Tom: Know this: that elements of the nature of energies may spread with great rapidity. As you have a media, a form of communication, of necessity it would only be a matter of days or weeks in transformation, if the energies charged into it were the highest. Know this: your planet Earth is on a verge of transformation.

GUEST: What are you calling a short period of time?

Tom: As a radio wave goes around your planet Earth, encircles it, or televises it from above your planet Earth, with proper communication the majority of civilised countries could come to understanding in three of your months.

JOHN: In the event of a nuclear strike, would you consider intervening on television and radio as was considered once before? Would that be one of your means of intervention?

Tom: I will consult... Yes, in some areas, but in the main it would come from an energy of a sound that you hear not, that would cause paralysis of mechanisms for a period of time.

JOHN: So, what might happen is that missiles might be fired but they might fail to operate and that would be a very powerful indication to all people that something extra-terrestrial was controlling the situation, is that so?

Tom: There would be a sound that would negate it, and the vibration would be felt by all, but not heard as sound.

JOHN: Who would initiate this?

Tom: Those of the Twenty-Four civilisations.

JOHN: Is Altea still in charge of this operation?

TOM: That of Altea, yes.

JOHN: There is a paradox that is going on in the peace movement: I'm suggesting that we should not be fearful of the Russians, but the peace movement is largely based on the fear of nuclear war, and I think the fear has a negative effect...

TOM: The fear will bring into existence that which is feared.

JOHN: How can we deal with this paradox, as peace campaigners are saying that we need to be frightened, because it's out of this fear that we will get people to do something?

TOM: You need to be aware; fear accomplishes nothing but destruction. Fear is the greatest enemy of all that exists on Planet Earth. Fear is bondage, fear is not freedom.

JOHN: You are, I presume, talking about a cataclysm being nuclear war, because there exists so much fear of it at the moment?

TOM: Yes.

JOHN: Can you give any advice on how to persuade people that they need to be aware of the situation and act on it, without being motivated by fear?

TOM: They must not be pulled into the blueprint of someone else's situation. It is like a magnet, suddenly all the filings have pulled towards each other and created a magnetic force field.

ANDREW: If it is mandatory that we survive, what will our work be afterwards, assuming that you will not allow total destruction, while there may be some minor destruction as a lesson..?

TOM: We would pray that even the smallest shred may not be the case.

ANDREW: Okay.

TOM: The importance is to inform others that energies of thought-forms are more devastating than nuclear warheads, for in your time now, in your future time, energies are being refined, for which thought is, and will be, the controlling factor.

ANDREW: Yes. Now, may I ask if in the course of evolution of human life on Earth, man has ever had this kind of technological possibility and capacity for total destruction?

TOM: No, it was localised. There have been shifts of crust upon your planet Earth. But that was not brought about by chaos of nuclear. In a sense it had at times the same type of radiation, but it was not created by humans. You understand the difference?

ANDREW: Yes, I understand. All right, so this is a unique event in the history of humanity?

TOM: It is the first time upon your planet Earth that it has been populated by so many, that there has been a form of communication with which all know information instantaneously, and it is the first time with generations of beings encapsulated in negative thinking – but also the first time that there are so many of those who exist in service to Planet Earth, working diligently to stop destruction, and to permit Earth's evolution as it should have been in the past.

ANDREW: Now let us assume, as one of the possibilities, that there will be no serious use of nuclear weapons: does this mean that natural catastrophes will still go ahead as a natural course of destructive events?

TOM: Again we will attempt to explain: If fear is instilled then it creates an energy that may bring that into being. But if there is enough positive belief in the future, then you humans also may relieve the pressure across your planet and release it slowly, so that there is not a need to have that amount of destruction. It will not be possible in every instant to eliminate all destruction, as it is nowadays that there are earthquakes in eccentricity. But it may be partly negated by relieving pressure across your planet Earth.

ANDREW: I was wondering how we could ever get rid of the threat of nuclear weapons, and obviously a nice way would be to dematerialise them and dump them in some black hole in space but obviously....

TOM: Man would then create more.

ANDREW: So that's not a real lesson, okay.

TOM: When the nuclear threat affects them directly, people of all nations then may suddenly come to awareness. Only people can change people. We cannot change people. Removing their toys does not change them.

ANDREW: Yes. Is this why you allowed the invention, the development, and the production of nuclear weapons to go ahead?

TOM: It was not like that. Let us explain to you. It has great value, this invention. It is what your peoples do with it − that is their path, their choice. They have choices, freewill to choose from one extreme to the other within their limitations. You understand that.

ANDREW: *Yes, I understand.*

MIKI: *What sort of use of nuclear technology has great value?*

TOM: That for generating energies for developing of countries, for a non-destruction situation. It is also possible for transportation in the Universe if handled properly, yes.

ANDREW: *One problem is the peace process in the world. As you know, some small steps have been made in the nuclear field, with a treaty between the USSR and the USA [1988]. Where can you see the next leverage exerted on the peace process?*

TOM: In the nation of Israel.

ANDREW: *This is the primary focus?*

TOM: Yes. As you know there is the attempt to establish the nation of Palestine in its own environment.

ANDREW: *Yes, I've been following that process.*

TOM: Then you know also that the most extreme people in both the nation of Israel and the nation of Ishmael will attempt a conflicting division. What is of the greatest importance is the intervention by Soviet Russia and the United States of the America to make it extremely clear to extremists that if either people permits its extremists to continue, then they will begin to intervene. Then the government of Israel will have the necessity of understanding its limitations and preventing the most extreme, and the Arafat [Yasser Arafat] will also have the need to stop that destruction. Yes.

JOHN: *Would you say something about what has gone on in the Middle East − in the Gulf War?*

TOM: This is the beginning of the time of the dissipation of division. It had taken time for the merging of the countries of the Cold War. As the element of division wishes to remain as it is, you now have a similar situation of division in the Crescent.

You had a concerted alignment of unity of many nations with purpose, in a focused direction and this has proven to the world that it can create a vehicle to bring about order on Planet Earth that is beneficial to all humankind. What must be exercised at this time is the strength of momentum to follow through and not to have discouragement – for there will be those that will attempt to utilise the situation for their own purpose. But in unity, planet Earth has proven that it can unify against what is not of benefit for humankind.

In the following transmission it becomes apparent that an important change has occurred in the aftermath of the Gulf War, as seen from the perspective of the Nine. This conversation, from 1991, does not benefit from the hindsight that we now have.

JOHN: *Was the Gulf War, [1991] in fact the final physical manifestation on the lower planes of the battle of Armageddon? It seemed to have so many of those lower elements in it?*

TOM: And continues, yes. It is now important not to let the old maintain its momentum in suppression and destruction.
   There is an element that you should know about which entailed a great debate and consideration by the Council of Nine, and the Twenty-Four civilisations, in connection with souls who transitioned [died] because of this great battle: those of the spirit, working for evolution of Planet Earth, have taken them into their bosom, and have taken them away in forwardness, so there is not to be a recycling of those who have undergone transitions.

JOHN: *You're talking about the hundred thousand, or more, Iraqis who were killed in the conflict itself, are you?*

TOM: Of all killed in this arena. And we shall continue.

JOHN: *After the 15th January 1991 [the deadline given to Iraq to leave Kuwait before hostilities broke out] was there any real possibility of resolving this conflict fully without military action? Had it been resolved without military conflict, the military power, the chemical and nuclear weapons, would still have existed, and I cannot see how there can have been peace with those in existence.*

TOM: It could not have been resolved by other methods, for those in the spheres are in battlement – therefore it was a case of 'As above so below'. The decision to bring those transitioned souls into light was because of that. It was not possible for it to be a choice on a human level.

JOHN: *There seems to be another difficulty, because there is some fear that the Shia population of Southern Iraq, if they were to gain power, would create another danger.*

TOM: What you must now understand is that that must not be permitted, as Saddam Hussein was not permitted. Therefore you must meditate for the united allies to remain united. Also you must now understand that those of Ishmael will attempt to overwhelm the nation Israel, not in violence, for they know that will not be permitted, but in wiliness. That also must not be permitted, for all peoples have a place in the world, that will help them manifest their uniqueness on all Planet Earth.

JOHN: Personally, I feel quite supportive towards the Kurdish people. Can you say anything about them?

TOM: They are one in more senses than one – they are straightforward not devious. As each of these representatives of different civilisations, who have manifested upon Planet Earth, are attempting to maintain their legitimacy, it is a part of the great mosaic of Planet Earth.

JOHN: You're saying that the different races in the region represent different   civilisations?

TOM: Yes, not of the Twenty-Four, but others. As it is in Yugoslavia, yes. And in others, do you understand?

JOHN: Yes. Now, there is a great problem in the Soviet Union [1991], and Mr. Gorbachev who seemed to be doing a good job, now seems to be in difficulty, can you say anything..?

TOM: You will meditate for him, for keep this in your memory: while the world was focusing upon the Hussein, the supportive energy was not directed to him. Now you must include him to help him again to maintain stability and balance.

JOHN: About the Middle East: the environmental disaster brought about by the continuing oilwell fires there, is there a real danger here? [Gulf War 1991]

TOM: There are many dangers. Remember it will affect your entire planet, not only the Crescent, and it will also bring into being a world order of rules and regulations, for in its vastness humankind must have order created, to abide by a civilised method. Your planet Earth no longer is a planet that has but a few million humans. It is no longer a planet that in order to see the other side one must incarnate. It is now a very small planet and must be treated as one skin. So out of this chaotic situation will also come the order of environment, and another benefit also, for those who support the environment also at times become dictatorial. So balance will be brought. Begin as much as possible to foster the elimination of those products that also bring other forms of environmental destruction.

JOHN: Yes. It seems that the act of destruction of those oil wells at the last minute was such an act of blatant evil, that out of the ultimate bad could come the ultimate good for the environment.

TOM: That is exact correctness, provided it is directed, meditated and kept in the mind, that out of that must come order. You understand the opposition is still in force.

JOHN: Yes. Recognising that there is a connection between the macrocosm and the microcosm, I feel that human unity, during the course of this difficult period, has taken a battering. I think that there has been some damage to the collective solidarity which grew in 1988 and 1989.

TOM: This is a truism. What is important in these times is setting aside one's own self and becoming a unity. If one is not able to do that, then there must be consideration of ways of creating more understanding. There must be great consideration. It is a simple law – and that is the Golden Law...

JOHN: Do unto others.....

TOM: ...as you would wish be done to you. And take into consideration all cultures, all personalities, and remove egos, become a true selfless individual or nation in times of need for Planet Earth, in unity and togetherness. Know this: all the civilisations that are in conjunction with the Twenty-Four are in readiness to help. It is time now for humankind to reduce competition with each other and to emerge as one unit of joy. That will take time, effort and love.

Most importantly it is based on trust, the trust that there are in the Universe those beings that are there to help you. As also is the unknown God. It is important to know that you must trust, you will be directed.

Also at all levels of consciousness you must trust yourself. Recognise the importance of understanding this and the necessity for generating this trust about yourself. It would be foolish of us to tell you that all that exist on planet Earth are equal, for that is not true – with one exception: you are all equal in that you come from the same

Source.

In the manifestation of your physicalness, however, there must be those who are leaders and who bring out the best in others. For there are those who wish to be led, and to attempt to force them to be leaders when they do not have the environmental, physical, emotional or mental faculties to do so, puts them in a detrimental situation. Therefore you humans must support each other, love each other, have respect, but be aware of those elements of humankind that are not in the highest state of evolution. They serve their purpose also. This does not mean that some are special and some are not.

The next transmission returned to the problem of peace between the Hoovids and the Ishmaels...

HARRIET: I'd like to thank you so very much for all your love and protection during this past Gulf War for the Allies, and for the nation of Israel...

TOM: That is for all nations, yes.

HARRIET: I'd like to ask you if you can give an idea of where the nation of Israel, together with the nation of Ishmael, stand in relation to coming closer to touching hands and making peace with each other?

TOM: When peace is made within, then it is possible for extension of peace without. What is important is this understanding, and we wish each of you to open your minds in clarity to hear what we say: it may not be acceptable to some, but there is a functional issue that must be understood, and that is that there are some that function differently to others. There are many cultures from different civilisations, and there are many differences between cultures. And in the process of their choosing, there is necessity for leadership and demonstrable   maturity.

You must understand this, we speak not of evolutionary level amongst leaders, we speak of the level of maturity. It is like this: you take a child, and when they do not understand the danger you make a rule, do you not?

JOHN: Yes.

TOM: You say that you must not pull [sic] yourself from a top-roof without a . . . .

JOHN: *A parachute. (Laughter)*

TOM: ....an umbrella.

JOHN: *No, an umbrella doesn't help much. We know what you mean – a parachute. (Laughter)*

TOM: You will understand that the nation of Ishmael is at times childish, which it is necessary to bring them through – however, this does not make them less than the nation of Israel, do you understand?

JOHN ¢ HARRIET: *Yes.*

TOM: It is important that you understand that. It does not mean that they are not as evolved: it means that that is the point of their choosing at this time. We speak now only of the masses. You see, if you permit a child to do as it wishes, it gets in confusion and does not know its safety-arena. Then when you tell to that child "You must not do that," it knows then that it is within the boundaries of safety, and that it is being looked after.

Therefore when there is a nation that does not have limits or guidance for the betterment of all nations, it is like a free-radical cell, is that not so? When radical cells go wild in the body, do they not create a situation of devastation? Therefore, with the nations of Planet Earth, what is important is to create guidelines to prevent them from hurting self, and to remove from them the ability to hurt others. This then brings them to a peaceful solution and takes away from them that ability to damage all, but what it also does for them is give to them a great relief, so they do not have to perpetuate what they think is their manliness.

You must include also the understanding that the nation of Israel, in past conflicts, has now learned that by not retaliating, they have grown in stature, not only in the world but in self. Therefore by taking away from those of Ishmael this ability, then it becomes their way, and they too will grow in stature. You do not give to a child the permission to stand in the middle of your most dangerous roadway and hope it will survive.

JOHN: *True.*

TOM: Therefore you put great barriers to stop it, is that not so?

ISRAEL ¢ JOHN: *Yes.*

TOM: When that is understood, and when opportunities for those emotional disturbances that keep people in bondage are taken away, the problem will begin to be relieved, and then they may begin negotiations.

Remember this: the people of the nation of Ishmael are very much like children, so today they love you and tomorrow they do not. This makes them not less, you must understand that.

LARK: Now, the Americans are very much involved in that peace process, and they don't look very mature to me either.[1991]

TOM: That is your way of viewing. You see, each culture has its own way. If the nation of USA did not stand in steadfastness, then at this time there would be a conflict that could not end. What is the greatest importance is the understanding that there are differences in all nations, and it is that mosaic that creates your Earth, and in each nation there must be understanding without condemnation of others. That is the important achievement to make. When also there is unity and holdfastness among all that are what you call 'civilised', not permitting others to disrupt other nations, then those children learn by example and by understanding, that they are not permitted to destroy themselves. When a child begins to understand that you care enough for it not to permit it to destroy itself, then it begins to feel safe with you.

This next transmission was given to a group of meditators in March 1991 :

TOM: Now we are moving into the period that begins the solidification and cleansing. In times past souls upon your planet Earth refused to leave it, and through your conflicts continued to recycle, as you recycle your trees. Your recycled trees have usefulness, but the soul-recycling of humankind does not create usefulness, but creates a bottlenecking of forwardness. You now have come to this time in which those who now make the transition – we speak of those who do not fulfill what they have come to fulfill, those who make transition [die] in accidents and in war, those that create their own transition either deliberately or accidentally, those live now in a different realm. Souls who have now transitionalised from the recent Gulf War and from accidents have now been taken into other, higher evolutionary states for releasing that anger and despair. Therefore there will not come a recycling of souls that have kept planet Earth in bondage.

This has come about because of the awakening of humankind to the reality of where they have come to, and the beginning of finding their divinity within. Is that not joyful?

Also humankind is now moving forward in increased unification, and in bringing about the ending of conflict and aggression — the world conditions that create the situation of bondage. That does not mean that there is instant change, but change has begun its great movement forward. This is shown by the unification of nations, that now understand that the destruction of one nation is in reality the destruction of others, and the beginning of all destruction. Also that the destruction of vital elements upon your planet Earth affects all. It is a time to be in great joy.

There are times when one would feel despair that there is not forwardness: what is necessary now upon your planet Earth is for each of you to understand that you contain within you that element, that cell, that atom, that molecule, that soul-part of you that is a part of the Creation and the whole, and that you in your evolutionary state of being at this time can create the energies necessary, by yourself and in conjunction with others, to stop further destructiveness.

For as in times past it was religion which led Planet Earth, (and it served its purpose) now it is you, the peoples of Planet Earth, that speak. You should be joyful for this and not feel burdened with it, as some of you seem to do. It is not a perfect time, we agree, but it is a time of greatness, and we are in gratefulness to you humans who are positive — for it is necessary for the completion and fulfilment of Planet Earth, for us to be in partnership with you.

We find great joy in this time, for the youth that are coming to Planet Earth in this time, and who have come in the recent past, are coming with the full understanding that they serve a purpose. Those who came and did not understand their purpose, it is now being revealed to them.

Most people have been upon Planet Earth in times past, in times in which you came for your learning: in this time many people have come to benefit Planet Earth in conjunction with us, in service. We bless you for that. Many of you also must understand that you come from higher evolutionous levels (that is not the correct term but we have no language to explain) of other civilisations that work in total peace and harmony with each other: and that have joined with all who are bringing Planet Earth to its rightful direction.

Know this also: each of you humans contain the essence of what you term a star — and we have not revealed that before. You have existed in all eternity and will continue to exist in all eternity. What is necessary now is to understand that, and the responsibility that goes with it, but it must be understood with joy, not with fear or despair. And it is now time to understand you must not flagellate yourself when you make an error, but move beyond it, and remove and peel off that shell and let another light of yourself come through. You must also understand that when you are in the presence of others, you emanate an energy of light that touches and begins their awakening also. And when you create jello [happiness, laughter — after wobbling jelly] in the Universe, you create great energy and the release of what you term darkness, and the removal of that which sticks in holes in darkness. Each of you humans is like a jellobean. (Laughter). Is there a jellobean?

LARK: *Jellybean.*

TOM: Is it wobbleness?

LARK: *It's very sweet too.*

TOM: Then people like you are sweet, are you not? Yes. It is important for humankind to understand that just because things are the way they are, that is not the only way they can be. It is time for humankind to understand it is the way it is, for perhaps humankind created errors. Yes.

It is time for humankind to begin to understand who they are, and it is time for humankind to understand that they affect the Universe, that the days of destruction, the days of saying 'That is their Karma' must end, for in both cases it is not a responsible way to think. You must also give time in your meditations to the beginning of elimination of human accidents, that entrap the soul in a non-functional vehicle do you understand?

JOHN: *Well, could you elaborate on that, please? What is it that entraps human beings?*

TOM: If there be embattlement and one is entrapped in a body that is injured, then that spirit-soul becomes very angry. Then it serves not the purpose it wishes. And if there be entrapment in the mind through ingestion, if it be deliberate or accidental, then that mind cannot fulfill its desired function, do you understand? Then that energy of despair is likened to an out-of-beat note, do you understand? It then needs special love and energy so in your meditations also to begin the elimination of what causes that. We have confused you now?

JOHN: I think you're talking about those people who are damaged either at their own hand or for other reasons sometimes described as 'Karma'. And that those problems must be eliminated so that the soul can live its purpose.

TOM: Yes. And they need help to remove anger, and it must be in your meditation that you wish for this. Yes.

JOHN: While we are all here together as a group would you like to say what meditations you would like us to do together?

TOM: We would wish each day, at your time of choosing, for you to be with us for eighteen minutes of your time, to bring about the ending of conflict in the Crescent, the elimination of the destruction of the environment, especially in the Crescent; and the acceleration of the return to a state of wellbeing, do you understand?

And you will also include the intention of permitting each nation and each group of entity-souls, to be allowed to be who they are, without being enforced by a nation that would wish to control them. Then will peace begin to really come to your planet Earth, and it will begin to be the paradise for which it was created. Yes.

While there are other meditations in this book for the ecology of the planet, at the time of the Gulf Crisis, Lark had asked this next question:

LARK: Can you give us specifics about how to solve the environmental tragedy with our meditations: what do we visualise?

TOM: You visualise all explosive smoke being eliminated quickly. For example: you will visualise a turn-off in suddenness. Also envision a suctioning off of that which pollutes land and water, for humankind in its higher aspect has an ability to create all that is necessary for its rapid elimination.

As we have said in the past and will continue to say until humankind is brought to awakening: It is important for humankind to understand its responsibility. It is time for this information and knowledge to be released. For humankind, in all aspects of its religious life – which has not supplied the understanding – is searching for the elements of their beginning and purpose. So with that information being brought forth comes the unlocking of forwardness.

17

Preventing Disaster

The main issue here is that we need to recognise our situation on this planet and then assume total individual responsibility for the outcome. The transmissions concerning the Gulf War and its effects are still relevant, for Tom shows us meditation techniques and demonstrates the use of the power of thought for good or ill.

TOM: Do you understand that if the awakening comes in its own time there is total destruction, and if it comes with acceleration then the world can be saved?

Those of you who have visualised acceleration have begun the acceleration. What you must completely and totally understand is your power. When you negate your power and your ability to bring change, then you negate the Universe and who you are – and you negate us. So what has begun [this was 1989] is the dedication to begin the process, so it is like a giant cannon that shoots out its bolt [sic], and it is going in great rapidity. Now we do not wish it to fall to Earth too quickly, do you understand? But it must continue. And know also that there is more fanaticism now, but that is slowly being dissipated. Yes.

JOHN: Is it that fanaticism had to come out, to be purged, that it couldn't be suppressed, it had to be released?

TOM: The most important thing is for it to be released, for in the suppressing it then grows more violent. Yes.

IRENE: But isn't it also true that as we move forward, those that oppose ....?

TOM: ...are moving in forwardness towards you, yes.

IRENE: And they are attempting to do whatever they can to maintain the balance on their side. Fanaticism is only one of the tools that they are using.

TOM: That is correct.

JOHN: Concerning the opposition and the rules that govern their behaviour, it seems to me that it is almost an arrangement: that if we can get ourselves unified and have clarity of purpose towards the positive, the energy of that unification can bring results and that's something that the opposition have to honour. Is that ....?

TOM: That is correct

JOHN: Good. That helps my understanding.

TOM: And also to remember that any of your strengths can be used against you, by the opposition. Therefore it is important to be clear with yourself. For example: if there is a problem with ego it is perfectly permissable to say,'Here is a problem'. It is suppressing it that creates the error. When coming to understanding of who you truly are there would be an elation in yourself. Now, if in that elation you begin to be fearful of appearing stupid in the eyes of others, then you will negate the joy in identifying who you truly are. This is how the opposition can use your strength. Therefore accept that it is understandable to be in joyfulness when you come into yourself, identify with it and the feelings of stupidity will disappear. Do not waste your time worrying if you will be considered in error. If you participate in your life correctly you will not be viewed in error. Do you understand?

JOHN: Yes. Thank you. Now, at this time [1985] We feel that there is a negative reaction as well as a positive movement on Earth. What is your assessment?

TOM: When there is a movement in forwardness, all that was, wishes to remain as it was. That is an element within a portion of human kind, for fear of not knowing the future, and also not wishing to give up the known factor. Therefore you have that aspect of negativity. You also have the aspect of negativity from those that be in power, that wish to maintain control and manipulation over others on Planet Earth. However, in our feeling we see that it is but a remnant that appears to be holding firm. Know this, that when its life is being threatened, this remnant maintains a stranglehold.

Now come some questions related to our improved understanding of the ecological balance on Earth.

JOHN: Is it not possible for us to generate sufficient energy on this planet for the use of the equipment that we need, without the use of potentially destructive things like nuclear power? I mean, are there not natural sources of energy that we can use to perform this job?

TOM: This planet eats itself.

JOHN: I don't understand that, what do you mean by that remark?

TOM: The peoples upon your planet eat up your planet in depleting its resources.

JOHN: But if we turn to the sun and wind, these are...

TOM: Your sun is a source of nuclear energy.

JOHN: What I'm getting at really is that there is quite a strong movement for the elimination of nuclear power stations in various countries, and I'm wondering whether you see any particular danger from nuclear power stations? I'm thinking of things like the Three Mile Island accident and so on.

TOM: We will explain: if you generate power with a natural source, this is the best option to save resources. But there are ways and means that nuclear power may also benefit humankind. It is only the introduction of the destructive nature of it that is the great danger. There are means and methods of using it without destruction, and with safe containing and refining of waste, yes. All things invented, all things brought into existence have value if applied and modified properly.

MIKI: How could the nuclear waste problem be solved?

TOM: We will ask Altea....It may be put to use as a source and form of energy also. It is just that your scientific communities have not attempted to find a way, except to isolate and bury it. It is an object of intensity of heat, and it in eventuality could be transformed and purified, if you have the will to create the technology. You understand in automobiles there is a circuit that is closed, that purifies the pollution?

ANDREW: Catalytic converters? Yes.

TOM: A similar type of situation...

ANDREW: ....can be developed.

TOM: It would lower the energy output, but it would not be contaminating.

IAN: One key issue of the past has been technology for the planet. Do you foresee it as necessary to transfer technology from your domains to our domains, or is it something that we can create ourselves now on the planet at this time? [1991]

TOM: It is important that the creation be brought about on your planet. It is important also to understand that those involved will be enlightened, as Edison was, by inspirational direct input, do you understand?

IAN: Yes, that's very clear.

TOM: We would ask you to continue your interest and forwardness. This planet was brought into its corruption by humankind, therefore it is important that humankind eliminates that corruption. And we say this also: not to hook you off, hook...

ISRAEL: ...get you off the hook......

TOM: .... that if it were ultimately necessary, there would be intervention, but then, you see, humankind could still revert to barbarism, for they then can say "We will do as we wish and still we shall be saved." Do you understand?

IAN: Yes.

TOM: It is not good to give all the answers, is it?

MIKI: Once you spoke about hydrogen being an energy form for the future. There is a person who is said to have invented a hydrogen engine, using very little energy – oxygen and hydrogen being separated for combustion, creating mainly water as exhaust. Is that possible? Is that the way for the future, or would it be better to have solar energy to generate power?

TOM: The utilisation of all the natural elements that are non-pollutionary are serviceable, and also use of sunshine is of benefit. One method may function in some arenas, others in other arenas. Both have viability. You understand that there are many on Planet Earth progressing in those directions, and that those inventors which are not pocketed by vested interests and have the future forwardness of Planet Earth at heart, will be those that will have the success – others eventually will down-tube. If you have a means of developing communication for encouraging forwardness – not to pollute and remove resources from the Earth, or collapsing the Earth — then we would ask each of you to be responsible to communicate this.

IAN: *Am I correct in saying that the key for an almost endless energy source would be magnetic energy?*

TOM: That is absolutely correct, yes.

IAN: *The big puzzle is that if you have a permanent magnet there is a constant force there that never gets smaller.*

TOM: You know that that is the force behind the transportation of vehicles from other domains? It creates a form that is like anti-gravity.

JOHN: *I heard that, counter to our thinking, the knowledge and understanding of gravity that we have at the moment is very poor, and that when we understand gravity, we will come to understand a lot.*

TOM: That is correct, as we explained that when you bring twelve together, that is four triangles — is it not? and when you use their electromagnetic fields (you know that humans have this energy field?) and weave together a canopy, then that is an energy that surrounds each person. Therefore it is healthy for you. Gravity holds you to the earth and those working with us on Earth that understand this force of energy, in sending out prayer and meditations can effect a change. For the mind is an energy field that is also a vehicle. You would see it as a living, whirling, wiggling field. As each understands and really 'knows' this, you can then weave a canopy similar to understanding the gravity field. It is a matter of shifting your mind-ness.

SUSAN: *Is a pyramid something that is useful for working energy?*

TOM: The energy of the pyramid has not yet revealed its secrets. By working together, people may find this out.

JOHN: *Tom, we humans seem to have got fixated on large amounts of force, and it seems that the future lies with weak energy fields, does that make sense?*

TOM: Subtle, yes. The scientific arena is now beginning to understand subtle energy in a form for using for Planet Earth and humankind. Also they are beginning to understand the interlocking and connection of all with one unity. Yes.

IAN: *So in order to generate energy — at present we use brute force —*

however there may be ways of using resonances and amplification at a very subtle level?

TOM: That is correct, yes.

MIKI: Is it necessary to use large amounts of energy to separate hydrogen from oxygen, or can subtle magnetic fields separate them?

TOM: The more smooth and subtle, the more beneficial. You have enough energy forms of destruction on your planet, do you not? Please remember also, that joy and jello [laughter] are also subtle energies that bring about change on Planet Earth.

Once again, the Sino-Tibetan conflict weaves a thread through the proceedings, underlining the points that Tom has already made...

IRENE: What's going on between the Chinese and the Tibetans? How important is it that this genocide be stopped, because as governments move toward providing a balance in terms of the ecology of the Earth (and we are getting closer, though it's by no means solved yet) if the Chinese were allowed to wipe out the Tibetans, that is an imbalance that could never be balanced again. Is that not so?

TOM: That is correct. What is of extreme importance is that humans of Earth must be made aware of the genocidal intentions of some governments of Planet Earth, and what is of great importance is that you have a legitimate structure through which to make people aware, so there may not be any censorship of that information, you understand that?

IRENE: Yes, absolutely.

TOM: When you permit extinction through deliberate elimination, as it is with an extinct bird or animal, it can never be replaced. And then that portion of the matrix is missing. Then other forces can move in.

IRENE: I had never thought about that. I knew that if an imbalance is created it could never be brought fully into balance again, but I didn't take it as far as you did, in that once an element is eliminated from the matrix, it allows other forces to move in and fill that part of the matrix, that's what you're talking about, isn't it?

TOM: Exactness.

IRENE: So it's more than just disappearing, it's allowing the opposite strength to take a larger, stronger place....

TOM: That is correct.

Then followed some more meditation instructions.:

In the nation of the U.S.A there are many petals of humankind, and what is of extreme importance is that people of that nation must now begin to understand that they do not live in isolation upon Planet Earth. In your meditations we wish you to expand them into a circle with the other nations.

And a particular question relating to the youth of this planet...

JOHN: I have a question about the violence of the youth in this and other countries. I'd like to understand more about this. I know they feel alienated, but can you explain more for deeper understanding?

TOM: They are the fruits of the war of Vietnam. These were those who died upon that soil on both sides.

JOHN: That's a very profound thing to get a grasp of, and I really appreciate knowing about that. What, if anything, can we actually do about it? Is it just a process that has to work itself through?

TOM: As it was in the war of Hitler, and then its passing, Except in this case there is even more violence for the training was of a different kind. And many of the people who died also had many addictions.

Back to the power of thought, its negative and positive aspects:

TOM: Understand this: in your physical world there are those who wish to be known of as gods, and that energy of godlessness creates devastation. For it devastates energies of goodness.

JOHN: Are you talking about the expectation and the predictions of earthquakes in California that came from some of the psychics. Is that what you're talking about?

TOM: That is correct. If they would but understand the devastation of their fear, their ego, their desire. Think upon this: when one continues to perpetrate only scandalous negations of life then do you wonder whence the earthquake comes? In your world, are there those that perpetrate goodness?

JOHN: *Not so many. Now, without making any predictions, we've heard that there could be some further devastation in California. Is this a serious problem?*

TOM: It is a very critical situation because of the size of roaring within the Earth, and its attempting to come back into balance. Would you be willing to meditate with us for the releasing of sizeable geological pressure?

JOHN: *Yes, of course we will do that.*

TOM: Total and completeness?

JOHN: *Yes.*

TOM: We thank you. We must explain to you about Planet Earth, its people and the energies bound within it and surrounding it. Planet Earth is a sphere – imagine a ball of clay. Now let us envision in that ball of clay that there has been a fracture internally and on some of the surface area, but it has been kilned so it is strong and it is firm.

If that ball of clay would move upon its path as a sphere without any bombardment, it may continue for the time of eternity of the Universe as it is. But if it should be in direct line with another body of great weight that could knock it, cause it to tumble or cause it to vibrate out of its normal path, then those faults could be weakened. As a whole it has a great strength and it would maintain, even though there be slight fissures of opening. By the same token, if upon this ball of clay there be insects that have antennae, and if those antennae continually vibrate with an energy of negativity, then that vibration in itself can weaken the ball of clay more than any external bombardment. So now we will attempt to equate the antennae of the insects to energies of humankind with thought, for the thought is your antennae of the insect.

Now you have upon your planet Earth a great many people whose antennae vibrate with negativity. When that happens it is stronger than when they vibrate with positivity, because beside the vibration of negativity of thought, there is a system within the physical body of getting the adrenal and the endocrine system also in vibration, so this emanates out from the body, and this in turn affects and weakens any structure. What humans fear, they may bring upon themselves.

But there are others who work diligently, knowing that this Universe, and particularly this globe, were ordained to fulfill what was created for humankind's purpose, so through their source of energy, they can negate the negative, to take the pressure off the globe.

In other words when the globe is stretched to the point where it may weaken, they, with their antennae of positive energy, solidify it and bring it back to strength. When you are in California, or just when you think of it, send a thought for release of pressures within the fissures, without destruction. Major destruction may always be averted in time, if there be only twelve that believe in this, yes.

We are in a crucial time. That time must now be utilised and developed for bringing forth awareness to people upon Planet Earth. Also there are those that oppose the changes, that come in many guises, and speak in an effective manner that causes confusion: the way to tell the difference between these and those who speak truth is their method, their personal style of existence, their motive in speaking out. You have upon Planet Earth many that will be in confusion, and many who will say that what they speak is truth and that only theirs is the truth. What must be made plain to humankind is that there are those who seem to speak truth who understand little more than average humans, and also it must be understood that there are those who write of beauty who live in corruption.

Each individual in relation to other individuals is a universe within itself. The motive of purity of spirit and heart, for the elevation of Planet Earth and for the youth of Planet Earth, is important.

We understand that Planet Earth in its density, in its stick-to-ness of the past, and in the energies of humankind, has elements within that bonds it, binds it and creates areas difficult to release. But when we speak to you of purity of motive and heart, we mean, we expect not saintliness, for that is not useful – for to be over-perfected is also to be out of balance, for you live in a physical world.

We mean only that your motive be pure for the betterment of humankind. To understand also the relationship of self with other humans, and the purpose of going into forward evolution, know this: Earth is in a critical situation, and we know that there be upon it dedicated souls who will benefit it and bring it into elevation and transformation; however, in the attempt to bring all of humankind forward, there will be those with whom it will not be possible. Therefore we say to you: do not carry with you guilt, when those that you would wish to understand perhaps do not understand – for guilt is an energy that stifles and stops your own forward evolution. For in their time of necessity they will come to understand.

Know this, that for those that are close to you, your energy is important. In your humility and your love for them, they will also come in forwardness. But we speak of those that you encounter in your daily life and who do not understand. It is a natural desire, when you are filled with joy, and when you know that a joyful time is coming in future, because of your dedication, to wish to impose your joy and understanding upon others. But this does not work. Other people must decide for themselves. They must decide, not from your desire but from their own.

There are many who speak of the ending of days. In the 'Harmonic Convergence', which took place in August 1987, began the element that has pushed this planet into a forward position – as you would say, you have moved from neutral into gear one. It is bringing up the energy.

There are still many around your planet who will think of the end of days, but what is now transpiring is that there are more who are beginning to understand that they are now in the shift for change, and they continue to pray, to bless and to be in joy. It is a time of great change, it is a time of forwardness, and it is a time of preparation. The manifestation of your love and purpose and energy for Planet Earth is as a great magnification that spreads outward and touches all. Humans have always looked to the stars and looked for where they have come from, who they are, how they have developed. It is time now to bring forth these answers, to give information that can begin to make peace in the hearts of humankind, and for them also to understand their purpose. You have wars upon Earth, religious disturbances, because humankind has not felt comfortable in the role that it has been placed in by religion. When humanity has the opportunity to view the essence of truth, that shift in consciousness will begin to bring about a peaceful order. Yes.

And know this also: there are those who have chosen to come to Earth who, as their service, will willingly cease to exist, as in the time of the holocaust, as there are those in Africa. Know that they are here in service of the highest order that they have chosen. For they know there is no death. The outcome will be the end of all the destruction of Planet Earth, of humankind. And Earth's true purpose will emerge, and also the decision of humankind in the Universe.

JOHN: So personal responsibility is a very important focus?

TOM: Yes.

JOHN: And the transformation itself, we need to be able to demonstrate transformation, through our individual nature?

TOM: And to bring forward those individuals that are concerned about the future – about nuclear waste, the ozone layer, destruction of forest – they will also bring the transformation.

The taking of personal responsibility – refusing to purchase a material that is destructive to the future. It is a small thing, but of the utmost importance. You have upon your planet five billion. Each one makes a difference.

JOHN: Yes. The difficulty is in portraying this in a simple enough way for people to understand. If it's done with millions of people it becomes too intangible, and I'm trying to get an idea of how...

TOM: We did not say with millions: we mean that you need to show those individuals who realise the importance of taking responsibility, and who do wish to take responsibility. Examples: if there be those who would wish not to use items that destroy trees, then find recycling methods. There are many different ways.

JOHN: In the end I suppose we have to look at what a transformed world would look like. You said before that it would be beyond our imagination.

TOM: We hear so much from your planet that "If everything is wonderful, it will be boring". That is not so. For in transformation there are continuous pursuits of understanding, learning and change. Humankind has been locked into the need for struggle. When it is understood that when there is freedom from want, freedom of time .... imagine all that exists upon your planet that billions have not yet experienced!

JOHN: Yes. So instead of trying to pull ourselves out of the negative, we will be drawn forward by the positive...

TOM: That is exactly correct. You will have the experience of joy of being. What you call upon your world 'peak experience' will be a way of life. Just begin, the rest will come.

You have throughout your planet pockets that are in dissension with each other, in the name of God. In your planetary situation many humans have attributed God-qualities to the beings of the universal civilisations. You are now in the days of the emergence of the spirit that was within the Nazarene, what you call the Christ. The acceleration of this energy being brought forth into the consciousness of humankind is of the greatest importance, for when resolution is brought into being, then other pockets of dissention also will be in resolution. You are on the point of tottering forward or backward. Now we wish you to understand this: to those who have committed to transformation upon Planet Earth, you have had personal trials, you have had great deliberations within yourself, you have at times wondered if your forward direction could be sustained on all levels of your being, in your consciousness, in your personality, and in your business life. There still exist, among some, difficulties in all three of those arenas. What is important is for you to view that you are coming forward and out of this, and you have grown in great strength. Now those trials brought to you were not from us, but it was from the Others, in the hope that you would forget your service and growth. But in staying upon your path, and creating energy-fields through meditation you see the results of who you are, do you understand what we say?

JOHN: *Yes, I think we all have a lot of difficulty attributing any of these effects to our humble human efforts.*

TOM: In each of your cultures, what is important is to understand that each of you is a complete unit, containing all that is contained within the Universe, and that each of you has the ability to change the necessary arenas to bring Planet Earth out of darkness into its rightful place. In your culture you believe humbleness to be humility: it is time to understand that it is now permitted to accept yourself.

JOHN: *Yes. Can you tell us what sort of practical resolution we are looking for, avoiding conflict on one hand, but on the other hand there are some major lessons to be learned, and it's difficult to see how that can be done without pain and conflict. Can you elaborate on that?*

TOM: When fanaticism begins to grow within a group it is like a cancer, but it is in actuality a compensation for doubt in belief. Therefore people must hold on to this belief, for to them it is their identity, whether it be with the Hoovids, or with the Ishmaels, or with those of the Nazarene. As it is also with the Hindu.

JOHN: *The only thing is that some people are opportunists, and even though they make religious claims they don't really represent that religion anyway.*

TOM: What you must evolve in your meditation is to send transformation energy, for each to understand their humanness and their identity. And keep in your mind also that the opposition is attempting to control. The balance is very fragile, and there will be conflict, for in reality at this time [late 1990], the Crescent arena is being used by the Others, by being fed the energy of power. But that cannot sustain — you understand. There is a saying in your world that if there is fire-playing then there is burning, is that not so?

JOHN: Yes... I suppose a major concern we have right now is for the hostages in Iraq. Can this be resolved without loss of their lives, or what?

TOM: You have several issues of great importance: You have those of innocence, and you have the biological weapons, which is the most severe issue. Hussein, in his thoughtlessness, does not comprehend that the releasing of biological contaminants stays in the atmosphere, contaminates and kills not only what it was targeted at, but becomes infused in Planet Earth and will continue its malignancy — that can be devastating for the people of his own, as well as for all Planet Earth, for the winds revolve around your world. This issue is not only an issue between the Ishmaels and the tribes of Jacob, it is a world issue, that the world has not truly viewed.

JOHN: Many years ago, there was discussion about a landing in case of nuclear war, and that you would never allow a nuclear war to occur, because the devastation effect of that would go far beyond this planet. Is this biological weaponry of a similar nature, and what are the implications of that?

TOM: What is necessary is your commitment in your meditations, so this meditative energy may then be utilised to blanket, to contain, and to bury this danger. What we want you to understand is that we cannot have that backfire, for in backfiring it also contaminates, you understand. Therefore it must be encapsulated, neutralised, and buried.

JOHN: Presumably Altea's technology is very involved in this addition to our, and all people's meditations — worldwide?

TOM: Yes. It is those committed to bringing Planet Earth to a solution of peace who have been maintaining but, as we have already said, twelve of ours are of vital importance: for that is the fusion, the knitting, the welding of the umbrella. Do you understand?

JOHN: Yes, thank you. The second problem that we are facing is the environmental problem, and there seems to be but a short time left for us to do something dramatic about changing it. Can you com-

ment about that?

TOM: Progress is being made. First you must resolve this situation of chemical, primarily biological weapons, and create agreement worldwide, by all parties on the elimination of all atomic weapons. For if that is chain-reacted then you do not have to worry about time.

JOHN: Which areas can we give particular attention to?

TOM: This is a vast question. You must first start with the seed to grow the food, is that not so? We ask that people on Planet Earth meditate for bringing a resolution: it takes but one step, as you have seen in the time of moving of walls and taking down of barriers. It can be resolved. True, there was preparation for months in advance by the energies of people. Know that there have been months of preparation in advance in your meditations for this situation. [the Middle East Arena].

You must have the understanding that you have the creative will to create that situation, and what we would ask is that you do not judge any in that region, if it be of Ishmael, of the Hoovids or of the Nazarene or anyone else, do you understand? For in your energy of power you can also unbalance the balance. What is that called?

JOHN: You're talking about balance and impartiality.

TOM: That is correct. Just permit your energy to flow, and this will be the most difficult. Now we will see if you really understand who you are!

ALL: [laughter]

SUSAN: Can I ask about atomic energy, if it's possible to blanket it, and contain it, and bury it – can it be used positively?

TOM: All that is negative may be transmuted to positive, yes.

We have come to a time of a grave situation as well as an opportunity for great joy. [1990]. It is time for each of you to remove self from self, to have great consideration, in all arenas of existence, for the future of your planet Earth, in preparation for the young humans to whom humanity is now giving birth. For you and they are the carriers and the future of Earth and, in truth, of the Universe. We would ask you to be in great joy, elimination of foolishness, elevational transformation of your self-centredness, to expand to compassion, to walk in the glorification of Earth, and to take complete responsibility for your environment, to bring to your consciousness information that creates future betterment for your planet. Create a working network of information so that you then can dispense to others. Do not become zealous. Do it with conviction but in gentle compassion. But most important, those with children must build the structure within these children of great love for all creatures, for all life upon your planet Earth.

We would ask also that for your own betterment, as well as that of the Planet, that there be daily meditation to find that time-space to connect with us, for we are in truth available if you connect with us for re-energising yourself. You may meditate on your own for eighteen of your minutes, but we would ask that you do it in a time that you do not have haste: it will help in your own movement through your day as also in benefiting Planet Earth. During you meditation we will not speak but we are there to infuse you with our love and joy. Keep in mind always that twelve people in commitment, completely and totally without ego, remaining in quietness about it, can bring great changes upon Planet Earth.

If it is not possible to make that commitment we understand that – that does not mean we love you less or honour you less, but if you should truly commit to the transformation to Planet Earth then it is time for you to walk in sureness, in joy, and in consciousness; to find the crystal within each one of internal knowledge and knowing, that is what is necessary. Remember this: knowledge is not wisdom. Wisdom comes from within and cannot be taught, and the person that is wise does not say they are wise. One who is wise detaches, steps back, observes, and knows when to go forward without the ego of exploitation. Most important of all is joy, kindness, compassion, to have charity, to have faith, and to accept there is always hope for uplift. Yes.

JOHN: *My understanding is that there are many souls on this planet who are going through their evolutionary process, and are not in service to the planet, while there are others who are in service, some of whom are conscious of it, and others who are unconscious of it. And then you also mentioned at one time that 98% of those that chose to serve, don't carry out their chosen service, although they may serve in some other way. Can you say anything more about that role of service, since we are all in that role in some way?*

TOM: That is correct, for out of every hundred who choose to return at this time to bring forth the Christ-energy, the Messiah- energy of the evolutionary state, two but fulfil their choosing – for souls become entrapped in their ego-personality or become competitive with the Universe. They have internal knowledge of who they are, and they misunderstand that this is not the ultimate reality, and that is the beginning of the misunderstanding of their individuality. Upon Planet Earth there are many that are in that state.

STEVE: *When I last talked to you, some years ago, there was a crisis [early 1980s], and now there is one again [Gulf War, 1990-1], while there has been in the interim a time when the world has seemed to be getting much more peaceful. At the same time there has been an emphasis on greed, personality-cults and selfishness. Is the human race at this stage able to cope alone or may it be possible that a direct intervention of some kind may be required in the present circumstances?*

TOM: What you see now is the thrashing of the tail of the negativity that knows it is on its way out — bringing forth cultism and fanaticism. There will be intervention if there were any people that would attempt to trigger the total destruction of planet Earth's environment. Also know that there surrounds the Earth many of what you call 'space beings' from lower civilisations that have come here, for they have destroyed their own planetary system and are looking for a place of survival in another. Planet Earth must survive: it is your energy that helps it to survive.

DAVID: *Is it appropriate to ask whether those space beings visiting us now are a threat to human civilisation?*

TOM: Some of them, yes. Council has said that I must clarify: These are not a threat to the survival of Planet Earth but not all mean it well... As you are in the state of transformation, so are other civilisations that are coming forth, yes.

VI

TERRESTRIAL AFFAIRS

18

Making a Difference

This chapter concerns our usefulness to each other on this planet and also our relationships – and how we deal with them.

Though concerned with what we can do to help the planet and humanity, Tom does warn us about getting too zealous. "It does not help your work for you to be too intense. It is important for you to have some form of relaxation or diversion, such as watching your television, or listening to music, to read, or to walk or to visit with gentle friends and talk of totally different subjects. In your physical world it is important to maintain a balance. You cannot do this if there is not diversion. You must relax in order to function at a higher level."

While there are visualisation and meditation instructions in the next chapter here is a practical, helpful thing that you can do to make a difference to the world that we live in. If some of these meditation tips are repeated later on, I make no apologies, it is to be helpful to the 'skip readers'. Meditation is among one of the most helpful things that anyone can do, both for themselves and the planet.

The Nine have suggested that we make a commitment and join together for eighteen minutes to meditate for the unification of this planet and also for the right of individual countries to exist and then to meditate that all these strengthened, unified countries throughout the world, use their solidification wisely. They have emphasised the need for group energy and cohesiveness, with synchronisation of the time of meditation and then a commitment to that arrangement.

The requested time is for eighteen minutes, co-ordinating with 21.00 hours in Israel (don't forget to check local seasonal time changes!) as a guide this should equate with:

    11.00 in the U.S.A. West Coast
    14.00 in the U.S.A. East Coast
    19.00 in the British Isles.
    20.00 in Europe

The selected day is Sunday. The Nine request that at least once a month a minimum of twelve people be together. On other Sundays if that is not possible, a minimum of three people would be required.

We are asked to keep our arms and legs unfolded during meditation, and to enter our meditative state in complete love, harmony and peace. If it is necessary for you to do something pre-meditative, be it with sound, colour, breathing, exercise or quiet – do this before starting .

Also before starting, the Nine suggest a colour cleansing using specifically – emerald green, royal blue and royal purple – visualise these colours showering down upon you, taking away all the disturbances of the day and allow that shower of colour to flow away into the Earth in purification before begining your meditation.

Tom: We each work in service together. Within each server there is an intuition that is the highest. It is your connection with us. Listen to the voice within you. Follow in directness whatever you have surety about. It is important that the peoples upon the planet Earth understand their responsibility for self, for each other, and in turn for the Universe.

It is important for people on Planet Earth to understand that in death they do not escape responsibility, that there is no death. So that each movement, each thought, each word affects the Universe. It is important that those upon Planet Earth begin to work in harmony, in unison, in balance and in peace with each other.

This book which we have asked to be written for us will help you to understand the purpose for each person, and for Planet Earth in relation to the Universe. Remember this: we are all one with you. We are you and you are us. We exist on your energy of love.

Understand that you are not an island alone, that you are part of a whole – and when I say this to you, I refer to all that are in service. Those that have desire to be alone and perform a service according to their own dictates, within themselves, are in truth not in service. To be in service is to give oneself for the love of the Universe and for the love of their fellow humans. It is also important to remember that if you begin to become trapped in looking within yourself, to have total understanding of your self, that is also a form of ego. It is time to put aside your self and go forward. We speak to all. It is the only way and the only form in which the Universe can evolve. We have no objection if looking within themselves can in truth benefit people, and they may then make a step forward, but to sit in a circle and look within, and constantly ask "What about me?" and "See what I have done" then they in truth are not prepared for service. When you can let go of "What about me?" and ask what can be done for the betterment of the Universe, and have the willingness to let go of ego, desires and self-pity, then what you have been trying to find within yourself will be shown in great clarity. The Council say that I should say this to you: the Others, if they can keep those that have desire to serve in a tight circle, and looking within at all times, then in truth they have succeeded, have they not?

JOHN: *Yes. It has been said in the past that the process of change and growth has to take its natural and somewhat slow course, and I feel that at this time of great change.*

TOM: We have not the time that has been said by men: all the souls that have existed, and now exist at this time, and those that are in the spirit world surrounding this Earth, have had their time. It is their selfishness, it is their egos, their self-pity, their physical desires, that they refuse to relinquish. They have had the time. They know within the core of their soul and their very being, that they have had the time. It is their egos that prevent them from change and progressing. If we would permit this, this planet would plunge into darkness, and it would take the greatest portion of the Universe with it. We have given this planet more than sufficient time. In truth we have given to this planet and those that exist upon this planet more time than we have given the souls that exist upon other planets. We cannot give more time. The time that we have given has not been used in a productive manner, but to feed egos again.

All people have potential. If you take a jar of oil and try to take it in, it does not taste pleasant, and you may take a jar of vinegar alone and it is not pleasant, but if you mix the two together, and then you take it in, it tastes refined. This is what you must understand about those with whom you work.

JOHN: *Yes, thank you, that's beautiful.*

TOM: What we explain to you now, we explain in all truth and sincerity. This is for all those who proclaim to be in the work. We wish you to understand that it is not possible for any people on Earth to escape responsibility for Planet Earth, in order to do what they say they must do. It is not possible for them to be of any service if they look after their own interests only.

Remember that all those that come to you from distant lands on

Earth, and would say to you "I have left all my responsibilities, desires, and all that I have had, and my mother, father and children, because I have come here to work for God." They are in error, because they cannot be working for God when they do not accept the responsibility for those that are close to them. They may in truth think that they do. It might be true a person is dedicated to what she or he believes is a dedication, but you do not remove yourself from what you are responsible for by doing it in a manner that causes friction or great hurt to someone else, because you are then responsible for the soul of that person.

We wish to explain an Earthly condition to you: you in truth have more understanding of the density of the Earth than we. We created the Earth, but we have not existed upon the Earth. Those that have incarnated upon Earth many times have more understanding of the weakness involved in living on Earth. When we say this we speak of relatively evolved souls. We attempt not to flatter you, we speak the truth of the position and responsibility of evolved souls. These people are teachers in service, for they have greater understanding of service than many that are in service.

JOHN: *Two difficulties we have with this subject of evolved souls is the dangerous feeling of elitism that it can create in some people involved in this work, and, if you are applying this notion of evolved souls to the members of our group, the strangeness that group members should have all come together at one time.*

TOM: It is not strange, for it is now the time. There has been great suffering amongst all of you in your past. In your previous lifetimes of service there have also been great failures, and there have been many that have come at this time that are also now experiencing great failures. It has taken great suffering to have reached this point. It has taken a long consideration among all of you to arrange to return at this point. It has taken great stamina for all of you to remain in your life-situations, to bring you together. And there are many others like you.

Please explain to servers on Earth that each of them has given all that is possible to be upon the planet Earth at one time or another. And in your situations, in not being world leaders, but in suffering, in despair, in anguish, you are not different from more ordinary souls. All that exist at this time on Earth have suffered in greatness in the past, though some have also been in great joy.

JOHN: *Would that imply that almost anyone on the Earth would have an identity that you could name from the past, one which would be recognisable?*

TOM: Not at this time, for there are millions upon millions of souls. Those that are gathered as servers now are those that were gathered also in the past to raise the evolution of the planet. They are now gathering again to evolve the planet. The Council say I have created difficulty in a system of belief.

JOHN: Well, the difficulty is not to give the impression that any one person is any more special or has any more special cosmic function than any other.

TOM: All people have a great cosmic function. It is important for you to relate that each has a responsibility to each other and to the Universe. They have come from many other planets, and they have served on other planets. They are now here to help Planet Earth, but also because of the attractiveness, the density, the physicalness, they have become entrapped in Planet Earth. Perhaps they will recognise that in themselves.

JOHN: I understand that those of us that have come back to serve in this way, made that decision before this lifetime. What I am not quite clear on is how we have come to be together and to work together in the way that we are, when we have no memory of that decision. How is it that we have all met, and have come to be working together?

TOM: That was your decision. If you had the memory, would you then be able to relate to the experience of souls on Planet Earth?

JOHN: Probably not. It seems that there was a sort of subconscious guiding thread that did bring us together, that remembered the past that we had shared.

TOM: It was your choosing. You are not here by accident. In your accomplishments, and in that which you will accomplish for the purification of the planet Earth, if you choose to be reborn upon the planet Earth in your next life you will then have memory, as those that exist upon other evolved planets have memory.

ANDREW: We humans on Earth seem to have difficulty in keeping to our commitment, in respect of inner resolutions we make. How does it affect you when someone ends up not doing what they said they would do?

TOM: We look over your scene and we choose those that we think are most beneficial to the work. They make commitments, they think within their hearts and they verbalise that they are making commitments, but we cannot truly interfere when all of a sudden the commitment does not want to be made. This has been the problem for thousands of years with this planet.

ANDREW: *Yes, I'm beginning to realise that.*

TOM: They will do that which does not interfere with their pleasures.

ANDREW: *I'm well aware of this and I think it makes you sad because it is for the benefit of humankind, on Earth. If we ourselves cannot help each other then it seems to me a very desperate situation as far as the future is concerned.*

TOM: We understand why you humans have difficulty with commitment, and we understand that we ask you to do many things. Then at times, when things do not happen, you understand why they do not, but others do not understand. People expect us to perform miracles for them. We can only do so much. We need your physical energy and your minds on your planet. That is very important.

ANDREW: *I hope to convey this to others as I get a deeper knowledge of this.*

TOM: You have worked with us for many, many years without proof, and for this we are forever grateful.

ANDREW: *I seem to be in a strange position where I don't have dreams, I don't have visions, I don't have insights.*

TOM: You have a knowledge inside.

ANDREW: *I seem to go on what's called faith — I guess it may be knowledge but, anyway...*

TOM: Knowledge is faith. Some people have a great desire to please us, but if in pleasing us it brings sorrow to them, then it does not please us. And if such a person is not in a position to bring forward clearness of complete commitment, we have great understanding, for we understand the nature of the Earth. We have said to you that there will be times of sorrow and times of despair, but they will be in the minimal, not in the most, and it will only come at times when there is a drain on your energy from those that surround you. Your commitment, if it is true commitment, will bring the song of the Universe within you. It will cause you to walk in a light of love, and to walk in lightness. If among any of you there is not understanding of this, then we would ask that you be clear with yourselves about service.

If your commitment is clear to the extent that it fills you with love, with joy and with the music of the Universe, by verbalising that commitment, it adds strength to it, for all those forces who are in agreement with you will be strengthened by your joy, and will surround you with the purest of love. But if your commitment brings not joy but sorrow and anguish, and not pleasure, but only a wish to please us, by verbalising that reservation it dissipates it, and those that love you may then give you the strength to filter it and to understand. Verbalisation in love gives you strength, and gives us strength. To be an ostrich, to be not reviewing, it is better not to serve the Universe.

Your motivation at all times must be the highest. Your purpose and direction must be as clear as is possible in the density of your world. Your generosity, your love, your heart, your joy in life must expand to touch others. There are no teachers, for all are students. There is an exchange that is given, and when you give yourself, if it be your physical, mental or emotional nature, if you give out that energy to touch and expand to others, what you receive is a hundredfold.

That is the secret of growth, the secret of expansion: the willingness to give yourself completely without question. But at the same time knowing not to give yourself to fools. You know that there are upon Planet Earth those that you call fools? They are there to see if you are willing to give yourself to a fool — that is their position. Only one who is willful and forces his way forward gives to a fool.

We must tell you also that zeal is futile. When you transfer what you know and become aggressive with this, and try to insist that other people should understand and agree, you are then creating a problem for yourself. You know who you are. It is often beyond people's comprehension, or it can activate their fears. You must be very careful to maintain balance and love and understanding. You are not special — though in truth you are, but this does not remove responsibility from you or give you special accounts in the physical world. There is no way that you can help others if you do not understand the joys, fears, sadness, despairs, loves and angers of the peoples that exist in the physical world. In truth you are to master these things, but one who calls themselves a master escapes from them: a master masters those things while existing among them — that is the difference between a master who does not claim to be a master, and those that claim to be masters.

If you remove yourself from the physical world then you have no temptation, no anger, no joy, no love. And by removing from the world, you can easily master those things because there is no temptation, no touching of other beings. You cannot transfer your beliefs or feelings to another: you can only plant a seed. And you cannot condemn others for the manner in which they live: you can only attempt to show them. Without being the highest example, they will not listen. Be gentle with people and drop a seed, and we will handle the rest.

There is not one soul on your planet that cannot be saved, if in truth it was handled properly with stability, maturity and love. It is important to have love, and it is important to give love and to share love, and it is also important to realise that you are not a perfect being, neither is anyone: but each of you has within you qualities that, blended with the qualities of others, make a perfect being.

After this there followed a discussion with a guest who had asked for guidance in his teaching of others.

There are no teachers. If you understand that principle, then you understand much. When one sets themself up as a teacher, they set themselves apart. We, the Council of Nine, are not teachers. The Nazarene was not a teacher. All are students together in the Universe, and when one has an exchange with another, then that that is called a teacher often is taught. That is what the exchange is about.

Another word needs to be utilised in your language. Yes. We mean there are no teachers of the Universe, you understand? Though there may be a teacher of a musical instrument.

You see it is now the time in the universe of Planet Earth that people must learn for themselves. The time of teaching such as religion, or another person's idea to another one, what is only needed in these times is a guidance. There are all means and methods and facilities of exchange of information to the far circles of the Earth. In times of past, leaders and teachers of Earth felt that the mass of humankind were not capable of thinking for themselves.

At this time of the forwardness of Earth, and of the acceleration that has been intensified upon the Earth, even that which you would call 'knowing' is being impregnated with the energy fields that are awakening the innermost voice within. And understand fully that there are no teachers, only facilitators.

Then an exchange concerning personal faith...

ALBERT: As a Christian, I am disturbed by the influence of other Christians, who criticise those of us who have a more mystical, meditative approach. Do you have any guidelines on this?

TOM: Surround yourself with a white light of protection, with the universal consciousness that is Christ, ask for direction and guidance, and above all else, ask yourself: what is my motive? Do I do this for gain, do I do this for exposure, do I do this to be different, do I do this for barter [money], do I do this so I may be 'someone' in my world? If your answer is yes to any of these questions then you are open for those to misguide you. If your motivation is only for love of humanity and to bring about peace upon this planet Earth, and you are able to be happily in silence with this, not to brag upon it, not to speak about those places or energies that have been used, then all good will come.

MIKI:I feel that I have become spiritually blocked, yet I still have the urge to make a difference in the world. Do you have any advice on this?

TOM: If you will discipline yourself to meditate for a minimum of nine minutes each day, but preferably eighteen when there is more allowance, to gather inner strength and guidance from your soul, all barriers to your spiritual path will be removed.

Know this: each and every human is in a position of great responsibility to bring about change in humankind, and that each of you does create a difference in the lives of those that you touch, even though you may not know it.

Therefore the importance of maintaining an integral self, and being honest within self and with others must be of the highest priority. It is important to know that each of you has within you a crystallisation of the spirit that removes itself from the ins and outs of your life, and comes outward as a beam that touches and inspires, and brings to those in contact with you the necessary energies for changing the self within and creating a difference in their own and others' lives.

It is important to bring the mind together with the spirit and the emotions, to bring them into a complete whole being. It is important that each of you be a battery for that to happen for other humans also. Know this: at times the battery just needs to be, do you understand? This lifetime is the most important that you have ever chosen.

Those of the past were past experiences for preparation for this one.

It is important to know that what is past is past, and what is coming in the future does not make a difference at this moment: it is this moment in time which makes the difference. Each moment is a new beginning. Each moment should be experienced and touched. The memories of those moments, as also the memories of past lives, benefit you, and it is in preparation for the future. But it is when you are in this moment that you are who you are, that you are at the centre of the Universe. Anticipation over the future causes anxiety. When you be with this moment, the future is but the next moment.

JOHN: I think it's our relative insignificance in society that makes it hard for us to believe that we are playing an important function.

TOM: That is your analysis of relative insignificance. A shoemaker may have more significance than the leader of a country.

The wear and tear factor of being in service can beset anybody. The next exchanges dealt with this specific problem:

TOM: In the expansion of your energy, in the etheric of each human, when it is extended continually in giving self to others, in forwarding service and direction, then you always leave a portion of your etheric along your path. What is of greatest importance is the retrieval of the etheric. You have in your world a gum-chew, is that not so?

DEE: Yes. Chewing gum.

TOM: And when it is new it is a full form, then you make it pliable by adding moisture. Then you masticate it. Then you remove all essence of the taste from it. Is that not so?

DEE: That's true.

TOM: Then you may take it and stretch it, and it will have holes. You may continue to put portions here and portions there, and then you cannot put it all back together. And then it not only loses its form, it loses the essence of what it was. That is when you over-gumchew, is that not so?

DEE: Yes.

TOM: The teacher that leads and develops cannot extend beyond what has been extended, when they are not of the substance to extend further. So it is necessary to make a complete break. One may curtail expansion of self in helping humankind to grow, until health and balance are restored. In this way it is possible to heal oneself while in service to humanity.

GUEST: *One of the major difficulties in my work is the sheer physical complexity of the matters that I have to deal with: can you suggest how, with the pressures on me, I can deal with this immense complexity?*

TOM: You have within you resources and energies. You have within you a mind, and you also have love surrounding you. To begin to think of great complexities in your hour of stress creates more complexities. To put things into action, do not attempt to do everything, but do one step at each time. Remove yourself from yourself, think not of yourself and your stress: detach yourself, detach yourself from your family, your friends and associates in emotion, detach from all in emotion. Think, for you have that ability, that you are performing a service, or that you are performing upon a stage, and do this with each step. It is important to begin, not to be concerned with difficulties. When you begin, you will see the great challenge it is for you, and it will occupy you, it will give you strength and fortitude. It will keep your mind in a situation of flux, not stuckness, so you may then think in clearness. You have created a situation that was created by you, therefore you can uncreate it, for you have that ability.

You will find that if you have difficulty in things that are morally right, care not what others attempt to do, or what benefit from your distress they attempt to gain, but know that you have done morally right, and if they attempt to earn more from you, to accuse you or to cover their own losses in making of you a scapegoat, then they in truth will be found out, and it is not your concern.

For if you are honest and morally right then only truth will come, and those that attempt to take advantage of you, or to use you, will be exposed in their own time and at a greater consequence. Yes.

There is not one that is better than the other. It is important to understand that amongst all that exist upon Planet Earth, there is none which is in truth more superior or less equal. When we say this, we speak of the soul. And if you look within the soul, you will find that each soul is a particle of divinity. While on the exterior, different people might not look equal, within their souls they are indeed equal. There is none among you that is not equal – and we speak of feeling and emotion. It is important to have this understanding.

All people have feelings, and feel everything as much as others, even if they seem not to. The difficulty with Earth has been not only the inequality of black people, yellow people, red people, but also of the females of all peoples. It is important to understand that you cannot set a rule. Neither a man nor a woman can set a rule, and say that "This is the way that it is to be". We do not set these rules: it was done by those on Earth in order to control, to manipulate and to use others. This has not been done by the human male alone: it has been done also, in some groups, by the female. We wish you to know that a man, regardless of his background, has the feeling that a woman also has. You cannot set aside a woman and say "This is a woman" and a man, and say "This is a man". For each is a woman and a man. This has been the greatest difficulty – as it has been with people's attitudes toward other people of other races. It is only at this time that both reach true blending, and that is why we have requested that there is work in unison between males and females. It is important to bring the ego into control, and to have the understanding that all others are equal. All humans have an equal claim. We cannot have ego and division in these next days: there must be cleansing within those that create the poison for all. There must be the understanding that if there is difficulty in your societies, it creates difficulty for the cosmos.

The female gender on Planet Earth has antennae of greater sensitivity to the knowledge of the internal workings of humankind. The male antennae view the surface, not always the inner reality.

IRENE: Yes. With reference to this, a project I am working on is about female sexuality, and where we have gone in the last thirty years in terms of the way that human beings have begun to deal with, or not deal with, this corrupted area of their lives. Is there something that you can tell me that could help in this, and do you think it's important?

TOM: It is important, and it is also what you call a Box of Pandora. For if it is not conducted with great sensibility, it can be misconstrued. But of greatest importance is to bring out what has been removed and suppressed from womankind: the true knowledge that in the past all power came from women – and now in recent years, this information and knowledge is emerging out of womankind.

At times they used their ability to control male humankind, and males have reacted to that – and now it is time for the elimination of the shadow of corruption in the utilising of women's power, to bring forth the purity of this power in its true form, concerned with creation and returning to the source. That creates a complication for you, but with sensibility and subtlety you can bring this knowledge forth, to those who will comprehend, and it will bear them fruit and release another freedom within themselves, which then also begins an acceleration in the world. This performance of sexuality has created bondage for all humankind. It is now a time of understanding and release of this bondage, without the corruptions.

IRENE: What has happened in modern times is that we have gone from a period of secrecy and control of the sexual act, done in the darkness, to rampant sexuality in the 1960s and '70s, to relative abstinence in the '80s, because it seems, humankind has not chosen to acknowledge any insight into this area.

TOM: That is correct, and it is important that sexuality now be understood. Understand this: the sexual plague was not created solely from mistakes in science: it was also created from the consciousness of humankind to break its habitual pattern, so it may review itself. However, as in most cases with your world all things are overdone.

IRENE: It's also a story of emotions, and it's also a story of understanding those emotions.

TOM: It is important to understand this, for the emotion in your bonding is the highest returning to the Source. It is the connection achieved on reaching completion, the feeling of oneness with the other and unity with creation. This is the drive behind the male continuously looking for that other side of being, the female, to make this returning to creation — but because of misunderstanding and misuse it is rare that this return is truly made. Do you understand?

IRENE: It's brilliant. But what is the drive of the female?

TOM: The drive in the female is to be given the power to create, and only when the female is charged by male catalytic energy is the creation formed. You see, this sexuality of creating acceleration in the female is, on a subconscious level, an anger at the population of males for the bondage with which it has encapsulated the female — for in its unconscious the male knew that all came from the female. The female has now awakened to the strength of her being. This anger emerged through promiscuity, to say to the males "You will not control my most important element, instead I shall abuse it", rather than make a commitment to self-control. It is like throwing it into the face, for the male had done the abusing in the past. Then within the collectivity of minds this abuse by males accelerated out of control, and the destruction of Planet Earth was the logical outcome. It began an inward tendency of devouring oneself. Humankind has brought about the breakdown in sexual relations itself, to stop its limitation and corruption of sexuality, through enforced abstinence and fear. Now it is time for sexuality to be brought out in true understanding, and for humanity to return to a sane understanding of its connection with creation, and of the returning to the light at times of coupling, to rejuvenate oneself.

IRENE: *That is also the beginning of the acknowledgement that Earth is paradise?*

TOM: Only on your planet Earth does this uniting come about. It is the ultimate unity. Yes.

GUEST: *I wish to ask about a statement you made in 1988, that "in the past, all power came from women". Now could you expand on this, and tell us how did this change in history, such that women have lost their power?*

TOM: It is not "All power came from female", but "All power comes from female". It was not lost: it was taken, for control. The male had recognition that this was power, and by controlling it on a level of instinct, believed they then controlled power. This is why, also, in the brutality, the clubbing of women, physical or mental, they can then attempt to destroy that power, rather than understanding that male and female, interchangeable, may be two pillars that hold up the world.

Now you also understand that there has been lash-back from those of female, and it is now beginning to come back into balance. Also, what was not permitted in the male was the identification of the energy of female that exists within them, for it does as a percentage, as a percentage of male exists within the female. It is only when there is complete understanding of equalness, that the world then begins to evolve to its proper place. In these times, in those countries not evolved – although you may think they are evolved – when they put less emphasis or love on a female child or destroy it, or continue to permit surrounding souls of Planet Earth only male vehicles for entering, then we ask how evolved are they?

You see it is equal, the power is women, female, and it must be utilised by the male. And the male to be utilised in forwardness by the female. That is the partnership. Do you believe humankind will understand   that?

GUEST: *In the course of time they will – some of humankind are beginning to understand, but it will probably take some time yet.*

TOM: Ingrained ideas are difficult to remove, are they not? For they make worms in the brain, and they nest in there, and they make eggs and siblings in there, yes? Therefore there are people of wormy mindness,   yes!

ALL: *[Laughter]*

GUEST: *Was there any omission or error on the part of women, and the female within men, which brought about this situation, which could have been brought about otherwise, in the case of the male controlling   the   female?*

TOM: In many many tribes there was understanding of this power. Therefore in the beginning equalness was accepted. Then there were those that regressed to the genetic animal state. It had not to do with what you call 'error'. It had to do with subjugation of one over another. It also had to do with the understanding that the female of the species produced the furtherment of species – and you know that in the early times there was not the understanding that the male energy was needed to produce the furthering of species. Therefore it became an ingrained idea, in mistakenness. The Hoovids understood this, for they know that was the outcome.

GUEST: *If we can clarify that: it became ingrained out of ignorance of the process of reproduction?*

TOM: Not in beginning, but when there was dispersion and moving into other arenas, and not having contact, it then reverted to animal-ness.

GUEST: *And there was no intuition or sense amongst females about the reproductive process either?*

TOM: They knew where it came from, but would they say to their chieftain? There was that knowledge.

GUEST: *Was that knowledge suppressed, therefore?*

TOM: That is correct. They were also impressed, subjugated with the idea that they had no value, except for aiding the productiveness of males. Do you understand how many souls were evacuated because of being a female, and attempted to recycle over and over?

GUEST: *No, I didn't understand that was a major phenomenon.*

TOM: It is still a major phenomenon, is it not?

JOHN: *In China?*

TOM: Yes. Also in the seven-gods nation.

GUEST: *Which nation is that?*

TOM: India.

Then some discussions were had on the role of youth

JOHN: *Do you have a message for the aware young people of today, who are now growing into adulthood?*

TOM: You are now completing the functions and lessons of children and have begun the identification of who you are. We would wish you to know this: you are not your personality, you are truly the essence of the whole universe. Therefore we make a request for the future, that you take upon yourself total and complete responsibility for yourself, the planet Earth and the cosmos.

When you were children, you played the game of children. Now you have entered the world of realness. This means that you know who you are, and you will not tarnish it by permitting yourself the games of children. You have entered a new phase. You have stepped through the threshold at the time of the beginning of releasing the bottleneck on Planet Earth. You have begun to enter into the chambers of the initiate. You have begun to identify your source, and if you truly think upon it, you know you can move a mountain, elevate Planet Earth and remove yourself from being stuck in yourself.

Know always you are loved, and walk in the knowledge of that love and who you are. Work in cohesiveness and love with each other, as we do with you. We have said in the past, you only need to ask. So drop the pride of children, and ask what you wish with sincerity and joy, and remove the personality that says: "we must sacrifice".

The sacrifices of the past no longer exist. It is not needed, we do not wish it. We only wish joy for you and the Earth. We are with you in the releasing of Earth from bondage: now at this moment release yourself also. Release yourself now completely, totally – accept who you are and go forward with joy. We thank you, we are in great joy and we love you. You are the manifestation of us upon Earth: hold that in the centre of your being and represent us as we represent you. We give you love, we bring to you peace. We are always with you.

DEE: *I'd like to ask about reaching out to youth: how that would best be done, individually, in small groups, in large groups, teaching, play?*

TOM: What is important is trust, and also to not underestimate their ability for understanding. On this planet at this time are souls who are now young who have come to bring Planet Earth into the future – that in truth is a glorious future for all Creation. They have come in trust, but there are some who are in great confusion, for they feel insecure. What is important is to place them in situations of security, trust, and love for the next few years, not to place them in situations of jeopardy – and for males who feel jeopardy is a part of their growing-up process, you must appreciate that jeopardy in this time is real jeopardy: the whole world is in question. Their world. There are energies that are not the best. We do not mean that a child must be pampered: we mean that good reasoning, understanding and ex-planation be given to your youth, for they understand more than you know. Also they know you better than you know yourself. They also know that they have boundaries, for they have come from a vast universe, and they need a boundary in your physical world, for that boundary creates their safety, and as they expand within themselves, the boundary then expands. But they must be in a spiral, in other words a boundary that helps them to go upward, growing outwards.

What is needed most, is understanding in the parents, for the youth of today come with a code of knowledge that has never existed before upon Planet Earth, and what is needed is for the parents to understand that all the books that are written cannot help these special youth – it must come from the heart. And the guilt of the parent also comes forth, because parents are not sure that they can carry forth this obligation that these youth have brought to them. Know this: they would not have chosen you if they did not believe you could carry things through, for you can.

JOHN: *We were discussing our concern that so many young people, boys, want to play with toy weapons, fighting and contending with each other. This seems to be almost a necessity amongst boys be-cause of peer group pressure, however much we might not want to give them toy weapons. How can we deal with this situation, and is this creating a problem for them in the future?*

Tom: It creates a great difficulty in future. There is on your planet Earth the illusion that if they are permitted to play out that aggression by attacking each other, then it removes aggression. That is not true: it creates more. You are the guardians of your youth, you must speak. Create ways and means through motion and exercise, and in creating games that have two aims: competitive with others and competitive with self. Create new ways and new means, and involve humankind's youth, and organise parents against weaponry.

When you force those who create weaponry to not create business through it, another means will be found. You must understand the energies that are created with weaponry, yes. You may be forced by the group pressure of youth, to give in.

John: Forced by peer pressure to give in – yes, that's what happened with us.

Tom: What is important is the organisation of small groups of parents against weaponry. Make your children proud that they do not need it. That they have other means of expression. Each of you has returned to this planet at this time for the betterment of Planet Earth. Utilise who you are: in your returning know that you have access to all knowledge. Do not limit yourself in what you can attain. Yes.

Miki: We were discussing relationships this morning, about each person being ultimately responsible for their experience, and about the possibility of one person being a victim of the other. Could you comment on that?

Tom: There is in your world a limited understanding of the overall view. It is possible for both people to be victims. Yes.

Miki: So, that means that one is not ultimately responsible for one's own experience?

Tom: Not in all issues. There are situations in which one is drawn into a pattern of another. Sometimes it is possible to clear this pattern, through working with each other's growth. Sometimes it is not possible, because the other is not able to become clear at that time. Each soul has to develop in its own way through learning and evolution. There are times when there is absolute victimisation by others, as it is possible also for one to create victimisation.

John: Yes. Is it true that, once you realise you are in somebody else's energy, that you then do regain your responsibility, because you then have the awareness, choice and ability to remove yourself?

Tom: Not always. If you are in someone else's blueprint, and their energy touches you on the periphery, it is easier to extricate yourself; but take an octopus – if it wraps its tentacles around you then you have a greater struggle to remove yourself, or to stop being eaten up. Recognising the problem does not help at that point, for it is too late, too big.

Miki: So is there any solution to it, not to be victimised?

Tom: In your planetary evolution there are stages as well as blueprints of life. We will take a tribe that you might call barbaric: in their state they victimise and are victimised because they live in a small framework, they do not understand the wider reality. It is only by experience and education that they extend and expand beyond it. The more aware you become, the less tendency you have to fall into the arms of an octopus. In other words don't take on anything or anyone you know you do not have the strength to pull away from. Or it has less significance because your ego is not so caught up in it, in the octopus-arms of your self or another.

Miki: It also seems that people who are very sensitive, psychically receptive, or open to others, or other energies, are more vulnerable than others. Is there any advice to such people, for them to be protected?

Tom: Yes. Upon waking each morning ask for a protection of light surrounding you, to keep maintaining balance, and constantly check on your reactions within – whose reality you exist within.

Can you be involved physically with other beings and not hurt them? Remember that you must have compassion, you must have harmony, you must have understanding, but at all times you must detach from the work. We will go one step beyond and explain if you wish.

In your physical world, in your physical desires and your emotional exchanges, can you in your souls and hearts become involved in a physical relationship, when you are involved in the work of consciousness? And if that person you are involved with is also involved in the work, can you in honesty say that when you go into the work you will be completely separate and objective, when you meet a conflict of priority between the work and your relationship? And can you be firm in your analysis of the situation? Can you say "No, in this matter I believe you are incorrect'', or will that physical relationship create a problem? Will you bend towards one side or another because of your physical relationship? Can you explain to your partner that, when you enter the portals of our world, that you must then be cut off from that physical being and act with detachment, completely objective and honest? You do not need to answer these questions to us, but to yourself.

GUEST: If one could not detach, leave that kind of relationship behind when necessary, does that mean it would contaminate our inner work, with your world – is that what the end result is?

TOM: It would contaminate the work, but not the relationship with us. Remember, in your physical world, people around you do not always understand who you are, and perhaps may never truly know who you are, but at times, in their own way, without meaning to, they will try to control you. And remember: because they might be in the world, this is their priority, so they may create problems for you. Do you understand fully?

GUEST: I think I do.

TOM: We must have complete clarification: you must not say you know, and later not know.

GUEST: Well, if I could paraphrase it, the work is to be detached from any other relationship we have outside of that work.

TOM: That is not a hundred percent. I will give you an analogy. We will put you in a situation: you have a business together, and the business is separated from your household. One evening you spend the time together, and you are very loving, very close and in complete balance and harmony in your physical life. In your morning time the two of you go to your business. When you enter that business, can you then detach from your partnership relationship? If your mate does something wrong in that business, or if your mate is not completely detached, or if someone comes into that business, and your mate does not handle the situation as it should be handled, on whose side do you go? Do you go on your customer's side or on your mate's side? Can you detach? Can your mate understand that in your correcting the mate, it was for the business and it was not personal? They say I am not making myself clear to you.

GUEST: I think we understand that very well, yes.

TOM: Can you not manipulate your mate, and can your mate not manipulate you? That is what we are trying to say. To the detriment of the work or your business. This is what you have to deal with. Can you stand firm and say you are wrong? Or will you weaken? Do you see?

GUEST: *Total objectivity and total honesty in these situations.*

TOM: Will it then create a problem in your evening?

GUEST: *(Laughing) Yes, it will! So you can't get into this unless your mate is carefully chosen beforehand.*

TOM: Will your mate try to then run your business? All areas you must investigate. Will your mate truly know better than you, or will your mate think that they know better than you?

GUEST: *Well, can you comment on whether there is any purpose or validity to the institution of marriage on this planet at this time, during this period?*

TOM: You speak of a marriage that is a legal contract according to the terms of the nation of your existence? A oneness is a oneness. If it is an identifiable structure to bring forth to those in your vicinity, to show to them that there is solidarity and oneness, marriage has value. However, many pairs of people are one, without a legal contract, and at this time they tend to be more at one in their hearts than those who are bound by contract.

GUEST/2: *My wife is now going to separate from me: how can I make her going away easier, for us both, and especially what can I do to let the least harm come to our children?*

TOM: Remove all past emotion as much as is feasible within you. Approach all from the centre of your heart. Be in gentleness, be in confidence with yourself, but be in loving kindness and sincerity. In every world, when there is separation from one who has been close, there is also great pain to many. For your children, always be in truth, in readiness to share yourself, to accept responsibility for them. Be a strength to them, but always in truth. Listen within and follow that. If you wish, call for help.

Humankind was not meant to be alone. Humankind has come to learn to merge the male and the female, the positive and the negative, the Yang and Yin, and then it becomes one.

We have difficulty understanding your nature. We are being educated by others in the ways of you beings. It is very difficult for us to understand your physical nature. We understand your emotional and your intellectual nature, but it is very difficult for us to understand your physical ways. We are aware of the problems that you are having on Planet Earth with the sexuality of the physical. We cannot remove this: this people must remove from themselves, or refine it.

ANDREW: *Yes, I guess we'll all have to work at it and do the best we can. Is there anyone who does understand the physical of humans, since it was designed and created by an intelligence?*

TOM: Are you referring to one of us?

ANDREW: *Yes, somewhere in your consortium there must be those who understand it.*

TOM: There are those amongst us that understand. I do not understand that emotion, so I will relate it in the manner that has been given to me. In regard to your physical bodies, the sexual desires you have – and we are speaking now in terms of your physical reproductive areas – these are similar to a safety valve. When you become involved in awakening, and this type of work of service, this is activated to a degree. If the being is not able to raise the vibration it becomes like a furnace that is stoked and the furnace must have a safety valve. The refined way of doing this would be to raise the energy level, or to work off steam in your way. Within all of you there is a pipeline and if the energy level is not funnelled upward so the steam can be released properly, it then becomes a hot burning furnace. The only release then is sexuality. I do not understand the emotion: it does not make sense to me.

ANDREW: *The emotion is a kind of feedback loop: if there is heat it wants more heat.*

TOM: As they are explaining to me, there is nothing wrong with this emotion, but if you let off too much steam, then it dissipates the energy of that furnace, and it no longer supplies and functions as it should. This is the problem in your physical world: there is too much involvement in the releasing of energy, rather than refining energy. It is important for this refining to take place... but they are telling me if you eat too much you will get sick. I understand not.

ANDREW: *Yes, if we eat too much we get what is called indigestion, we cannot handle the load, and I take it this refers analogically to this physical desire.*

TOM: This is true. If you eat too much, you dissipate energy gained from eating. If you act too much you dissipate the energy of action. Energy is important, it must not be dissipated and thrown into the ether, it must be channelled properly. We also would like you to know that there is nothing wrong with your physical relationships. It is when they become the central issue of your being that the energy is dissipated.

CHARLES: *Masturbation: is it a normal form of behaviour, or shouldn't it be at all?*

TOM: It is in your world of physicalness, because of the desire in genetic factors within the human body, that has been generated down through generations. We have no objection to masturbation, for it was a form of masturbation that seeded the Earth. But it spills what is of great importance to us: we do not object to the youth, if it releases them of pressure within their physicalness; but in older people, and those who work in service with us, it can be a wastage of energies, which may be utilised otherwise. When it is not utilised, in equality or blending of etherics with one of the other gender, it is not in its best essence. But if it would bring to you the releasing of pressure, then we have not objection, yes.

MIKI: *I know we are not supposed to kill. But when a female is receiving a baby which she does not want to receive, till which month after conception is she allowed to terminate this small one's gestation?*

TOM: We wish for you to know that there will be no extinguishing of a life that has a right to live. That is governed by the universe. When we say a right to live, we mean a soul that chose to come back to serve, or chose to come for the lesson that it needs. Those that are stopped before their birth, in the great majority, are willful spirits that need a longer time to exist in the before-birth state, before their returning to a physical existence. Most of them also should be born in other civilisations. You have used a term of 'kill' – it is not correct. It is a very serious problem upon Planet Earth, because your religions have made it a serious problem in order to control people. We say this to you: a soul that is meant to be born in its proper method will not be extinguished. Those that should not be, in some manner will be not brought forth. There is no death before there is life in the physical world. What is murder in your world? It is the extinguishing of a life that has not yet served its full purpose in the physical: it is not a removal of life, but it is a complication of the process of evolution on

Earth. But in reality there is no death. It is wrong to extinguish a life that has not fulfilled its purpose. We mean one that has been brought forth fully to the planet Earth – it has been born. Altea has said that if you want a term, it would be not be past three and a half of your months. For up to that time the soul has no memory of its being in a cocoon of the womb. Therefore it does not get hurt within.

GUEST: *Is there such a thing on this planet as natural or true soul mates? And if so, is there only one true mate, or other half, for each person?*

TOM: When you speak of soul mates we come into an area that is difficult to explain, for there are those that you have existed with in the physical past in other lives, that you may have an affinity for, if they pass your path again. But when you speak of a true soul mate, we speak then of a relationship that is made up of two but is in reality one. In that instance you cannot have several possible ones: there is only one. There are those that exist that have integrated as one whole into one being – as in the civilisation of Altea there is no male, no female, but only one gender. On your physical planet, because of its situation, it is necessity to be male, or to be female, but you are in essence one.

And on the subject of homosexual relationships:

TOM: There are very few souls who have come to Planet Earth but one time. But those who have come in what you term homosexuality, are beings that have lived many existences, and repeated them in one sex-identification, then came through in the opposite sex, and have confusion. Each of you, you must know this, at one time have lived in this situation. Know this: it is the connection, the coming together of male and female energy, which brings oneness with creation. Man has always innately known that power comes from women, and in your heterosexual relations males who go from one woman to another looking for that connection with the Creation, and they do not take time to understand the energy. They only know, in the darkness of the recesses of their mind, that they have this desire, and it overtakes them, and instead of bringing elevation it degrades their being. As in the case of the religions upon Planet Earth, in the beginning people had knowledge, and then men became dogmatic in their attempt to control others. Even though, in the basis of their knowledge, there was truth, it was lost in misuse. You may not wish to hear what we say, but when there is a person that is homosexual, it is a being who has lived as the opposite sex for many lives, repeatedly. What is needed is more understanding of this. For all souls have been of the opposite sex. When you humans understand, then we have a great step forward. Each soul who elevates themselves to understand humankind has lived in this situation. There is a saying in your Christendom that says "But by the grace of God go I". What it should say is "But by the grace of what I created go I".

19

Adventures in Consciousness

Explorations: of ourselves and our attitudes towards ourselves. Helpful hints on meditating and changing mind sets. A chapter full of loving caring advice from the Nine, that we may choose to adopt if we so wish.

JOHN: Is there anything you observe is being neglected by people who are trying to make a positive difference on the planet now?

TOM: Education about self-worth.

JOHN: Any advice on how one does that?

TOM: Part of this difficulty lies in lack of education among the masses on the question of inferiority. If you can begin to organise to change the majority who feel inferiority, then that will have great benefit. It is a primitive state, yes.

MIKI: What is the reason for this massive inferiority?

TOM: People's inhumanity to each other.

MIKI: But it seems to be so basic in nearly everybody, this feeling of inferiority.

TOM: Part of it is sense of inferiority, part is real disadvantage. There are important areas of life where people are not sure of themselves. But at times those inferiority feelings create the impetus to become better. It is different for people who have a real disadvantage, a lack of what they need. When you are strong your soul knows the area that you need to overcome to be in greater strength.

JOHN: But the lack of recognition of our potential or our self-worth is prevalent in society.

TOM: Yes, because religions control people's beliefs. Religion has the primary   responsibility.

JOHN: *Because that reduces our power, our capacity to act?*

TOM: Yes. Some would say that when they die, when they make the transition, they are transformed. But that is not what we mean by transformation. For if in their transition they take with them their problems which they maintained upon Planet Earth, then they have created a transformation that is heavier than what transformation is on Planet Earth. Therefore we wish them to know the importance of transforming who they are during their life on Earth, their direction and their understanding of their responsibility for Planet Earth, its inhabitants, its life in all forms, including the seas and the minerals within the Earth — to have respect and to bring about transformation of Planet Earth by elevating it out of darkness. That begins with the individual. Is that explanatory enough?

JOHN: *You once said that if human beings would learn to be kind to each other...*

TOM: The singular most important word in your vocabulary is kindness. It is not love. For kindness is love. And the word 'Love' is used and misused to bind, to control, to manipulate. But kindness — who can resist kindness? Not any. All can resist love. For it is misunderstood, love. Kindness is love in action. It is also a matter of acceptance. If there were understanding and acceptance, there would not be difficulty. But there cannot be acceptance with only a portion of acceptance. For acceptance is total removal of self: if you remove your self, then you have 'yourself' but if there be difficulty between two of you or all of you, then you have not removed yourself from 'yourself'. It has to do with how you 'see' another. Can you place yourself in the shoes of another, and see things from their viewpoint? Can you see the whole of life from a wider viewpoint than your own?

MIKI: *Could you draw a distinction between change and transformation and enlightenment? Especially this question: is there an enlightenment to gain?*

TOM: Before one can become transformed you must be given the tools and experience to bring this about, or you must find the strong need within the self to bring it about, or experience the total collapse of that person who you are, to bring it about. Out of chaos comes order.

So when a person, or a country, is in a situation of chaos, if the tools are there, or if the desire is there, or if the push from others is there, then it can be transformed almost instantaneously. It is like a shift on the crust of the Earth: one day it is like this, the next day it is like that, and it is never the same.

MIKI: Thank you. To fundamentally shift, we do need to have the will to do it. And this is not just a mental statement that "I want to change", it is a feeling of necessity. It has similar symptoms to death, but it's a psychological death-rebirth: we become something utterly different.

TOM: You have within you, each of you, the ability to change the Planet, but you must begin within yourself, by loving yourself. You can only love yourself by respecting yourself. Respecting yourself means removing from yourself all those areas which you disrespect in others. It also means removing all those hidden things that you disrespect in yourself. When you humans can walk with your head high, when you can look upon yourself and say "Yes, I may live with myself, I may live with my thoughts, for my thoughts are pure and my thoughts are love, so therefore I love myself". Then we give you our promise, Earth will begin to move forward rapidly, in a way that you had never envisioned. You have chosen to serve, and that service is not just to us, it is to all that exist upon Earth and in the spheres of the spirit.

Begin to serve by loving yourself. Remove contamination from your physicalness, remove contamination from your mind and heart, permit your soul to show you the way.

Remember that within you is a seed of power: if you do not maintain a balance, the ugliness of power may appear. It is the desire for power. But remember to forgive. We hold no animosity within us, and you need not either. Even though you exist upon the densest of all planets in the Universe, remember that all souls may be saved.

JOHN: Yes, I think there have been occasions we ourselves have been guilty of that attitude.

TOM: This is a truth.

JOHN: For which we ask forgiveness.

TOM: Forgiveness comes from you, when there is true recognition of what has happened. May we say to you, to voice a feeling is one thing, but it is the act that is important. There are many actors upon the world stage that play a different part from what they feel. It is when they begin to feel, and to act from the whole of themselves, that they make a difference. They may say they love God, and they may say that they have understanding, but if they do not act as they say, then that is a grave error, because it is not done in ignorance. It is the same as when you give to another because you believe that what you give you will receive – then what you give is not gold.

If you have the wish to cultivate perfection, we will teach you how perfection is attained on your physical planet. There is but one law of perfection – there are no complexities, it is a very simple law: treat each and every soul, every animal, and every plant as you would wish them to treat you. In that way you grow to perfection. That is the golden law, it is a law of the Universe.

Understand this: the importance of exercise. As a physical body ages, if it does not continue in movement and exercise then it becomes limited in its movement. That also then begins to affect the mind, for the mind then becomes limited in its expansion. All things are interconnected. Therefore it is important for those peoples who are moving into the age of forwardness to maintain physical exercise and to develop exercises to keep the body in mobility. Otherwise portions of the body become locked in iron stiffness, which lock portions of the mind. It is important to know the value of order within, of formulation within, patience within, and the value of balance within.

Order is important, for in order one begins to understand the nature of Planet Earth and the Universe. Formulation is important: through formulation you may present a plan, a system to bring forth the greatest progress and productivity.

Balance is important, to experience your physical Planet and to experience the Universe. An example: If you consume your food in great impatience and in great haste, it is not chewed properly enough for your digestive juices to be activated to digest it properly, for it to be free to go through your system. If you consume it in haste, in a gobble, without proper attitude and releasing of digestive juices, it will cause you to have difficulty in your physical body. It will poison you. We are using this as an example, for patience should be in all phases of your existence. In patience you will see the nature of the Universe, you will digest it and not lose it. You will grow with it, and you will appreciate the beauty of it. It will stay with you in joy. Do not be like those that are in great haste. Move in gentleness. It is important for the evolution of Planet Earth. Teach yourself patience.

We do not give to you flattery, for flattery brings forth the essence of those who do not comprehend truth, but accept only their own greatness. Always come from the highest motive and essence. It is as if, in human robes, people strangle themselves in the robe, are not able to remove themselves from themselves, to give a brief moment to returning to who they really are. It is because people are frightened to find out who they really are, for when they know that completely, they feel the responsibility is too great. The truth is that when they find out who they are in completeness, responsibility is joyful, and the energy emanating from each person touches others and soars to us.

JOHN: *I have to say, for myself, that I have a strong feeling of inadequacy – and whilst on one level I can see what you're saying, on another level I am so aware of my human limitations.*

TOM: But if you would get out of your own way, and not be concerned about that, and simply move forward! Look upon what you have already contributed to Planet Earth. It is not humility to continuously berate yourself in being guilty. When you create order and follow the direction you have chosen, then all things begin to move along with you. It is that first step, as a baby has fear to take that first step, for fear of falling: but as it doesn't know the consequence of that fall, it takes that step. Forget the anticipated consequences of your falls. Do you not trust enough, that if you begin to create happiness it will come in greatness? Do you see the competition you have created for yourself?

Express yourself in words of love and words of joy, for that makes the Universe happy – for when there is happiness, joy and laughter in the Universe, it is a time of great celebration. This is what Planet Earth must do: humankind must not take itself so seriously! It must begin to experience within itself the joy of its divinity, the joy of its oneness with the Universe. It must pull itself out of this bondage, it must stop living in a situation of victimhood. We have never asked for victims or sacrifice, but humankind, in its guilt, creates its victimhood, for it knows that it has passed and has crossed that valley that it should not have crossed, and now, together with all, we are bringing it back across the valley for it to be one with the Universe. We love you, we will walk with you, we will be with you. Limit not yourself, any of you humans.

If you can visualise the Nazarene within yourself, then you can be like the Nazarene if you wish. If something or someone hurts you, it is your ego that hurts you. We love you. We encircle you and we bring you peace.

When the day arrives that we may communicate with you, and you may communicate with others in a form of mind language, those that exist upon your planet will begin to truly evolve. We have been in observation, and the sadness that we feel is because there is so much difficulty in the mode of which you communicate. We have observed that what you speak is not what you think. It is tragic that your mode of communication is used in the manner, but the day will come when what is in the mind of one will be directly understood by another, because then no one upon your planet Earth will be able to speak in a manner that is not truth.

IAN: In previous communications you said that language was brought here to the planet in order to evolve human beings, so I want to ask about the significance of language in the future.

TOM: It is critical and crucial. Verbal language is the only means at this time for one human to have a means of communication with another. This also is important: how a word is used releases energy into universe, how a word is dignified releases energy into universe. The sadness of humankind is that they banter this and they banter that, and they do not understand that what they banter creates a difficulty for the Universe, for it dissipates energy. However we caution in this manner: you cannot go from the language of your existence to a completely new language, for humankind has tendency of resistance, and when people resist, they become immobile and rigid. Therefore you humans must find a bridge, in other words you must begin to educate in the nature of language, not just bring out new language without people understanding the reason. In your world humankind does not hear what is said, so therefore listening is of great import.

Now here are some specific instructions for meditating which were given to the group at various times...

IAN: Would you give the group a simple technique to use in weekly meditations? Any guidelines for us?

TOM: We would ask you to be in your chair in preparation for three minutes of your time before starting. Take in deeply within your system, breathing great depths and releasing. And when you do it think that one of us is now with you. And with each exhalation a disturbance within yourself is removed. Then you become a vessel of purity for identifying your true self, knowing who you are, your connection with us and the Universe – knowing that you have all that is instilled within you, encompassed in all that you are, your spirit, soul and mind, which continue on in all eternity. You contain all that is. Identify the power within yourself to create and bring into being the necessary changes for Earth to evolve to its state of paradise.

Be one that is ahead: not as an elite, more intelligent or wise, but ahead in being able to remove yourself from yourself, to step back and view the truth of your being. When you have done that, then in your thoughts, infuse all humankind and its youth with the purity of love and kindness, and all those things that have been entrusted to you – the woods, plants, flowers and animals that create your para-dise – infuse them with the essence of your being. And in your thoughts, bring the message to all people that they contain within them the ability, with you, to bring about the necessary changes upon Earth, by protesting when a human is not in humanity to humankind.

You may incorporate that into a program that may be given to others as a form of meditation from us. Within your mind is great power, and within your mind you can produce the greatest of en-ergy. It is not your physical energy that is great, it is your mind energy that is great. Your mind can bring things into existence, if it has the knowledge of how to do this, but it can also unconsciously bring into existence many things that you do not have desire to have.

If there were thirty-six with one mind, focused together, then the entire world, even the Universe, may be changed.

If there be twelve on the Planet with one mind, with the power of concentration, there is nothing that cannot be accomplished.

This is a repetition of the instructions in the preceding chapter, but the use of these colours has such results, that it's worth it...

Enter your meditative state in complete love, harmony, and peace. If it be necessary to do a pre-meditation, use any method you would need, if it be breathing, or sound, or colour, or exercise, or quiet, for you to cultivate that state before entering meditation. We wish you not to look at your time-piece and say "Now sit and do". Also, you may visualise yourself, before entering that state, as being cleansed with the colours green-emerald, royal blue, and purple, showering down upon you: this will take away all disturbances of the day.

Take that cleansing into the Earth in purification, and then you may begin your meditation. And then view people with their light-energies consuming the dark and letting it filter out in light streams. Like this method: if you do it with a plant, have a plant in front of yourself, give it to it and it will osmosis it. That is a strange sounding notion?

IAN: Osmosis is an exchange with the plant.

TOM: That is what we mean, thank you, yes. Remember this: you are all from us, you have within you our perfection. You cannot in truth attain perfection in the physical upon Planet Earth because of its density, but you can attain perfection within your soul and your mind. Limit not yourself. Any philosophy, any civilisation, any religion upon the planet Earth gives to you a limitation. For example, if you have a belief that it would take you one of your years to accomplish something, you can concentrate for thirty-six of your seconds to remove the belief, and then you may re-learn a new belief in thirty-six of your seconds.

JOHN: I'd like some advice on concentration.

TOM: We will give to you an example. If you concentrate on what you wish to remember, to remember things in both your conscious and your subconscious, concentrate for thirty-six seconds, and it will not be erased from your memory. It may be brought forward from your subconscious. If you wish to erase what is undesirable within your mind, or your subconscious, or a thought that has been placed in your mind, or a personality difficulty that you are trying to eliminate, if you will concentrate for thirty-six of your seconds it is cancelled within your mind. If you think for thirty-six of your seconds that you are ill, you will become ill, if you think for thirty-six of your seconds that you are healthy, you will begin the way to health.

The masses that have been programmed by society, by governments, by religions, to believe in a rigidity of their prayers, have brought many things into effect. As an example it is a mass thought upon this world that all must age, that all must have illness, or that difficulty leads to further difficulty. These are the common beliefs that have been programmed into humans.

JOHN: What concerns me most is that the capacity to concentrate totally, I understand, is only for about fifteen seconds. I personally find it very hard for more than about six seconds. Is that also a program?

TOM: You have understood your program!

JOHN: Could you give us what you would define as enlightenment? I think it's a term that's very poorly understood on Earth.

TOM: Do you have consideration of yourself as being enlightened?

JOHN: No.

TOM: May we ask why?

JOHN: Because I have qualities in my personality that I need to get rid of before I...

TOM: You are then equating enlightenment with perfection. There is not perfection in the density of Earth. To explain what you asked about: enlightenment is what you are. Enlightenment is constant reaching, constant searching, constant consideration of what ever needs to be removed or modified or purified, but with total accept-ance of yourself. Also acceptance that, since you are part of divinity, anything you desire you may accomplish, if it is for the betterment of the Universe. But you think that you have to constantly reach to heights that you have been programmed to believe cannot be at-tained, to be searching not only for yourself, but also for your relationship to the Universe, however, this is your personal feeling.

To have understanding that you are responsible for a portion of the Universe, to have understanding that it is your love that has created us, that sustains us and that feeds us – this is enlightenment. To understand your negativity or the planet's or the Universe's nega-tivity, and the way that power that seeks to control is created and uncreated – this is enlightenment. You are on the path. Yes. This does not mean that you may stop reaching, yes.

There is the greatest power in clear thought. It is as close to supreme power that a soul on a human level may have. Be aware that your thoughts can put things into action for the greatest benefit, but they can create much difficulty when thoughts are in error.

We will begin in smaller matters: if you wish to totally remember something, concentrate upon it with the greatest concentration, without any interference, for 33.3 seconds – the Council has said I should give to you thirty-six, but in truth, it is 33.3 – not less, but you may do more.

If you concentrate with total elimination of anything that would interfere, it would then be in your mind, it would be in your higher self, in your lower self, and in your conscious self, and in your subconscious self. It would not be able to be removed, except with similar concentration. If you wish to remove an error from any portion of your mind, concentrate on removing it for thirty-six seconds, and it is erased from your subconscious and cannot be recalled. If you take this one step further, build a pyramid in your imagination for 33.3 minutes, and then it is within your mind in the strongest possible way, and you have then created an energy which has the power to make things move or change in the way that you wish. In order to remove error it would be necessity to reverse the process for thirty-six of your minutes. The mind brings its own reality into being.

As an example: the nations upon your Earth have a mass thinking or belief that permeates the atmosphere. It is a collective belief. It is like a chain of thinking, and it brings into the Earth whatever thought has been created by the members of the nation. A government creates thoughts in its people, and the management of a company creates thoughts and beliefs in its employees. That process may be erased, if necessary.

If you concentrate for 33.3 of your minutes – which is a great difficulty for the conscious mind, it takes practice and habituation – you may release much that has been done in error. For not only the Earth but for individuals, whatever they have done to themselves or to others. If you take thirty-six people with one mind, with one thought, with one love, for 33.3 of your minutes, you may in truth change the Universe . If you take twelve people for 33.3 minutes in healing or in any area that needs purification, it can be done, but remember also that the Others can intervene if this is not set up properly, with sound motivation.

In the physical world upon which you exist, as is known within your world, you use only a portion of your brain. Is that not so ?

JOHN: Yes, that is so.

TOM: Also the full capacities of your physicalness are also not in use. If you wish to use more, the more you use the more you develop.

JOHN: There are many arguments about the percentage of our brain that we do in fact use. I know it's very small, could you give us an accurate figure on that?

TOM: We would say it would be between 18% and 22%.

JOHN: We do know some of the things to do to develop brain capacity. Is there anything in particular that is not known to man that would be helpful to know?

TOM: It is of importance to increase the oxygen supply into the brain at intervals. It is also a great deterrent to the brain to take ozone into the lungs. It causes difficulties within the lungs, and causes a breakdown within the valves, then in turn it causes a lack of oxygen in the brain.

JOHN: To get oxygen to the brain, is it mainly physical exercise which will do this?

TOM: Physical exercise is important, because besides the oxygen which is carried into the blood stream, it also supplies other nutrients. But if it were possible on occasion to inhale oxygen by breathing exercises, it would be of great benefit.

JOHN: Now I imagine yoga and meditation are both good. Is standing on one's head valuable for increasing the blood supply to the head at all?

TOM: We are having a consultation... They have said the standing upon the head... The value that it has... I understand not if they are in seriousness or not... They say you would view of the world upside down. Yes.

ALL: [Laughter]

JOHN: Yes. But behind that I imagine it does have some increase of circulation in the brain.

TOM: Joseph of Aragon has said that exercise would be of the same benefit.

JOHN: I see. I have great difficulty in meditation in stilling my mind. I hoped that over a long period of time, as it's now been, this would change, and I'm still not able to do that...

TOM: May we ask you, who gave you the idea that in meditation you were to be still in your mind?

JOHN: Well, that's my own wish or understanding...

TOM: If you are in a meditative state, you are meditating upon something, is that not so? Then how may you have a blankness in your mind?

JOHN: Well, I imagined that if I could hold it on whatever I was meditating on, the meditation would work better. I find that my mind moves around a lot and so as a result of that I repeat and change my prayers and so on, is that just as effective?

TOM: When you are in a state of meditation your power is tenfold.

Here is more useful advice on visualisation techniques:

CHARLES: If one would wish to have a beneficial emanation on subtle levels, whilst going about one's daily business, do you have any suggestion of what can be done?

TOM: Most important, upon your rising and your retiring, you need to cleanse yourself, mind, and body, and spirit, of those energies that may have touched you and attached themselves to you. And if it is not possible to be in an area where water is available for cleansing completely, then visualise yourself standing under a fountain of water, and then in your state of purity, and when you have the real water or the imaginary water, visualise that all negativity from yourself is being released and cleansed, and that your purity of spirit remains.

If you are in an area where there are healthy trees, you may also take your solar plexus, and wrap yourself around the tree, and release the negativity to the tree, so it in its turn may transform it into pure clean energy, oxygen, and send it into the ether, so that there is no contamination.

Then go forth and do your daily work, knowing that your heart has the utmost pure motive, and does not seek ego-recognition for self, but quietly desires peace on Earth and goodness for those you are in contact with. You will then emanate such energies outward from yourself, in a circle.

Know also that, throughout the day, other energies will attach to your energies, which will shorten the span of expansion of your energies: you may then repeat the process of cleansing your body, mind and spirit, by showering with water or cleansing through a tree, and begin again. And silence is the word, for to speak too much shortens the expansion. In other words: go quietly with peace and love.

MIKI: Is there a way for us to be reminded of our purpose on this planet in our daily life?

TOM: If you would come to agreement with yourself that a day not pass without giving yourself the gift of meditation, you would come to that awareness. Is it much to ask of humankind to give nine or eighteen minutes daily to themself? It is not for us, it is for you.

MIKI: *In our professional lives, we find it difficult to coordinate our meditations with the others joining us. Is it possible for us to meditate individually and still contribute to our work?*

TOM: It is of benefit for you to meditate. If there can be three, then the energy for the Earth is better utilised. If you cannot meet with all and you arrange a time for three of you to meditate at the same time in different places. Then you would cover the globe with triangles — would that not be glorious?

One of the most important arenas is the development of methods of movement control. In the martial arts is a form that brings control, and therefore the mind has opportunity for expansion. Another form is the inhalation of the breathing apparatus for periods of time, to cleanse the mind. The most important but in truth the most difficult to attain is letting go in a state of meditation, but you may practise it upon yourself using devices to help arrange your mind to let go of the mind. You understand that?

MIKI: *Yes. Recently, I have met a teacher from Yogananda in India. Do you feel the practices they teach are of value? Is there any thing else you have to say about meditation?*

TOM: There are many from the Yogananda who may expand the mind, but we ask you to be in great care to understand the Hindu. The exercise of yoga is of great benefit, for it teaches discipline of body and mind. But enlightenment comes when you are able to let go and trust totally and completely who you are in connection with the Universe. Then the ego is released — when we say ego we mean the ego of non-importance, the personality ego. In your practice of evolutionary development for bringing Earth into its transformational light-vehicle state, it is good to do a form of meditation each day.

When you understand where any human truly is at any moment, then you will know how best to function with them. This is on all planes of existence, in every arena of life. Yes.

If you expand the Earth and its consciousness then you make it light and extensive. And then the Planet becomes a light-space vehicle.

ANDREW: *Now, does that expansive mechanism stretch out in space? Will that help the problem of ultraviolet penetration (in connection with ozone layer depletion)?*

TOM: We would ask you to do this: to visualise that you are weaving a... I am trying to find the word. It is like a cheesecloth...

JOHN: Filigree.

TOM: Filigree, yes. Make one in your mind in your meditation, and visualise your cover in the ionosphere becoming repaired. You can create the alchemy with your mind. Re-create those particles of disruption into atoms needed for balance.

ANDREW: What starting material should we use to carry out this exercise?

TOM: Your mind.

ANDREW: That's it?

TOM: Pure mind. The highest form − the Council has said to use crystallised   consciousness.

In 1991 more questions about meditation were put to Tom:

JOHN: One question I think we all would like to know is what meditations we could join in future?

TOM: What you now need to focus upon are the necessary changes in government, in order to deal with environmental stress on Planet Earth. In your meditation, please bring into the consciousness of humankind the need for worldwide protest against the elimination of disadvantaged people on Planet Earth. The Others and their servants attempt to eliminate different strains of humans upon Planet Earth through genocidal methods. You dedicate yourselves to stopping the elimination of endangered species of animal but you do not protest the extinction of species of humankind. That is also important.

JOHN: Yes. So is the suffering of children, through parental abuse, that is so prevalent in society at the moment.

TOM: It is only now being brought forward. Meditate for exposure of this. You see, what is important is bringing forth that knowledge into the conscious viewing eyes of humankind, for then they cannot turn away. When it is not spoken about, or when it is not viewed, when it is pretended not to exist, then it can continue.

However, it must be said, that if we, in the last few months, had to depend only on you, our group, then your world would be inverted and would become a black hole of darkness – for there has not been unification or solidarity. We asked and asked, and when we came to realise that the Others has also reached many of ours in diversion, we were grateful that there were small numbers who had accepted and continued.

If you understood the importance, you would never miss a meditation. If you choose not to understand the importance, that it your will.

We shall speak of knowledge if you desire. With knowledge comes responsibility. We need to speak about one step beyond this, about the knowledge that we have transferred to you, to help you understand the difficulties within the Universe. We are also responsible, inasmuch as we have imparted this to you. Remember that with this knowledge comes greater responsibility, since you have become a part of a circuit of souls and energies, such that each one of us is responsible for the other, and that knowledge which you have makes you more responsible because you are now responsible to us, as well as to your own soul.

JOHN: *If people have absolute freedom of choice, how are they not going to be tempted to be self-indulgent still? I mean, we know that choice exists, but we still want them to make a... full choice.*

TOM: Choice is not the end, it is the means: for there is a due, is there not, a payment to be made?

JOHN: *You're talking about consequences, essentially.*

TOM: That is correct, for if you see your planet Earth in destruction, that is the consequence of ill choice. There is well choice, and ill choice.

In 1994 Israel Carmel, Phyllis' husband, was given a meditation process from the Council of Nine for the good of planet Earth and Tom requested that it be included in this edition.

ISRAEL: *We can practise a very effective form of meditation for the environment of the planet. The recommendations of time and place are the same as have been mentioned in the preceding chapter. Linking up by using the same day (Sunday) and co-ordinating with the Israeli time of 9.00 p.m. enables a worldwide link to be made. The Council of Nine request that a minimum of three people be gathered* physically together and thus triangles can be formed around the globe. (These would become circles if there were more that three people.) The total length of the link up phase is of eighteen minutes and the meditation consists of a tour of the world visualising the governments of the countries on each continent or land-mass; then visualising the peoples of those countries and the trees of those countries. Thus are the minds, hearts and bodies on the planet united. This is how it works: some might like to imagine a stream of white light as they travel through this meditation, and it is helpful to spend three minutes on each land-mass. However don't get fixated on timings, for with a little practice it will become easy to move through the meditation at the correct speed.

For this meditation it is vital to have the hands placed on the legs just above the knee, with the palms upwards and the fingers relaxed but not touching each other, in order to keep the energy circuits flowing and not closed in a loop.

1. We are going to start the meditation by focusing on the rainforests of Brazil, and this is the essential theme − the devastation that is being done to the trees − and by extension, to the whole Planet.

a. Focus on the governments of the countries involved in the deforestation process and meditate on their becoming aware of the damage that they are causing to the environment.

b. Focus on the peoples of these countries: that they become aware of their responsibilities and press their leaders to call a halt to the chopping down of these rainforests.

c. Focus on the trees themselves and send your energy to these magnificent forests, and they will transmit that energy from tree to tree.

2. From the rainforests of Brazil and the countries of South America travel to North America and repeat the process, applying the same principles, to government, people and the trees. While holding the rainforests as the priority, visualise all the trees of North America sending their energy to each other and then travel up to Canada and Alaska, until they are all linked.

3. Then follow the energy across the Bering Straits and into Russia, repeating the process as you visualise the countries of Europe.

4. Then travel through Asia, which embraces the Middle East, India and China.

5. Then visualise Australia together with New Zealand.

6. Finally we leap across to Africa, closing the circle that we have made around the globe. The world has been bathed in loving energy,

which has linked the people to their environment and created the need for responsibility towards their planet.

This principle of meditation could be applied to many aspects of our lives on Earth and with the Earth, but, in 1994, it is the predicament of the rainforests that the Council of Nine have particularly asked us to concentrate on – indeed the predicament of the trees throughout the globe. Their branches reach to the Heavens and their roots interlock with the Earth, that we would do the same....

GERI: Do you think on Planet Earth, people as a whole will always be in a state of imbalance, is this necessary?

TOM: This is the tragedy of Planet Earth, this imbalance, for it has stopped the forwardness of the Universe, it has bottlenecked. It was not meant to be: it was meant for a soul to come to experience this balance of the two and then to expand itself into other realms. We would pray with you that with enlightenment of understanding through your modes of mass communication, the inner spirit would identify and understand the importance of the choice of responsibility – you see when humankind evolves and Planet Earth is able to fulfil all that it was created for, then you release all other civilisations in the Universe, for them also to be in choice. Do you understand the importance..?

IRENE: Yes.

TOM: We've never told this to you in the past.

JOHN: So you're saying this is a test? We are in fact a test-bed for free will?

TOM: That is correct.

JOHN: Wow, that's an incredible concept. That's amazing.

TOM: It's only on Planet Earth.

JOHN: You have said in the past, that right now is a crucial time.

TOM: The most crucial, for in giving up the will, we give up the Universe. Yes. We will leave you now. We give you love. We bring to you peace. You will please tell to our Being of our love for her.

20

Soul Matters

Once, when Phyllis was in deep trance, she was taken before the Nine. At first they had manifested as venerable old men but when she asked them to show her what they were really like, they turned into "Balls of light that were like, pure energy, but with a soul".

"Perhaps that's what a soul looks like", Andrew said when he heard of this, "perhaps that's what they are, all soul and no body". Phyllis then explained what they had shown her: "They took ... like the negative and positive forces or energy and they showed.... Now, if you're so positive and you spin.... they showed me this energy spinning and it keeps spinning so fast it gets light and it disappears.... And the negative also spins, but with its spinning it picks up other stuff and it gets dark. It's an energy that gets dark and then it falls. And they showed me that neither one of those was good, because the way they were going, that soul was out of line".

"Or balance", Andrew had suggested.

"Out of balance, right". Phyllis agreed.

"Hmm," Andrew said, "that's interesting." And he tried to make scientific sense of Phyllis' imagery – in terms of spinning leading to increased velocity and eventually to disappearance into another dimension.

Once Tom was answering a question on reincarnation when he said: "A reason that you do not remember your preceding times is because of the atmosphere of the planet."

The following exchanges concern matters of the chakras, birth and death, reincarnation and healing and all in relation to the soul, with which we start:

ANDREW: *We do not understand the way in which you use the words 'soul' and 'spirit'. I wonder if you could clarify the distinction?*

TOM: There are actually three.

ANDREW: *Is that what you call mind, soul and spirit?*

TOM: Yes. And when you blend them completely, then you are pure energy, which is pure soul.

ANDREW: *I see. Now what is spirit as differentiated from the other two?*

TOM: Spirit is the soul that manifests both in your physical world, and in the atmosphere of your physical world.

ANDREW: *In other words.....*

TOM: ....it is a vehicle.

ANDREW: *Does that have any relationship to an 'astral body' or the 'etheric body'?*

TOM: Yes. It is the astral.

ANDREW: *Right. . . . now, 'mind' — is that part connected with the brain, or is that part connected with the spirit, or with the soul?*

TOM: The mind is connected with the soul.

ANDREW: *I see, from previous discussions we understood that the etheric body seems to be....*

TOM: It is the soul-cover.

ANDREW: *The soul-cover, right. So these are distinct functions of the human personality: the mind related to the soul, the spirit related to the body, and the soul of course is independent, if it is not in the body.*

TOM: Yes.

ANDREW: *But if it is connected with the body, it is connected to the 'etheric body'?*

TOM: Right.

JOHN: *Could you go a little further on the relationship between mind and soul?*

TOM: Mind is the intelligence of the soul.

ANDREW: *This sounds like a stupid question, but I have no idea what the etheric body looks like. Is it something that is wrapped around our physical body or is it alongside our physical body?*

Tom: There are two bodies – the astral body and the etheric body and including the one you see, which is physical, there are actually three bodies. The etheric stands outside the astral and is similar to an envelope, but that is not a correct term. I will explain in another manner: If you had an egg, inside that egg would be a chick, which would be a physical thing. Then around that chick would be a membrane which adheres to that chick. That would be the astral. The shell would be the etheric.

Andrew: Very good, so they are envelopes. Thank you very much, that helps enormously.

Tom: We would like to explain something to you in relationship to the life-energy that must be funnelled upward. There are not, as you understand it, seven chakras. This is not true. There are truly nine chakras. When these chakras and the root chakra is opened this creates the furnace fire, when you generate this upward, there are those who think they are sending it up and out and it is going into the ether, and then they do not understand why they have cravings and desires. What is actually happening, the energy is being trapped in their astral body and then it is flowing downward all over their body, and this again creates more of a furnace. It is necessary to get this energy up into the ninth chakra and project it out through the etheric body.

Andrew: May I just ask, the location of that ninth chakra?

Tom: It would be at the top of your head – it is where... what you call your 'Silver Cord'... but that is not where the Silver Cord is truly located.

Ron: On this subject, I have some rather esoteric questions. What I'd like to do is to read a portion of something that came through my head and ask if it is correct, and then ask further questions – is that all right?

Tom: Yes.

Ron: In the beginning (it's kind of a Genesis) the One breathed breathless by itself and turning inward upon itself the tension was one and became the manifold all. Varying densities and intensities of matter and spirit, with the potential to become one union. The Nine, the Civilisations, humanity and the Other kingdoms are each part of all that is. The infinite creation in its totality is the One Infinite Being. The One Being which is aware of itself to the extent that its different aspects are aware of themselves as part of all that is.

The Nine is the crown chakra, where God's will is known. The hierarchy of the civilisations is the heart chakra, where God's love wisdom is expressed. Humanity is the throat chakra. What the whole is — is unknown, it is the mystery. As the head, heart and throat chakras open completely to be their becoming for God, so it is a process of becoming aware of Itself.

TOM: At this stage of your knowledge we cannot explain to you the true understanding of the Universe. What you have received comes not from us but from the civilisations who also do not have full understanding. It is in portion of truth but it is not complete and it would be very difficult to give you an explanation. For knowledge can be conveyed in words but wisdom sounds foolish and it is not able to be conveyed in such a way. But it is acceptable to us that you convey these thoughts to those to whom you speak.

RON: Yes, thank you. What I would like to know, is the significance of the throat chakra in terms of the great Solar One-Being, in terms of humanity and in terms of the individual human being.

TOM: That deals with your physicalness. I will have a consultation... Council have asked that I convey this to you: In the need to have tangible structures that they can relate to, human beings in extending their understanding have used the term 'Chakra' but it is really a matter of different levels of the soul. Do you understand?

RON: The different chakras that are opening, are different levels of soul...?

TOM: Yes.

RON: Manifesting through us?

TOM: How can we explain? We are not of the crown chakra. When a soul is born it is in the first chakra. From that moment onwards it strives to reach that that is of us — do you understand?

RON: Yes.

TOM: In each of its reincarnations in different civilisations and also upon Earth, it goes through a process. There are those that may remain in the first chakra for many incarnations and there are those that, in their understanding that power for self accomplishes nothing, may generate and go into the third chakra, bypassing the second chakra. All are striving to return to us as fast as possible.

Individual humanity is not of the throat chakra. It is only when all of humanity has understanding that together it can become of the fourth chakra – Council have said that you spoke of the throat chakra. I am sorry, but it is of the *fourth* [the heart chakra] and then humanity may evolve in mass. Do you understand what we are attempting to explain?

RON: Yes, I think so.

TOM: Also, understand that a soul could be in what you would call the first chakra and if it has only the glory of the Universe in its life, in its motivation, then it may come immediately to us.

Since you must have something that you can relate to in order for you to have understanding in your world, let me just say that there are not pigeon holes, therefore please do not attempt to pigeonhole. You have an essence of truth. It has limitations but it will be of service, yes.

JOHN: There was another question we were talking about. That is about humour. We have humour in our world: I'm wondering if in your reality you have humour yourselves?

TOM: God could not have survived without being able to laugh at himself!

ANDREW: When God laughs what happens in the Universe? Is everything shaken...?

TOM: Everything shines!

ANDREW: Shines! I see. Now, to which function is humour related, to the mind, soul or spirit?

TOM: It is related to the mind. Which then in turn feeds energy to the soul.

JOHN: Most of our humour is based on our physical existence and the funniness of its situations.

TOM: We have cosmic humour. The Universe is funny!

ISRAEL: I would like to know the difference, if there is one, between ego and pride.

TOM: It is ego that creates pride, and it is pride that makes ego. In the Universe, there is no difference, but upon Earth they create a difference. We will attempt to explain: if you do not ask for help, it is your pride and your independence that keep you from asking, is this not so? It is also your ego, saying "I am independent and I need no one" — is that not so? It is one and the same. It is necessary to have ego for existence, but remember that there is the negative ego, as there is the positive ego. And ego must be in a balanced state. It is pride that takes the ego out of balance. It is necessary to have ego, it is of spirit. It is when the ego becomes a pride-filled thing that it becomes a problem. And if the ego becomes limp and like a dishrag, and permits itself to be stamped into the ground, then that is not good either.

PETER: I have been working on the split between what I would call body, mind, heart and soul and it would appear that an enormous number of people allow the conscious mind to overrule the heart continuously. This seems invariably to lead to a path away from consciousness.

TOM: You have come upon a truth and an awakening. You see, when science became strong then it eliminated and ruled out the true self of humankind, its intuitive self, its self of love and heart. It is time for the returning to that, for science placed humankind in holes of pigeons, categorised them, labelled them, and put them in a situation such that all people began to think of them in that way. Those scientific beliefs then led to a pattern of mass thinking.

PETER: What I have observed is that if people make choices, often it is the mind that tends to make the choice rather than the intuition or soul. Thus one comes into life for a purpose, but the mind overrules the purpose of the soul.

TOM: Because science and humankind conditioned themselves to fear to appear foolish, science made the decision that belief in universal love, consciousness and the Creator — for the truth is you are the Creator — was not realistic. Thus they lost touch with reality and humanity was then conditioned to permit its mind to rule it.

PETER: The continual question for me is, that given these two points, is it possible to offer the opportunity of consciousness to people who don't wish, in their heads, to seek it? Or is it possible only with those who are willing to take a step towards consciousness by becoming more spiritually aligned?

TOM: There are those who do not comprehend, neither wish to know: do not waste your time.

JOHN: *With regards to reincarnation, it's sometimes said that we have an overly simplistic concept of a soul entering a new body on a number of occasions, and it seems to be rather more complex than that. I wonder if you could possibly describe the point at which the separation takes place? What reincarnates and what does not, in terms of the relationship between the personality and the soul?*

TOM: That is a great elaborate dissertation, it is very difficult to explain in human terms because of your egos. However we will give you a small sample. As an example: your son is now begot from you. Therefore a portion that is you is within him. Therefore if your son had been begotten from you many times, in different lives, then there would be a stronger proportion of you within him – then perhaps next time it would be as if both of you were the same person. Do you understand?

JOHN: *Yes. So a little piece of each incarnation goes along, so there are complex patterns. . .*

TOM: It is as atoms grow with atoms. It is not that this soul is encapsulated, and then it floats away on its own and encapsulates itself in another physical entity.

JOHN: *Is it possible then that if one takes someone like Napoleon from history, two or three people might think they are a reincarnation of Napoleon, because they each have a piece of that?*

TOM: That is correct. But there is also a symptom upon Earth which arises when there is not good health in the mind: they may tune into that consciousness and believe they are of it. There is a fine line, as you say.

JOHN: *Is it also true to say that there's probably one person who carries more of that than any of the others?*

TOM: That is correct. Yes.

JOHN: *Okay, that helps very much.*

TOM: Who of humankind would want to understand that? For the ego of humankind resents the fact that somebody could be a portion of them.

JOHN: *It seems that the concept of reincarnation would be very important for people to understand, in order to grasp their full responsibility; but religion, or at least the Christian tradition, resists that. How can that be broken down?*

TOM: That is one of the processes that will be of great importance to develop in the future. It is important to prepare this information for those who wish for it.

MIKI: How important is it to understand our past lives in order to go forward?

TOM: For some, it is of great importance, for others it is not that important, for it is as if they had the internal knowing and they step in another direction. But for some, knowing their historical background then gives an insight into the personality of this life.

GUEST: Why do humans forget their previous lives when they incarnate on Earth? If they remembered it would be much easier for them to see the light to improve themselves.

TOM: In the beginning there was rememberance then it became necessary to structure society for the progression of what you would call 'civilised behaviour'. In those societies that have not entrapped themselves in intellectualism without sensitivity, their peoples have awareness of other realms of existence. These societies are largely dismissed by those in the arenas of the world in which there are the main technological, scientific and intellectual advances, and when children of these 'civilised' societies were born with memory (which was often) it was not considered acceptable and therefore it was suppressed. Now, however (1991), there are many in your world, in those 'civilised' societies, that have come with rememberance, We ask of you and all upon Earth, permit your youth to remember their past, to understand that there is continuity of life, that there is not death of the spirit or soul, that what passes into a form is only that of the physical and that all soul, all spirit, all that each of you are, contained within thyself – all the essence of the Creator contained within you – continues in continuity.

The time has now come to this planet when there is more and more rememberance. In the past, some religions had not benefited humankind, for they also suppressed that internal knowledge of other worlds. It served its purpose for a period of time, but now it is time to let the true essence of humankind come to the fore. Yes.

GUEST: Is it true that every soul in the Universe needs to live on Earth at least once?

TOM: What is of great importance for humankind to know, is that in all the Universe, Earth is the only planet of free will and choice. This does not mean that other worlds of existence, on other planets of physicalness, there is always a control. What it means is that on other planes of existence one may choose a physical expression in a collective consciousness in agreement. All souls in the Universe must experience this planet Earth at least once in order to learn of this balance between the physical and non-physical – what you would term the spiritual. Planet Earth is for that purpose, therefore the importance of bringing yourself into balance on Earth is vital. When souls are born into this planet and begin to experience such things as the ingestion of your foods, those of your liquids that control the mind or those drugs that also affect them, then humankind forgets the essence of who it is and begins to believe that it is the only reality. That is because, in the past, humankind was attempting to elevate and come to an understanding of itself and then it entrapped itself and recycled over and over again, instead of going to other places of existence for further experiences. This became your reality but it is not the true reality. However, because souls recognise that this planet is of Paradise, in their confusion they entrapped themselves. Not that planet earth entrapped them, they entrapped themselves, and this recycling bottlenecked the Universe. A soul chooses where it will be. When they do not go beyond the earth boundness of this planet, they choose to recycle here. That does not mean that if a soul has made an error, in the past or in another civilisation, that they may *not* choose to come here, for often they do. However, know that there are others in the Universe that also tempt, and attempt to control souls and create a corruptive state. Then, that soul, when it is in its state of purity can identify that problem and chooses to visit planet Earth or another planet, in order to overcome that corruption. Yes.

Now follows a discussion on birth and death,

GUEST: May I ask about transitioning into and out of physical life? One thing that concerns a lot of conscious people at present is the quality of birth and the birth experience, for souls transitioning into the body. Do you have any advice for people who wish to give a good birth-transition to children coming into the world now?

TOM: You know that in past days there was not this great difficulty that exists now? In days past, what was created in sound-waves was not discordant. People did not have mechanical sound-patterns and waves, did not have electronic fields of energy, and birth was accepted as natural. What happens in these times is that people who want to give life to a developing spirit in a peaceful way unintentionally create confusion for a child, for they speak to it in gentleness and lovingness, and then they proceed outside, where there is a very noisy environment. Therefore this new-born spirit is not even knowing what kind of world it is come into.

Therefore that must be explained. For can you imagine yourself in a warm cave, and then suddenly you feel the vibration of a volcanic explosion: you would not know if you could survive this warm cave, would you? Then you receive assurance from the mother, and then that assurance is taken away, so it causes great confusion. What needs to be arranged is this: if one who is in gestation could be in a calm environment for this birthing soul, with soft music, lighting, educational input. You know that you may read an encyclopaedia to one that is waiting for birthing? As that is assimilated also is this noise assimilated, discordantly. So when you are in that swing from calm to disruptive, would you not be jarred also? You see, if one spirit chooses to come back and it really should not, and it is forcefully returning, and then is creating more discordancy, and the nutrients feeding to it are discordant also, then can you see why it then discordances the Planet? Now if that one came back wilfully and had opportunity to have serenity, it then has a chance to perform in its human role in the method that it should.

GUEST: *There are a number of people who now understand this, but it has yet to develop in a larger way throughout the world.*

TOM: What must be done is the creating of arenas of safety that a female enters for that time.

GUEST: *Around the time of birth, or during the whole of pregnancy?*

TOM: Through gestation, from half-through.

ALEX: *I believe that this is one of the few planets where we are able to sexually reproduce in the physical being. How would the experience of having a family, or the experience of a family unit, aid us in our spiritual evolution on this planet?*

TOM: You are correct in that it is the only planet, not one of few, where that of the sexuality for reproduction is the method that is in sexuality, and in that, you see, humankind searches continuously —

this we have explained before. Therefore we will attempt to answer the second part of the question. It is bringing forth, and it is not always a necessity for humans to have a family – that is the first premise that must be understood. When a soul chooses to come forth to benefit Planet Earth, then it is important that it chooses those elements necessary for its development into its divinity-potential. In times past there were souls that forced conditions in two humans, in order for their reproduction to come into being, for they wilfully wished for the elements of either or both humans.

This has been so in times past, and is now in change, because no souls will recycle that should not [1991]. We are now moving into a planetary state upon Earth wherein that method no longer applies, so in your future, not immediate but soon, a soul will then choose to come forth with the agreement of the male-female vehicles. Therefore the importance of that family is to bring forth a soul, for it to nurture them and for them to nurture it, for it and you to attain evolutionary growth, the removal of barriers, and to peel away the density of Planet Earth, and prepare for its blooming.

JOHN: *The concept 'there is no death': we hold some beliefs about reincarnation, but I sense that it is a little more complex than a simplistic view which many hold.*

TOM: Those upon this planet can understand that in the times of their coming they chose to come to Planet Earth. If they are in a state of despair, the elements of the Universe can be explained to them.

For Planet Earth brings about the desire for the individual to be an individual, and what is frightening for people is that when they begin to believe that if they relieve and purify and evolve, they merge with the Source and are no longer an individual. Therefore there is the rejection of reincarnation and the continuity of life. In truth, those who exist upon Earth are from the gods. There are those who have forgotten this completely in differing degrees – particularly in the civilised world, as you term it.

We know not how to explain, to you and your humankind, the energies that exist and merge with the Source and still be of one individual. It is quite complicated.

GUEST: *The ending of individuality and the end of free will for many people on the Earth would be as bad as dying. It would be very difficult to get over the concept of merging into a universal consciousness because that is felt to be like dying.*

TOM: Exactness. Therefore what must be understood is that the individual identity of the personality does not die. That is what we mean when we say "Humankind upon this Planet are from gods". We mean from the civilisations or the sub-civilisations. Do you understand that? Somehow the means must be found in your world, to convey this concept: that death does not bring about individual destruction.

GUEST: *Is free will ego then?*

TOM: When we say 'free will' we will speak now of the physical planets. For example: if you choose to go to another planet, you know in the going that you have given up your individual free will, to become part of a collective free will. Only on Planet Earth is each individual totally one of free will. You asked, "is free will ego?" Perhaps you could say it is. But it is more than that, it is choice...

GUEST: *May I ask whether you can give advice to people moving close to the end of their physical life, about any ways they can meditatively prepare themselves for the transition?*

TOM: There is only one way, and that is the acceptance that it is only physical demise which takes place. The soul, spirit, mind, and emotion energy continue to exist. If they understood this when they make the transition from physical to spirit, they would not be in shock-state and sleep-state at the transition.

GUEST: *A lot of people in our world anticipate that nothing will happen to them after they have made their transition, but we have a great lack of understanding of what a soul may expect or visualise after they have made the transition...*

TOM: There is much written about that from spirit sources, you are in error in your thinking, for in your world, for example ... all Hoovids understand life after and life again, all Indians also, all of Shinto also, all Islam also. It is only in your misinterpretation of the Nazarene, of the sleep-state and then the rising of only the good people that creates lack of understanding.

Now those who have followed the Nazarene are becoming more enlightened concerning that. For the non-God believers (atheists) it is their sadness, as they will not know they have passed on and they will be confused, for they were not prepared, as most Nazarene followers are not prepared. For when you pass you are who you are. You do not become enlightened through passing.

GUEST: *I was asking this question for these kinds of people, who get lost, when they cross over...*

TOM: Then I would say to them: when you have passed on and you are confused and do not know what has happened, then recognise that you have passed on and you are alive!

JOHN: I'm concerned that the Church seems to be taking such a counter-productive   position....

TOM: You know there are people demanding. Is not this the time for people to demand from their religious leaders? And those religious leaders who do not evolve, then this will be the end of their religious movement, for people will take possession of their lives.

JOHN: So is it true to say that all the major Earth religions have some belief in the continuity of life after death, so this could be the one common theme between all religions?

TOM: That is correct, yes. There is this knowing in humankind. The religious, those who head religion, utilise that knowing for controlling the masses.

The next questions were asked by a scientist, interested in the subtler aspects of healing...

IAN: I want to ask about the energies that are working on the DNA, when a healer is healing someone. It is known by science that only 5% of the DNA within each cell is used to build a physical body. So about the other 95% we don't know anything. I think the other 95% has a certain specific function, in relationship to energies and in relationship to healing, the low frequency fields and the magnetic fields. Is that true, or am I off-course on that?

TOM: That is absolutely correct. Know also that the ability to heal is within all, but it is more available to some than to others because of the mechanism of their understanding. A portion of the DNA is used for collective consciousness, streams of energies, and if it is not understood someone may believe they are someone they are not. If it is not refined within them they may believe they are Napoleon.

IAN: So it is something like the genetic memory of the mind?

TOM: Yes, and if they were in that time-period or had some brief connection with it, if it is not completely understood, they may believe that they are of it, for it has not been defined correctly within.

IAN: *So it seems, that in these 95%, that in each cell, there is physical manifestation in the DNA of all the past lives, experiences, of the cosmic knowledge, the cosmic connection?*

TOM: Yes. Of the archetypes also, and how they began to manifest from that.

ANDREW: *When healers are working in threes with you, that is three healers and the patient, what is the nature of that healing process? What is it that flows from the healers, and what is it that is triggered? [In this instance Andrew was referring to a situation of two male and one female healer] An enzyme or some system in the human being who is worked on?*

TOM: What in truth transpires is, that in the case of healers connected with us, the energy comes from the civilisations Ancore and Aragon. It is similar to your laser beam: there is not in your world or language the nature of what we have.

ANDREW: *But it is some kind of a coherent beam, I take it?*

TOM: It is a beam that then goes through the male healers, and then penetrates through the female healer and then in turn purifies the body of, what you call the patient.

ANDREW: *Yes, right.*

TOM: However, when the healing is between two (the patient and the healer) the polarities being male and female, and when the two are placed close to each other, their two etheric bodies blend and in this blending are refined and the refinement then creates a funnel or a focus for us to generate through. It is also possible for healers to work as pairs, two male and two female that would work as a team, particularly when working on severe cases. All energy then would be funneled through all four beings in order to reverse a deteriorating process in a being that is ill.

ANDREW: *Well, that's very good. Now is any specific enzyme system triggered, or is the oxygen worked on, or the red blood cells... ?*

TOM: It is the entire etheric body which is brought back into balance.

ANDREW: *I see, the action is etheric, which in turn of course acts upon the biochemical mass, I see.*

TOM: It removes from the etheric. It is like a laser beam that removes poisons. It is a giant filter that purifies and removes impurities. It is as if you took the patient and turn them completely inside out, and then scan them, and remove from them all the poisons, all of what you would call a tumour, all the things which do not belong in the physical body, and then you would right side it up. It would be as if you had a doll that had within it a very fine silk cotton filling, that then in turn a bug had crawled into, and the bug then made a nest, and then you would take it and would cut it open and turn it inside out, and purify it and sew it back, and then the bug would be removed. It is of the same nature.

DAVID: *To what extent is sickness caused by either emotional stress, karma, wear and tear or learning experiences with other people in relation to these causes?*

TOM: What we see upon Planet Earth in this time is the creation of a new belief, we call it the religion New Age, which is a belief that one brings forth from the past an element into this life. It is also said that one has chosen in order to teach others.

Know this: that most of the illnesses upon this planet are brought about by the peoples of Earth in their error of thinking, their foods, their pollution of lands and waters, by contamination from ingestation, by those who make business at the expense of humankind. There is a portion created by stress of emotion, there is another portion created by stress involved in pleasing others, we speak now of youth. There is also a portion created by conditioning in the brain during the time of youth, but the greatest portion is created out of Planet Earth. I will explain: humankind was meant to be born to live a full, fruitful, healthy, non-diseased life, and in the passing of the physical body, not to have ageing or suffering as now exist, but to pass on quietly in sleep, after a good portion of a hundred years. It is always in the last years that knowledge and wisdom are brought together. But humankind has lost that for many reasons: those that we have spoken of, and also it has become a collective thought that all must be ill and ageing. It is difficult to override that. Yes.

DAVID: *When, for example, a body has created calcification because of a bone spur, is it possible to alter matter just from thought?*

TOM: Yes. It is possible through proper nutritionals, through supplements of vitamin, through your elevation of thought and dissolving of this calcium, and also with healings. It is possible. It is best in the process of removing it not to have the ingestation of animal for a portion of time. For the body will begin to consume the calcium then, yes.

IAN: *You said in the past that errors in thinking cause diseases within the human being. So I wondered what the relationship is of these energies, what the process is, from thought-process to physical manifestation. Because I guess there is a relationship also with magnetic energies and low frequency energies, and also with the etheric energies. So how does this all fit together?*

TOM: In the beginning there was purity and purity of thought. When you do a major thing that is against self or Universe or the Creator, the internal knowledge of the cell begins to react. You call this guilt in your world, but we know it as a form of opposition destruction. Altea and Aragon have said to tell you that all of it comes from a base of fear. Therefore it penetrates into the etheric and it tarnishes, so the magnetic field is dimmed, and it then can then be penetrated or contaminated – and what you call Scalar F, ELF...

IAN : *Yes, extra low frequency waves.*

TOM: ...these pick up energies, and they can then penetrate and contaminate the etheric. If you place upon your body a crystal consciousness with crystalline structure then ELF cannot contaminate. What takes place with contamination and the dimming of the magnetic, and the penetration of the etheric, is a wild cell. And it then bores a nest within and begins to drain life energy force.

IAN: *Yes, so this is like the beginning of a cancer, in our words?*

TOM: Yes, also cancer can be brought about in error of thinking by mass humankind, which is connected with contamination of environment.

IAN: *You mean, if the mass of humanity is thinking in error, it reflects in the environment?*

TOM: Yes. If environmental contamination is brought about by visual contamination, this also then penetrates the etheric. So it may be this: you may not be in error of thinking, but the etheric is bombarded and penetrated – from the collective. Then contamination can come into being. That all comes from error in thinking because humankind thinks that they can do as they wish with Planet Earth. By creating destructive devices. Humankind was not created for suffering, humankind was not created for disease, humankind was not created for destruction. Humankind was created for the joy and glory of the Creator, who in truth is humankind. Do you understand that you created us?

IAN: *Yes, in a very abstract sense, we can understand it.*

TOM: You also understand that you created the Creator?

IAN: *Yes.*

TOM: Therefore you are the Creator?

IAN: *It's hard to get, but we have a sense of that, yes.*

TOM: So what is important is to know that upon Earth you are the Creator that created you. What is also important then is that there are those [elements] upon Earth that were created by the Other created. And that can contaminate and create error.

IAN: *Yes. That's the difficult part for me.*

TOM: For the basic element of humankind is attempting at all times to strive to its higher self, and it is confused because the density of Earth helps the power in opposition to the higher self.

IAN: *Yes, they mix it up.*

TOM: That is correct. You also know that with your power, which is infinite, all can be changed. You know in science that if you place a drop of one item it can change the properties of the whole.

IAN: *Yes, I wondered about that, and it's great you confirm this, this is absolutely how it goes, yes.*

TOM: Therefore realise that those of ours can change the whole. You as a scientist understand it when you analyse it: you must now understand it when you cannot analyse it.

IAN: *Yes, that's the difficult part. But I see the importance, yes.*

TOM: Also realise that who you are creates the ability in you to change all things. Yes.

A portion of the bottlenecking on Planet Earth now comes from the New Age movement, from the releasing of inhibitions and the desire to be again upon Earth, in the belief that the physical reality of Planet Earth is the only reality – and then becoming subjugated to the desire. Therefore the New Age, which is to teach Planet Earth to go forward into growth, has actually stopped it.

JOHN: *Is it also cutting off contact with you? There's some idea in the*

New Age movement that we can go do it ourselves, do our own thing.

Tom: It is not possible to go it alone. The problem in the thinking of the New Age is that, "if you think something away, it will go away". Therefore it invalidates others for whom it did not go away. What it then implies is that you are not pure enough, your thinking is not clean enough, you do not have the techniques. This is in great error, and instead of supporting, enlightening and being joyful, it brings about more guilt. It also is an example of the belief that if you have knowledge of the mind, you can overcome all possibilities. Those of humankind who have lost a child that are in New Age, they have two choices to assume: one that the child was not deserving to live, for it perhaps came in with a predisposition of debts owed, or that its demise came about because of some inadequacy within them, not being able to sustain it.

Both thinkings are in error. If you become trapped in the past then your understanding of the future has no value. What is also important, is the understanding of the cosmology of what you term the hierarchical situation of the Universe. We do not like that term 'hierarchical.' But to understand that there are other physical civilisations that are attempting to bring benefit, that there was also the seeding, and to understand that the Twenty-Four civilisations are what they call the twenty-four elders in the Book of Revelations. What is important is to begin to clarify the errors that have crept into the religious aspect that holds man in bondage. It is only in the asking that you do the receiving. Know also: it is time for humankind to understand that they are of us, and must be freed from the burden of poverty. Remember it is some religious leaders that have created the idea in humankind that it is more worthy to be less, to be poor. It was their way of controlling humankind. If you must continuously struggle for existence, then those who are close to you, and the environment that surrounds you becomes less – this does not give you the freedom to serve properly. We would that all of humankind be joyful. We also know that because humankind can believe and understand that your earthly realms are the reality, the error creeps in, and the confusion. But know that if you focus yourselves with each other, the burden of error can be removed, and the understanding of the true self and your service can be revealed for utilisation. It is a time of celebration, in the beginning of its opening into the reality of its rightful position in the Universe. It is the planet of free will, of choice, and it has been kept in a form of density which has entrapped souls in rebirth-recycling. It is now coming into a state of true consciousness.

There are those amongst you that have great joy for Earth, and there are those who do not have, who relate in discomfort to the planet. It is time for humankind to understand that Earth was created to be the true paradise, and for that purpose the variety and beauty were created, for experiencing your physical with the spiritual aspects of humankind. In times past the density upon your planet earth helped to influence an entrapment and soul-recycling.

PHILIP: You mentioned about our no longer having the excuse that things are the way that they are, and my question is around how I, in my own life, often say "Well, I do that because I'm human". And I was reading in the Bible a passage which said "We should be like our Father in heaven who is perfect".

TOM: Is that not what the striving is for? Is it not a religious element that has entrapped humankind and given a rationale for out-cop? I have confused you?

PHILIP: I'm not sure about your saying that religion has caused that to happen.

TOM: There are those forms of religion which say also "it is human to err" but within the human being is contained the divinity of creation. Therefore it is not a truism that it is human to err — it is a mis-truism.

PHILIP: What is it that we can do if there has been a shift to become more aware of our divinity — that I am divine and focused more on that than on my human nature?

TOM: You insist you have a human nature! (Laughter)

PHILIP: I don't want to insist, it's just what it seems like.

TOM: You know you have a divine nature?

PHILIP: I'm aware of it.

TOM: You know?

PHILIP: Yes.

TOM: You know when you have created error?

PHILIP: Often.

TOM: And just as humankind creates habitual methods of living-identity, it is necessary to attempt to remove the habitual nature and to replace them with the divine being that you are. This acceptance of the divinity within you is a beginning. Do not blame yourself when you have erred, but make a position to not repeat it. Always function from the centre of your being, in integrity. What is important is to attain a state of being in which you cannot view yourself with dislike. Also it is important that honesty is functional. You see, there is confusion in humankind, and we have hesitated to speak of honesty, for they then will utilise it in error. It is important to understand that in honesty there must also be wisdom. Therefore, in one form of honesty, you must never take what is another's — you all know this. Humankind makes an error by embarrassing others and then saying "I am honest, they are not". That is not what we mean, do you understand?

PHILIP: *Yes, you're saying we need to be appropriate as well as being honest, is that right?*

TOM: That is correct. And find a method of communication and behaviour that is consistent with your integrity, and with wisdom. That is difficult, is it not?

ALL:*(Laughter)*

TOM: Know this: as you now understand your divinity, you must also understand you contain the elements of wisdom. Knowledge is gained from educational methods, but wisdom is innate. Therefore the development of your wisdom is also important.

PHILIP: *Yes. Also, earlier, you mentioned that each of us contains the essence of a star. I wondered if you could perhaps explain that more, and what you mean by it?*

TOM: This is difficult. Each being exists upon Planet Earth, and each is a total individuality, containing the energy of a living star. It is the light of your soul, do you understand?

PHILIP: *I can understand when you say the "light of the soul". But when I think of a star I think of a body in space that exists...*

TOM: Is that not light?

PHILIP: *Yes.*

TOM: Is it not energy?

PHILIP: *Yes.*

TOM: Is it not living?

PHILIP: Yes.

TOM: Are you not light?

PHILIP: Yes, I see where you're going.

TOM: Therefore you are a star.

DAVID: So is each of us representing a different star?

TOM: That is correct, do not ask us which one.

ALL: (Laughter)

SUSAN: But that star is not the same as the civilisations?

TOM: That is a different point. The civilisations are physical planets. There are stars and planets, and stars that can be created in eventuality into planets. As you have a civilisation of millions, they also have a star. Each one is represented.

21

The Next Millennium

In May 1994, whilst at a meeting with our publisher, Alick Bartholomew of Gateway Books, he suggested that this revised edition would provide an opportunity to update *The Only Planet of Choice* with information for the next millennium. Gateway had received many requests asking for more information.

It appears that many mediums, channels and psychics have been giving conflicting prophecies and predictions about the changes that are going to take place in the coming century. Needless to say, Alick's suggestion was valid and timely. Among other subjects this chapter sets out a transformational arena that now seems to be the focus of The Council of Nine's attention and it concerns the relationship between the Celtic Nations and the English. While parts of this chapter may be uncomfortable reading for some of us who live in the British Isles, we should be courageous and realise that the time to start on these transformational processes is already here, we cannot wait until the year 2000. We are on the threshold of the next century. Hopefully what Tom and the Council of Nine have to say will provide us with some insights and guidelines for a new way of life.

I had the privilege of sitting with Tom for these communications and consequently I have been able to emphasise certain words, and indicate the pauses – because I was there. No amount of writing, however, could adequately convey the very special energy that was present, or the multi-level communicating that went on. I do not know if this is the usual experience, but while Tom was talking, ideas and complementary words and images were being given to me telepathically, which has led to a rather different style of writing than the preceding communications, at which I was not present.

IRENE: Greetings Tom and to the Council of Nine, while we would like to ask you some questions concerning the next millennium, do you have anything that you would like to say to us first?

Tom: The Council has asked that I convey to you that we understand the difficulty of removing self from self in your world of density and of propensity for self. For the past three decades there has been interest in self for self and interest in decadence.

It is now time to let go of the past three decades of decadence before moving into a new transformational arena.

And as you know, anytime that there is a forward movement, the old entraps and strangles like that of the Octopi....they occupy you...is that right?

IRENE: Yes, we understand what you mean.

Tom: And they also attempt to hold tightly to systems of belief and the necessity for change is then covered in darkness. We would wish you to understand this: in the past we had explained the importance of the nation of Israel as a microcosm of the macrocosm. Now, in the nation of England, that is considered as the most civilised of all nations, what is of the greatest importance is the settlement of that that is the Celt with that of the Anglo, for only in the settlement of that difficulty can we move forward in correctness. Consider this: this nation of England, in its considerable acceptance of its civility, also creates the most barbaric weaponry, because of the repression of who it is. Therefore it is important to include the English in your meditations for until this problem is resolved it is very difficult for the rest of the world to move forward – for they look to this of the civility, ... not servility....with a 'C'...not an ocean, you understand?

IRENE: Yes.

Tom: Yes. Then there is a great opening, for we may bring the brothers of Abraham together.

IRENE: Yes.

Tom: There is no growth without struggle, is there?

MARY: No, there is not!

Tom: There is no strength without struggle, on your world, is there? If you would lie upon your bed and not move, there would be weakness, is that true?

IRENE: Yes.

Tom: If you lifted weighted things, there would be strength, is that true?

IRENE: Yes.

TOM: Therefore you are in strugglement.

IRENE: Yes, thank you for that, we really appreciate it!

TOM: In the nation of England the civility stops the truthfulness. What is needed is a courageous breaking through − that breakdown in correctness − for do not those of the nation of England tend to put everything "under the carpet"?

MARY: Yes.

TOM: We are sorry, Mary, for it is your nation also.

MARY: I accept what you say, I understand it, I think that it is so, and I am sorry that it is so.

TOM: It is simply because the male energy has ruled for dominant times and it is feeling threatened now, for it knows that it must have equality with the female or it cannot survive. All the source of power comes from the female. By controlling the female, keeping her in bondage and in servitude he can then own that power, do you know that?

IRENE: Yes. It's no different from what the Chinese have always attempted to do with the Tibetans.

TOM: Exactly. Now that the time has come for equality, those of the male geneticalness are frantically trying to rearrange their molecules in all of their energy fields and wanting to maintain in their relationships that it is the god. Think about this: of all the nations upon your planet, the nation of England has what you call significant corruptions of sexuality within its government, does it not?

MARY: Yes, it does.

TOM: The male power knows that it only maintains its power by taking the energy power of the female. It believes that. Instead of it being partners, it is total control, and from another viewpoint, it knows innately that in the act of copulation it is returned to the Source. Yes?

IRENE & MARY: Yes.

TOM: Very complexional those of the nation of England, in their shuttered   minds.

MARY: This recalls a conversation which was held previously [Chap-

ter10] concerning the preparation of this planet for humankind. You had said that the Others were trying to cut the ley lines, when they were being prepared, and that they had succeeded with the Serpent. I feel that that is a dual reply, for in cutting the Serpent, [also known as the Michael and Mary line in England] they then managed to create the imbalance of power in this country and this affects the entire planet. This energy is now being brought back into balance. So the Serpent not only refers to the ley line but also to the male/female relationship as depicted in the Word Book.

TOM: That is correct and of importance.

MARY: So, if the nation of England manages to correct this male/ female balance, then the energy of this country, the way it spreads out through the planet, via the Serpent that goes across England and all around the globe, but only around the northern latitudes (which was the area of the original seedings of humankind). Is this how the energy balances that male/female power throughout the planet?

TOM: Yes, for it sits at the top, does it not?

MARY: Yes.

TOM: It balances it in the civilised world, for in the societies that they would consider as 'primitive' in spite of appearances, this connection is understood. We pray that all extremities be brought into balance, be brought to consider what it has brought forth.

If you understand the singular importance of this time: there is one movement forward and another that is trapped, so that the forward movement is blocked. It is as if there is this division, between that that is, and that that wishes not to be. There is a churning in the oceans of your lives on planet Earth that the Octopi wishes to oc-cupy. Do you understand?

IRENE & MARY: Yes.

TOM: Council has said I must stop asking if you understand, for you are not children is that not so? [we laugh] Now I must...yes. There-fore the Octopi attempts to occupy by strangulation of thinking in clarity. The way forward is across the threshold and in that threshold is the occupier of your planet at this time.

What does one now do to disentangle, on your planet Earth? You could gently remove the tanglements but if they are strong and fierce, they will only hold stronger will they not?

IRENE: *Yes, they will.*

TOM: If you would wish to axe them off, you might axe of yourself also, is that not so?

IRENE: *Yes, it is.*

TOM: You are in a quandary.

IRENE: *Yes, thank you very much!*

TOM: ..... You must be flexible – in time – do you understand?

MARY: *Yes, because if we become rigid in our beingness then it is back to the same problem and we break. Flexibility of crystal understanding.*

TOM: Yes.

IRENE: *Is this a new bottlenecking of the souls?*

TOM: It is more than that. It is a strangulation and in the strangulation there is no releasement.

MARY: *So, relating this to the preceding conversation, that means that as the English don't express themselves fully, and this nation represents this particular aspect of strangulation on our planet, if we keep expressing ourselves in truth and integrity, that this will also help to eliminate the strangulation.*

TOM: It is vital. You are correct, yes. It is advisable to keep bringing forth gently, to the males of this nation of England, the importance of releasing the suppressed...repressed.....and that they find within themselves the courage to bring it out, to view it properly. When it is repressed then it manifests in your male/female inversions.

MARY: *I was going to ask you if the situation in Israel now [May 1994] and also the recent election in South Africa was a reflection of some resolution in that previous aspect of bottlenecking referred to in earlier years?*

TOM: It is the beginning. However that does not mean that there will not be an attempt at strangulation. But you see, when it is verbalised, when it is written, then the crystallisation begins to become fluid. That is of great importance. What must be recognised by the nation of England is that rigidity. We speak now, to those that your society would call the 'ordinary' people. They must begin to change their ability, to think for themselves and not permit the government and municipalities to control them in their thinking, concerning these two nations of Celt and Anglo. It is of vital importance they understand that they have created a bigger tragedy in the name of the Creator. For the English identify themselves as civilised. What they do not understand is that they identify all others as non-civilised, therefore they do not give the opportunity for growth to the Celt or to any other.

Think upon this: What is this Anglo nation? It has a triangle of Celts, does it not?

BOTH: Yes.

MARY: *Symbolically the Celtic lands are to the left hand side and the Anglos live to the right hand side of our island, which reflects the intuitive processes as against the rigid intellectual processes and the melding of these two aspects would create a balance throughout the planet, as we said before. So is that why the crop glyphs are mostly in a triangular area in the center of this particular nation? Has it been to start this process?*

TOM: It is a movement, an awakening, of asking "Why?" Why in this nation of England is there this stuckness — saying: "That's the way we've always done it." We ask, how many years does it take before being able to say, "Why is there now something new?"

MARY: *There are groups of people who walk the country's ley lines and try to get these energies balanced. Many are very linked to the Arthurian legends and it occurred to me, after our conversations, that the symbolism of the sword Excalibur is that of balance: Ex Calibre.*

TOM: That is a form of correctness. It *is* calibration.

MARY: *Thinking further of this nation's landmarks, can you tell us anything about Stonehenge that we don't have in the traditional guidebooks?*

TOM: What do you have in the traditional guidebooks about pyramids? Also all of animal pictorials were points of reference for those of the sons of God, you understand.

We then went on to ask if Tom had any special message for the U.S.A.

TOM: What is important in that vast arena of the nation of the United

States is to bring forth the awareness to the youth of the power of their thinking. And the determination to remove from their nation this violence, corruption and destruction of the planet of beauty, the paradise of Earth. It is important for the youth to insist upon their elders that they will not permit the destruction.

It is important for the youth also to understand that being bombarded by violence [mass media] implants a violence that is then out of their control.

It is important for the youth to join together with their elders in going forward in meditation, in love and in joy.

It is important for the youth to understand that it is joyful to be joyful...and not at the cost of another.

Also, in that vast continent — if they might set up three meditators, so that there be four corners, creating twelve people meditating. Perhaps they can start...how do you say....pen pals?

The following day we continued with our questions:

IRENE: *I would like to ask the council and yourself to clarify what is going to happen as we move into the next millennium.*

As you know, there have been endless questions as to how the changes are going to take place for humankind — is it going to be internal, pyschological, spiritual, geophysical — what are the changes that we can look forward to as we get closer to the changing of the millenium?

The second part of that question is, how best can humankind prepare themselves?

TOM: It is in this manner: Humankind holds within itself the means of forwardness and also it holds within itself the direction. Listen in carefulness, with openness and understanding :

The next thousand years are those of the years of the *mind.* Energies of the mind which will be brought to understanding of the true power of what is created by a thoughtform, a visualisation or a strong desire formed of it. It is in this manner: there has been many predictilations.....predictions which bring a predictilation... is that correctness?

IRENE: *No, but its a new word!*

TOM: Yes? What I meant to say was, it is in this method: in the past many upon your planet Earth have made predictional which have created a predilectional.....

IRENE: ....yes, very good......

TOM: ...and what they have done, by programming humankind, in truth they have actually created that event.

IRENE: Yes

TOM: Now, there are several areas, that those who create these events need to observe and look upon, within themselves (those who still exist, for thou knowest some of those have now transitionalised). It is like this: they have either been predicting from sources surrounding Planet Earth or sources of civilisations that do not have all knowledge, nor a doorway to all knowledge or even that of a window. What they are seeing is like looking upon Earth and seeing the different paths and routes that humankind may take at any given time in the historical aspect of humankind. What they are also seeing is at times, if humankind is moving in a direction that appears to be confrontational they then believe that it is a given, ordained, when that is not true. For humankind has within it the ability to bring all changes within its own parameters and to bring all peace within.

Also there are those of the Others that have in a form, corrupted information in order to create diversion and anxiety in making situations of chaoticness. Now again we say this: there are those upon your planet Earth who did not believe that in their time of existence upon Earth there was the possibility of East and West in communion, is that not so?

IRENE: Yes.

TOM: That did not happen by chance, for many, with their visualisations, their prayers and their actions brought that into being. For it also takes action, you understand.

IRENE: Yes

TOM: Most humankind would believe that that barrier [wall] came [down] suddenly, in one day. It took much time to bring it to that. In the same manner as the changing of the situation in South Africa. It took much effort by many quiet workers. Also as you see what has happened with the nations of Israel and Ishmael. There are those workers who are attempting to disrupt and to bring them down. Therefore it is held within the faculties of humankind to bring to themselves what it is that they wish.

Humankind does not want to hear this, for is it not more dramatic for them to feel that it is out of their control and that all will happen. [that everything is predestined].

Then there are those who believe that the planet must be purified and cleansed of the humankind who are not worthy of it, in their opinion.

This then creates another energy of negativity and those who have the audacity to believe that their predictions are correct and rightful have created a great difficulty, not only for themselves, but for Earth. They have given their power to another energy you understand?

IRENE: Yes.

MARY: There are a growing number of people around the world that are interested in the 'Ascension' philosophy. Can you tell me where that information comes from, and then, whether there is any truth in the concept that a few chosen ones will help the planet in its evolution, or coming back into balance, after what they term 'chaos'?

TOM: We will explain to you again about those civilisations that do not have full information, and then attempt to create an elitism amongst those of humankind, in order to give them the feeling of specialness and uniqueness – in that way they keep them blind to other realities. At times, or in some instances, some of those sub-civilisations believe that they have the truth. It is not complete and they do not understand that when they speak of the 'Ascension', it refers to the energy fields creating the means for Planet Earth to be a light space vehicle in upward movement. It does not mean that humankind will ascend, nor that a portion of them will ascend.

It is also of importance to understand that the fear of destruction keeps the planet and humankind in bondage and serves no useful purpose. It only creates a lack of balance for the planet and imbalance and depression in humankind. We speak to all of humankind who live in this concept of destruction when we say that you hold within you totally and completely the ability to stop the devastation, the destruction of your Planet Earth. If you are someone who wishes to be right at all times, and in your error of thinking believe that your planet will be destroyed, then you take the responsibility of creating the destruction; and if we were in your place, we would be in great caution [very careful]. For you do not know what you bring upon youself.

MARY: Thank you, so just to clarify a little, these sub-civilisations are not from the Others, then? They are just a bit confused, is that correct?

TOM: And [Sitting] on the fence, some of them. Do you understand what that means?

MARY: Yes, thank you very much. That is most helpful.

TOM: Therefore, we say: take hold of your own life, your own planet, take time for reflection, take time for prayer, take time for action, each be responsible in a small way and your planet will come to its peace.

As you would feel that it has turned into chaoticness it can also turn into joyfulness. And it is a natural situation at times, for there to be small eruptions and conflict for there are evolved souls and those that are new souls without understanding totality but that does not mean your planet is heading for total destruction.

There is in your world a belief that there is a thousand year reign, is there not?

IRENE: Yes. [The Bible, Revelations Ch.20 v 4-7]

TOM: It is [up] to you and in you are the conditions when that goes into effect. It is meant for your next thousand years and there will not be a sudden, but a gradual change with acceleration – for humankind must now take a stand for living upon Planet Earth. You hold this planet completely and totally. If you wish to give your powers to those who would destroy it, remember that you destroy yourself.

Also remember this: It is true there is not death, so there are some who say "It does not matter, for there is no death" but it *does* matter, for if you cut off a life before it was meant to, if you cut off your own life by that which is not correct – by incorrect thinking, action or otherwise – then your choice and that of others has not been fulfilled, and there is a payment that you will extract from yourself – and you might not like what is due. Is it not better to fulfil what you have chosen for this planet?

Earth can be in greatness, for each humankind is a potentialness of greatness. Do not be afraid of that or of the responsibility, for it will bring to you great self respect and great joy. Do not permit others to own your soul. Move forward.....and we are with of you. Did we answer your question, is there any clarificational?

IRENE: One question that I have concerns this whole notion of technological revolution and computers. You were talking about the next age of humankind being the age of the mind. How will that interact with what's happening now – with our society becoming so completely computer oriented. Are there things that one needs to be aware of?

Tom: What is important to understand is this: Remember we have said that your Earth is the planet of the physical and the spiritual. Humankind has also been burdened with laborious means of working and that has held some in bondage, is that not so?

Irene: Yes

Tom: So, in the millennium of the mind, the balance would be a millennium of *technology*, is that not correct? Therefore is that not a gratefulness? For then humankind has freedom to fulfil its promise to itself.

Irene: So the millennium of technology frees us from the laborious work of the past however it also frees us in terms of our pursuit of the spiritual.

Tom: That is correct.

Irene: And that's the thing we mustn't forget as we become obsessed with our new found toys.

Tom: That is absolute. Do not get out of bounds. As that of the mind begins to understand its power eventually that of the technology will be merged. But you must not lose sight of the spiritual aspect and the balance. Otherwise a corruption will set in again.

*   *   *

This chapter is so vital, that Phyllis, who rarely writes commentary on the transmissions, has felt the need to add these words of clarity:

For over twenty years, Tom has consistently reiterated that if the Messiah/Christ consciousness comes in its own time, it could mean some catastrophic upheavals but if the Messiah/Christ consciousness comes with acceleration, planet Earth, including humankind, will be transformed. What does Tom mean by this, and how does it work?

Tom and the Council of Nine have explained that if the Messiah/Christ consciousness comes in its own time it would mean that the earth and mankind are in such despair and agony that they are crying out for help. Only then can outside influences, such as the Creator or other civilisations, take action to help us.

Acceleration of the Messiah/Christ consciousness means that if there will be enough consciously aware humans working diligently to bring about change – on all levels – government, education, prayer, meditation, environmental issues – taking responsibility and action – then humankind and planet Earth can begin the transformational process that Tom has referred to throughout his communications.

In our lifetime we are beginning to see all of this happening in pockets around the world. Our thoughts and actions are means of bringing about transformation for the coming millennium. Today, science has begun to prove and legitimise the powers of the mind, especially in the area of health. We could expand this concept and consider the possibilities that would come about by using this creative energy within us to accelerate the Messiah/Christ consciousness – it is worth a try ..... just "what if .....?"

The choice is ours.

Briefing

How it Came to Be

by Phyllis V. Schlemmer

Before I knew who Tom was, Tom was already a part of my life.

Since my earliest memories I have seen angels, spirits and strange looking creatures, later on I realized that they were beings from other dimensions, and humanoid entities. I played with spirit native American children and watched as native Americans tried to defend themselves or plotted against the white man. For me they were as real as my brother.

I was raised in an area of Pennsylvania which had experienced many Indian battles, and many of the towns were named after them. My mother was quite ill after I was born, so I was raised by my father's parents. I adored both of them. Much older than my Grandmother, my grandfather was a tall robust man, whom I called Popop; they had nine children, most of whom were still at home. My father was the eldest. It was the time of the Great Depression and the family grew all their own potatoes, corn and vegetables, and Bessie our cow gave us milk which my Grandmother turned into cheese and butter. With all this and the wonderful home-made bread she baked daily, we were quite well provided for compared with many people.

I was the first grandchild and I was loved, joyful and cheery. My grandmother would take me with her everywhere she went. She was the local midwife, and when she was called out and no-one was around to look after me, she would pick me up, wrap me in the large grey shawl she always wore, and off we would go to deliver babies. She would also take me with her when it came time to pick the vegetables; that was when she taught me about nature spirits. One of my jobs was to pick the potato bugs off the potatoes and the nature spirits helped me with this. They also helped me when I went looking for mushrooms which could be found in the local cemetery.

I would see many people in the cemetery, some trying to talk to visitors, who did not respond. Once I asked my grandmother why they were crying and why no one paid attention to them. She told me that they did not know they were dead. Sometimes they would loom up in front of me as if to play a game, and I would go chasing after them or hide behind tombstones. They seemed so happy that at last someone was paying attention to them. My grandmother would explain to me who they were, why they were there and how their families kept them Earth bound. She also explained that although I could see them, they were not so solid as I was. But I would try to hold their hands and sometimes I succeeded.

When I was around five years of age, my grandfather became very ill. My Aunts told me that he was going to die and go to heaven to be with God. I recently had a kitten that died, we placed it in a shoe box and buried it in the garden. I was very disturbed about this dying and going to God. For me, it meant being all stiff, placed in a box and put into the ground. That night as I was saying my prayers, I asked God not to let Popop get all stiff and die. I then began to pray that I would not die. I asked God to please tell me I would not die, that Popop would not die, and I would do whatever he wanted, but please not to let us die. Suddenly I heard a voice saying "Hush child, hush, you will never die, I promise you". I looked round. No one was in the room with me and the voice seemed to come from the ceiling. I said again "Promise me God that Popop will not die, I will be a very good girl". Again the voice said "Hush child, hush, your Popop will not die, I promise you." I had such a wonderful feeling of peace, space and light. It was as if I was filled with such joy. God was my friend; He gave me his word that neither I nor my grandfather would die. I told my grandmother about it and she just smiled and said, "Yes, child". After my grandfather did pass on, I insisted he was not dead, because I saw he was well and happy, standing alongside this very big doll that looked like him lying on the bed. When they took the doll out of the house later, he and I were playing hopscotch outside. I asked him if he wanted to go with the doll. He said no, so we continued to skip and play. I was so happy he was no longer ill.

Both my grandmothers were sensitives and recognised that I also had this ability. The two of them were involved in my training, for each had unique abilities. My father's mother taught me about the little people and life after death. She was born in Ireland, had a wonderful spirit, loved to sing and I never heard her say a negative word about anyone; she was the least judgmental person I ever met.

My mother's mother was born in Italy and she was a medium. Her family was known for their healing abilities. She read the oils, was very good with psychometry, found missing people and communicated with spirits. She was very strict and taught me to be responsible and to develop my own abilities. Both grandmothers were very strong on ethics and discipline which they instilled in me. With this background, it was inevitable that some day I would open a school to teach metaphysics, which I did in 1969. I had been told by my Italian grandmother, who came from a family of kabbalists, that one was not ready to teach until the age of forty.

I opened my school in Orlando, Florida on my fortieth birthday and began to teach a select group of seventeen potential mediums and psychics. I would go into deep trance, and the class was taught by one of my spirit mentors called Dr. Fiske. I had created a special window-less room for this class with a microphone hung from the ceiling. Outside the door was a tape recorder which was turned on by one of the students using a remote control after I had reached a deep trance state.

One Monday evening several months after the group started, an-other entity came in to talk to the group after Dr. Fiske had finished. When class ended and we were all sitting and eating, the students told me about this wonderful being who had come in. They liked him very much, he was very gentle, loving and softspoken. He spoke of univer-sal things, he was completely opposite to Dr. Fiske who was strong on discipline, spoke in a loud voice, and was very authoritarian. I suggested we listed to the tape. Dr. Fiske spoke first, but after he said goodbye the tape was blank, and it continued blank for about twenty minutes before we heard me coming out of the trance. This went on for several weeks. Finally I told my group they should ask him who he was and why they could not record him. Up to this time they had never asked him questions, but just let him speak. So the next Mon-day evening one of the students said: "May we ask you questions?" He replied, "Yes". They asked him what his name was. He said "My name is Tom". When they asked him why they could not record him, he replied, "You did not ask permission, is it not correct to ask if you wish to record someone?" They agreed and asked his permission.

From that time on Tom's voice was always recorded. I channelled Tom for approximately four years before he was identified in 1974 as one of the Nine, their spokesman.

I believe I am one of the few deep trance mediums still around. Many mediums find it difficult to give up complete control, which is necessary for this kind of work. I am able to surrender myself com-pletely and let Tom and the Nine take over. I have not channelled any other entities since Tom first came, with the exception of a few occasions on which Dr. Fiske came to alert the sitters to help bring me out of trance because my physical body was in distress. Tom and I have had a deep relationship for the last twenty-two years. Strangely he always refers to me as 'Our Being' and never uses my name. Since my experience of the voice that said "Hush, child, Hush". I have always had a strong internal knowing of the existence of God – the one and only God, for which I have felt very grateful.

Tom and the Nine have not detracted from that; they have reinforced and enhanced it. I feel so very, very fortunate and appreciative that I have had the opportunity to know Tom, and through him the Nine. I do hope you will find them as helpful on your journey through life as I have found them in mine.

The Process

by John Whitmore

Channelling, sometimes known as mediumship, is neither a new nor an uncommon occurrence. Phyllis Schlemmer is not comfortable with either the term 'channeller' or 'medium' because of the general impression that these words convey to the vast majority of people and more importantly, she feels that for her at least, they do not describe the process correctly. Phyllis considers herself to be a transmitter – as indeed does Tom, who says so, further on in this chapter. This point having been made, for the sake of the reader, we shall continue to use both the word 'channel' and 'medium' throughout this chapter.

Channelling can be found in every culture and in a variety of forms, such as 'automatic' writing or artwork, and voice communication, where the channel appears to speak for another mind than her own. (The majority of channels in our culture are women so I will use the feminine gender throughout.) This may occur in light trance, where the channel is aware of what she is saying, or in deep trance, of which the channel will have no recall whatsoever. In deep trance the channel may use speech, language patterns and tone that are completely different from those of her normal voice. Even foreign languages totally removed from the channel's experience are not uncommon. Some people have never heard of channelling, and many more would not give it a second thought, because on the surface it is easy to dismiss it as an act or hoax consciously perpetrated by the channel. Hoaxers however have to have a motive. Could there really be so many hoaxers, in so many cultures, whose only reward is often physical and psychological pain and, at least in 'developed' societies, a fair amount of ridicule? The payoff for manipulating people in channelling is not significant enough to attract widespread hoaxing. However, institutional psychology is incapable of producing an explanation of channelling that fits within current scientific orthodoxy, and therefore ignores the subject, in the same way that physics ignores dowsing – even though most water supply companies and mineral and oil prospectors employ dowsers with profitable results. Channelling work is anathema to the very assumptions upon which our society is based – individuality and the ego are sacrosanct, and the thought that larger influences can come through an individual draws in many other major questions, such as those of reincarnation, the soul, the transpersonal roots of the psyche and the very meaning of life. Channelling has been going through a resurgence in recent years, particularly in America, where sittings with channels have, to a degree, replaced the psychiatrist's couch. As with any phenomenon or fad that grows to popular proportions, the quality of what is available is likely to decline and greater discrimination is required by those who wish to avail themselves of transmitted guidance. Some of the aspects and pitfalls of channelling work are addressed here.

It should be remembered that many of the statements that follow refer to the particular case of the transmissions of the Nine by Phyllis Schlemmer and do not necessarily apply to other practitioners of the art.

*   *   *

GENE: *If people can accept the reality of channelling at all, they are then faced with all the problems of interference in channelling and in receiving these messages, coming as they do from a different dimension. Can you comment on the possibility of how much of the messages we are receiving from you are garbled by static and interference, and whether or not it is possible that we are occasionally receiving misinformation because of difficulties in communication?*

TOM: Misinformation would be in the interpretation, and in limitations within the mind of the channel – in the usage of words, of which we do not have sufficient in the mind of the channel. There is not within the minds of humans the language to even attempt to explain our knowledge or the knowledge of other civilisations. But the channel is in our control.

GENE: *Can Phyllis be unconsciously affecting any of the communications from her own inner self? How certain can we be that our method of communication avoids all thoughts and needs and so on, that Phyllis herself has?*

TOM: Do you understand that our Being is not in the body at the time of communication?

GENE: *I didn't understand that, but I understand what you're saying.*

TOM: Do you understand that the functions of the body in most areas are in a state of stoppage?

GENE: *No, I –*

TOM: Do you understand that the heart and the circulatory system is kept to a minimum of function?

GENE: *I underst-*

TOM: Do you understand that we are in complete maintenance and control? There is not a word in your language to explain, except for the word that we totally possess the body.

GENE: *I understand. I think that answers my question completely on that.*

TOM: If our Being, did not give us total permission to take control without creating difficulty or objecting to us, we could not – for the sake of non-interference of free will – completely control our Being. Our Being's mind, her soul, is not in the body when we are communicating. Our Being had great objections to computerisation. That was the original plan, but out of the fear of being controlled by a computer, she created great difficulty for us, herself, and for the civilisation of Altea, that was attempting to communicate in that way. We would not be communicating in this manner if our Being had given herself in completeness to a computer.

In many thousands of years of communication from the other planes of dimension to species and beings upon the physical planet Earth, there has always been great difficulty. There have been but few that we would call perfect, as anyone possibly could be perfect upon your planet. The reason being that there have been but few that would permit complete control.

ANDREW: *I see, that is absolutely basic in the process, is it?*

TOM: It is primary. Without the control and without relinquishing the personality of the individual it is not in truth clear communication. We have cautioned you many times to be of extreme caution with the conscious mind of those with whom you work, whom you use as a communicator. It is important for you to understand that in order to communicate, and I speak now, not just of my operating as a spokesman for the Nine, but also for other civilisations, to be able to communicate, we will use an instrument. We use this term, 'instrument' because the one through whom we communicate is in truth a physical transmitter.

When we use a being it is important for you to understand that we must truly control that being. We take over the subconscious. It has to be a being that is willing, that becomes passive in order for us to become active. We have never had a difficulty with our Being. That is because our Being removes her individuality. But that is also the reason for the fear of computers. She understands in her subconscious, and has made a commitment, but the fear of a computer is the fear of a loss of soul.

Do you then understand that we must with great effort maintain a balance in the physical body? It is important that when taking over the body, that at the moment that we are taking it over it is in a sense like a computer. We must cause the body to have its heart operating, its lungs breathing, all of its major organs functioning. That is the reason that many times there is a drain of energy in the two of you it is because we are using your energy maintaining the body in a suspended state.

ANDREW: *Is this carried out by a computer or is it by a being?*

TOM: With our Being it is another being; that is the difficulty. We do not violate the agreement with our Being. She is the only one on your planet who was able to do this, and it was from an earlier agreement, that she decided to give completely to the Nine – it was not an agreement with computers. At the time that we communicate with you, we wish you to understand that we do not have a vocal language.

ANDREW: *You communicate by direct mind-to-mind.*

TOM: We communicate with the mind of our Being, and then her subconscious transmits into words.

When we maintain our Being, it is as if we take a million threads and we weave these threads together to communicate with you. If there is a situation where she is not physically in condition – if for example, she has difficulty of digestion, or difficulty of elimination, or difficulty in emotions, or if there is a negative vibration within her, or a negative or doubtful vibration within either of you, or an anger in you, or a disturbance – we cannot then use the energy from you because it would cause a breakdown in the threads which we weave with her to communicate. And so we communicate at times with great effort, which then in turn causes more of a depletion upon her. Also, when conditions are not proper, it is very difficult to present the images so they may be related.

Through thousands of years other civilisations have worked very diligently to perfect and to refine a system of communication, so there would not be the necessity to transmit and to control a being, to relate what other civilisations would relate to you. We are telling you now, and we pray that you have understanding of what we tell you: when we speak to you, we speak through this Being. That is to be clearly understood. Communications which you receive through other beings and species come through a different sort of communication. It is relayed.

JOHN: *Could you answer one question concerning the means that you use to speak through Phyllis, because the Tibetan [who channelled through Alice Bailey] and some esoteric schools give advice not to pay much attention to deep-trance channelling. It is considered lower psychism, and of course this gives us credibility difficulties with those in those esoteric schools.*

TOM: Do they feel that taking a pen in a hand [automatic writing] is higher psychism? What is the difference?

JOHN: *Well, I believe that what we do here is a more pure way, because of the lack of interference.*

TOM: You are in truth. In this manner there is no mind, there is no consciousness, there is no unconsciousness, lower consciousness or higher consciousness.

JOHN: *But why did the Tibetan give that advice? In that case there must have been some reason?*

TOM: Remember this: in those times [the earlier 20th Century] there were many that were used by spirits. Those in such schools must change their thinking, for this is a changing Universe. It is not static; they are remaining, in staticness.[sic]

From time to time during this period we worked with other channels who seemed to have access to specialist information that complemented the Nine. However they would at times relate things outside their specialisation that would conflict with the Nine or would lead us off track. This caused confusion and occasionally conflict within the group. We asked the Nine about it.

ANDREW: Can we discuss again the human problems of some of our other channels?

TOM: We have difficulty in understanding your nature. We are being educated by others in the way of your beings. It is very difficult for us to understand your physical nature. We understand your emotional, and we understand your intellectual, but it is very difficult for us to understand your physical. We are aware of the problems that you are having with some of your beings with their physicalness. We cannot remove this from them, this they must remove from themselves, or refine it. I will try to explain, but I do not understand that emotion, so I will relate it in the manner that has been given to me.

In regard to your physical bodies, the desires that you have in your physical reproductive areas are similar to a safety valve. The conscious mind of others may have desire to use of you. When it would be one of the opposite sex that would use you, be careful of their communication. We are not saying that you are not allowed to communicate through others; but it would not be direct from us – we want you to be clear of that.

ANDREW: Yes, I'm very clear about that.

TOM: But it is when they wish to use you that they may not speak to you what is the truth. It may be that the civilisation that speaks through them is trying with great difficulty to relate a truth to you, but for them it is an opportunity to use you. We wish you to know that the most destructive element is the ego that controls.

JOHN: Some other channels, here and elsewhere, are producing a lot of cataclysmic predictions, and other sorts of messages that do not seem to coincide directly with yours.

TOM: We have related in many of communications, we will continue to relate to you, there are many civilisations that have communication with humans on Earth, in which that would be a consideration. We will use a term that is not a term that we like, but perhaps it would give to you understanding. There are those that are in a higher echelon, and those in a lower echelon. We communicate not through any but that of our Being. Only if our Being is returned to us, would there be a decision to communicate through another. In the civilisations that create great chaos within many, they are giving their point of view of seeing.

In relationship to catastrophes, we will not permit catastrophes to completely remove souls from the earth. What we are attempting to say to you, is that those that communicate in the strictness of negativity are in a realm that is using their emotion, their drama; it is not of the purest. Do you understand what we are saying?

This particular case of confusion, which had arisen within the group in the early days, is recounted here to demonstrate the kinds of trouble which are easy to fall into when exploring a new world such as channelling. Also, it gives some interesting background into the dynamics of some of the groups of channellers which exist today. Apart from lesser civilisations with lesser knowledge of the whole, there was always the question of whether some non-terrestrial intelligences were deliberately destructive or had evil intent, and whether they could interfere with communications with the Nine.

ANDREW: *Since there has been so much talk of positive and negative forces, is there any sign or method by which a person could confirm that he or she is dealing with positive forces? Some religious people might be frightened by our communications and insist that they could only be negative.*

Том: By their knowledge, by their benefit to Earth, you will have the understanding. We have explained that there are those civilisations that could create difficulty, but that their power cannot sustain. Within your ear, within your heart, within your mind, if it feels not right in the essence in which they convey to you, then we give to you our assurance, it is not right.

The Nine also warned us that Civilisations that did not have the best interests of Planet Earth at heart could exploit the weaknesses of some channels.

Том: There are two ways in which your channels can receive and get into problems in your physical world, One would be when the channel is weakened, either by lack of rest or illness. The other will be when the channel is willing to be used negatively because of the desire for power. Our Being was not a willing channel for negativity.

In this particular case we may interfere and we help. In a channel willing to channel negativity we may not interfere. When a channel is willing to be used negatively there are many factors that ·you must take into account. And because a channel is willing, it does not mean that that channel cannot become unwilling...

JOHN:On the subject of being willing, is there a difference between being consciously willing and unconsciously willing?

TOM: There is no difference. An unconscious desire for power is the same as a conscious desire for power.

ANDREW: I have a feeling that xxxx has the potential to become a channel. What is your advice with respect to this possibility?

TOM: This is possible in the future. But she must learn discipline before she may work. And when I speak of discipline I mean this in the sense that she must learn to balance in this physical world. Without the balance in the physical world it is difficult. As you know, for every hundred that come to this planet to do the work, who have chosen for themselves, ninety-eight do not make it. It is because of non-discipline in your physical world.

You must be extremely careful with whom you deal. And when I speak of this I mean contacts that you make with sources from other civilisations or the spirit realms. Not always are such contacts valid, true and honest. Because a contact is made, it does not mean it is a true contact. When I say this I mean a contact that says it is working for us.

JOHN: Be careful because there are all degrees of spirits. Is that what you're trying to say?

TOM: This is correct. And we are not a spirit, and this is what we speak of. We do not wish to be involved with the spirits. The spirits are those who have passed on in this world and are hanging around this planet earth. We are not spirits. Spirits of your world that are in the atmosphere and around the bands of your world, are as confused as the physical beings on Earth. There are those that are evolved but most are not. We are not spirits. We are trying to save the Earth so that these spirit beings also may be released and be evolved. Be careful whence you work. Remember this: most of the groups and most of the organisations using channelling are working with the spirits. As I said there are those that are evolved but there are those that are also confused. When they left Earth they also took their desires with them, and one of the desires that manifests on Earth is the desire to control.

ANDREW: This constitutes some difficulty for people in distinguishing what is going on when they have inner or psychic experiences. We felt this was happening with the young man that we spoke with today.

TOM: It is of a different nature. Those that exist at this place at this time are in truth with their souls, and have great love for the universe, and their motive is in the highest, so therefore the energy will be used for the benefit of the universe. Confusion comes from non-experience, but it also comes from a great desire to have....How may we say this to you? ...

As in your world there are those that believe all of the words that are written in your publications (is this not so?) Similar to the nature of those that accept that all that is written is truth, there are those that have contact with spirits and civilisations that also believe that because they may make this contact, it is of the highest and of truth. But often it is not. You understand the nature of the spirits existing upon the Planet earth? You also understand that in other civilisations that have what you would call periods of transition, they would also be spirits?

GUEST: Yokatow, is that a spirit or is it one of you?

TOM: A spirit but a good spirit. When I say good spirit I do not mean there are bad spirits, I mean they are just more evolved than others. And on this planet there are those spirits that are working very hard and very diligently to raise the level of this planet. He is one of those.

We just would like to clarify that we are not a spirit, we are spirit in the sense that all beings are spirit, but when we say spirit we mean a physical spirit attached to the Earth.

JOHN: I have another concern. Phyllis' use of the English article word 'of' has increased about ten times from the first to the latest communications. In the earliest communications with you, the language was quite colloquial. Now, in recent communications I find the word 'of' being used in many ways, and is now used as many as eight times in a simple declarative sentence. Can you help me with my confusion regarding that?

Most of these 'of' words and similar language flaws have been edited, in order to ease the flow for the reader. The following paragraph has been left untouched:

TOM: We will attempt to explain to 'that of' you. In 'that of' working 'of' communications with 'that of' our Being, it is 'of' an adaptation from 'that of' us. In the beginnings of 'that of' the communication with 'that of' our Sir John and 'that of' our Doctor, it became 'of' important for us to have 'of' clarification of 'that of' whom we would speak and 'of' what it would have meant. Perhaps we are not using in 'that of' the terminologies that are 'of' correctness, but it became 'of' more 'of' clarification to us with 'that of' our Doctor Andrew, our Sir John and 'of that of' others, and 'that of' our understanding that we were communicating to 'that of' them. They say I have not clarified 'of that' for you.

ANDREW: Could you ask Altea for the linguistic basis for the use of the article 'of'?

TOM: Yes... It is 'that of' you. It is not 'for' you, it is not 'to' you, it is 'that of' the essence of you, as it is 'that of' the essence of us. To answer your question, the physical is deteriorating.

ANDREW: Is this a direct consequence of the work, or is it age?

TOM: It is communication. The draining of the physical body causes difficulty. The area of the brain which we may use for the words has been having a lack of energies. Therefore we must be careful not to drain our Being. This Being was chosen, and chose to do this work, and this may be difficult for you to understand, but in our world she is considered a genius in communication. She can relate and communicate and get across to those that do not understand. But in our miscalculations we erased part of her memory, and it is very difficult for her to find and to choose the proper words. Part of the programming that we were doing when we instituted this process in 1963, was with this device that was placed into the brain to translate our language into your language. Because of this error that we have made we are now having difficulty in translating into the language. If you will please tell our Being to place your dictionary under her pillow. If a dictionary is placed under her pillow, part of the programming then can be programmed in.

In practical terms this has resulted in slower transmissions but the quality of the communications has not been impaired. This section was included to outline some of the difficulties that can arise in this type of work.

TOM: There are many in this room with us now.

ANDREW: I wish I had the vision to see them there. There are so many times I look around and I'm sure they must wonder why I am so blind I cannot see them.

TOM: You are not so blind, it's just you do not have the X-ray vision eyes that some have. They call it seeing with vision or clairvoyance. It is not so, it is X-ray vision eyes.

ANDREW: Well, I offer my love and my peace to all those who are here. Even though I cannot see them I accept their presence.

TOM: At times they touch you.

ANDREW: I thank them for paying attention. It helps, it helps.

TOM: They are always attuned to you and many times we weep with you.

On various occasions, questioners have drawn out some insights into how to deal with the crucial problem of the reliability of the transmitter's source.

TOM: When you open yourself for communication with other dimensional beings it is of great importance to have understanding of purpose and motive, for there are those who come forward proclaiming one thing and being another, and there may be a slipping through of information that may be truth, but may also be a method of manipulation and control.

ALICE: Then how can it be clarified: how can the channel be cleared so that there is no question?

TOM: In your world we have not known of the existence of any that has not had partial self-involvement, for it is very difficulty to clarify. You must continuously search self in your direction, motive and method. In the past there have been many who have communicated portions of great truth and not other portions, spirits of mischief, or thoughts of collective conscience. So it is difficult to categorise or place it in proper perspective.

When you are asked to do something which is not compatible with your physical surroundings, or with practical provisions, then it is necessary to detach, to stand apart, and to view it. When your communicator demands or relates to you, that if you do not do something asked for, then there will be great difficulty in the world; then it is important to understand that that may be something that is fulfilling a need within you, or it might seek to control you.

JOHN: *I'd like to ask about two other channels, one who seems to be producing some important communications, but she claims that they come from the Nine. Can you clarify who really this is?*

TOM: It is not from us in directness, but from civilisations that are in service. So if she would wish to say it comes from us, it would be in an indirect form but also remember this: there is a Board of Directors, a head who has knowledge of all, and there are those underneath who have departments, and there are those underneath that who carry out production. It is of the same manner here, but that does not mean that it negates what comes, but it is always not in true clarity and in directness, do you understand?

JOHN: *Yes. Therefore, perhaps she should not use the term 'The Nine'.*

TOM: She must ask whom it is in that name, do you understand?

JOHN: *Okay. The other person has had some communications recently, also claiming to be from the Nine. I presume this is a similar situation.*

TOM: Yes. As we have explained to you on numerous occasions, we come only through our Being. I am Tom, the spokesman for the Nine, I am the only spokesman for the Nine, and I do not speak through any other. That does not mean that what they bring has not value for those that work in conjunction with us.

Some years later, this same channeller came up in conversation again, though the situation had evolved by then:

MIKI: *A medium we know of is channelling information which claims to come from the Nine. Can you tell us where it comes from?*

TOM: Our Sir John asked us that question over two of your years ago. We explained to him then that it was not from us, that it was coming from a lesser civilisation that had not all knowledge. Since that time her ego has become obsessed and it is being used by those that would wish for destruction. It must be understood whom she is with. It came to her in writing, and now she is attempting to channel in a similar way to our Being, but it is not true, it causes discomfort in the world, and it causes us to be appearing as a clown. It is best not always to hide the truth.

MIKI: From which source comes the Seth materials channelled through Jane Roberts?

TOM: Her higher self, yes.

MIKI: I don't really understand that.

TOM: You have your self, have you not? You have your consciousness, have you not?

MIKI: Yes.

TOM: You have your subconsciousness, have you not?

MIKI: Yes.

TOM: You have your higher consciousness, yes.

MIKI: So, she is not connected to any hierarchy in the Universe?

TOM: It comes from the reservoir of knowledge within her high self. Do you understand?

MIKI: Yes. Most of the material I find is very valuable but still then I find sentences which are contradictory to what you say, especially the information about Jesus. How is this possible?

TOM: It is because of connection to the reservoir of knowledge. You understand that there are streams of reservoirs of knowledge, what you call collective unconscious? In the seven planes surrounding earth, that in truth are nine, there are within each a portion of truth. It is when you go into the ninth chakra that all truth is, not all are capable in this point of their existence.

JOHN: A person I met is interested in channelling, and I was concerned about his lack of discrimination...

TOM: The singular most important thing to know, which you have a natural instinct for knowing, is the checking of your own internal source. This you must convey to him. There are those who channel that are not the best for humankind, however there are those with great intelligence upon your planet who accept all forms of channelling without discrimination. It is important to continuously check yourself and challenge also. It is permissible, in fact it is important, that there be questioning.

There are many channels that in their hearts believe they are doing the things that are correct, when they are simply being tools of the negative, you understand? If they can understand that this is possible (even though they may not accept it) then those that go and utilise this can be brought out. The singular most important thing that may come forth is that you must check your inner source.

You know that all humankind, no matter what environment brought them forth or what education fulfilled them, have an internal check on the balance within, yes.

BACKGROUND

Dr. Andrija Puharich, a medical doctor and inventor, became highly interested in extrasensory perception in the early 1950s. While studying the subject he came across the Council of Nine. It wasn't until 1974 that Phyllis Schlemmer, Sir John Whitmore and Dr. Puharich were brought together by 'circumstances' that Sir John recalls:

"In November 1973 I met Andrija Puharich in New York to invite him to speak at a conference to be held in London in the Spring. He accepted, and agreed to use "The May Lectures" to reveal his extraordinary experiences with a previously unknown psychic, Uri Geller. In January, Phyllis Schlemmer, who ran a psychic development school in Orlando telephoned Puharich about a remarkable healer she had discovered. Soon afterwards Phyllis, Andrija, the healer and I gathered at the Puharich home in upstate New York to investigate his abilities. To everyone's astonishment the healer began to channel information from an extraterrestrial intelligence. Later, when the healer showed signs of instability, we decided to seek advice from one of Phyllis's spirit guides. The guide told us that he was not a spirit, but the spokesman for the Nine – and thus a great adventure began."

In the early 1950s a doctor of medicine cum parapsychological researcher, while studying extrasensory perception, came across the Council of Nine. It wasn't until 1974 that Phyllis Schlemmer, Sir John Whitmore and the Doctor were brought together by 'circumstances' and began their transmissions with the Nine. The story of their first years together: *Prelude To The Landing On Planet Earth,* was written by Stuart Holroyd and published by W. H. Allen in 1977. This was published in paperback by Corgi and Doubleday in 1979 under the title: *Briefings For The Landing On Planet Earth.*

The transmissions in this book *The Only Planet Of Choice* date from 1974 through to the present day. Since those early days, various people have, at one time or another, been present during the transmissions, serendipity being responsible for most of them being there. This has been voluntary work, sometimes requiring much energy, time and personal expenditure. First names of the different questioners have been used in this book in order that the reader can see how the different personalities invite different types of interaction and information from the Nine. Some first names have been changed at the request of the individuals concerned, for they already have extremely active lives and wish to be able to continue their work with The Nine, without public attention being diverted onto themselves.

It has frequently been pointed out by the Nine that, in the past, enlightened information has often been corrupted or lost in the propagation process. The emphasis shifting from the teachings to the teachers, who incorporated their own doctrinal modifications.

The Nine wish that the information they have transmitted be shared with the people of Planet Earth. They do not wish for a cult, religion or any form of elitism to grow around them or the information. The people who, at the time of writing, have shared in the process of channelling have done so with an attitude of service, to support and facilitate the process. Since the members of this group were from various countries they usually convened at twice or thrice yearly reunions, while smaller sessions involving specific individuals occurred throughout the year.

Following a procedure developed over the past fifty years that she has been channelling Phyllis counts herself down into deep trance. To the observer it seems as if she is falling asleep on her chair. Then she suddenly becomes animated, raises her head and her hands and a different voice – Tom's – announces that he is present and offers greetings and blessings. His voice is high-pitched, slow and the English is somewhat archaic. As explained by Tom, Phyllis' body and mind are taken over by the Nine, and bodily functions are maintained by Altea, the leader of one of the Twenty-Four major civilisations. While Tom is transmitting through Phyllis her hands move about in a series of Mudra-like shapes. Channelling through a unique transmitter not only maintains the integrity of the message, it also underlines the enormous amounts of complex preparations and training that are involved in making them. The transmissions usually start with Tom making an important statement. Otherwise one of the sitters (most often it is Phyllis' husband Israel Carmel) asks Tom if there is anything that he wants to say before they start on the question and answer process. Tom does not transmit words, he uses the transmitter's brain as a translator, dictionary and syntax-organiser. Tom calls it the servo-mechanism. The length of a transmission depends on many factors and it is always Tom who announces when the channelling must end, whereupon conversations are finished and goodbyes exchanged. Phyllis goes quiet and then counts herself out of trance. This is sometimes a difficult procedure and awareness, care and collectedness are required from all the people present.

Phyllis has no knowledge of the transmission when she resurfaces – and in fact she has not even read most of the transcripts that have been made, in order to keep her mind uncluttered.

At the end of each transmission Tom always says "Tell our Being of our love for her". And if nobody tells her – she does not know!

Tom's Prayer

From the Council of Nine for the Nations of Earth

We pray that the nations of the Earth come to peace within themselves and come to recognise whence they came.

We pray that all the civilisations of the Universe that are engaged in the balancing of the Universe, be given strength and peace within, to carry on the work to which they are committed.

We pray that the physical beings of the planet Earth come into a state of awareness and understanding, in order for their souls to evolve, to raise the level of the planet Earth and to cleanse the heavens around the planet Earth so that the Universe can progress.

We pray that those beings and civilisations that are opposing what we do come to the light of understanding, so that they also come into perfect balance.

We pray that the day may soon come when all in the Universe have the knowledge and the understanding that will make them whole.

We pray for understanding among ourselves, and for the strength that is needed so that each of us can guide the others to become perfect beings.

We pray for the souls of the children of the Earth to be brought out of the dark and into the light.

TOM

Editors' Notes

I: HISTORY

1. "Compared with the preceding Neanderthals, who displayed virtually no technological innovation during more than 100,000 years of existence, the Aurignacian [Cro-Magnon] peoples were able to realise with increasing rapidity, a wide range of social, technological and mythical possibilities. Having surveyed some of the key developments of the Aurignacian in technology, body ornamentation and representation, one is led to ask whether there is any way to tie them together... Close to the heart of these developments is an increased ability to think in – and communicate by means of – specific visual images". This quote is from 'Visual Thinking in the Ice Age' by Randall White, *Scientific American*, Vol 261, No 1, July 1989.

In the last few years, information that the Nine supplied twenty years ago has been corroborated by new evidence. As one authority described the findings: "After an evolutionary struggle lasting millions of years, our species emerged as top hominid. And then, in one spectacular moment we became human. As recently as 35,000 years ago, western Europe was still occupied by Neanderthals – primitive beings for whom art and progree scarcely existed. Then there was an abrupt change; anatomically modern people appeared in Europe and suddenly, so did sculpture, musical instruments, lamps, trade and innovation. Within a few thousand years Neanderthals were gone. Insofar as there was any single moment when we could be said to have become human, it was at the time of this great leap forward. 35,000 years ago". From 'The Great Leap Forward – Dawn of the Human Race' by Jared Diamond in *Discover the World of Science*, May 1989. Refer also to: 'The Search for Modern Humans' by John J Putman, *National Geographic Magazine*, October 1988.

2. The beginings of Egyptian civilisation have been a perpetual source of mystery for historians and archeologists, for the elements which made up later Egyptian civilisation suddenly seemed to appear at once, in the fourth millennium BC. Egypt moved straight from a stage of pre-civilisation to the government of large areas, without the usual era of city-states intervening. The ordinary logic of historical development does not apply to Egypt as it does to Mesopotamia.

3. The Sumerian civilisation, in our historical records, began around 6,000 to 5,000 BC in what is now southern Iraq,

4. Around AD 1,200 There was a close relationship between the Mongol Emperors of China, Mongka Khan and Qubilai Khan, and the Tibetan Lamas Sakya Pandita and Karma Pakshi. However, Srongtsen Gampo, a powerful Tibetan King in the early 600s and the first Buddhist monarch of Tibet, had a Chinese wife and a Nepalese wife, both of whom were responsible for converting him to the Buddha-Dharma.

5. Ioannes, also known as Jonah, was half-man, half-fish in mythology, the God of the water-depths, and a friend to people. He brought culture, literacy and sciences to the ancients of Ur, and was looked on as a potter who shaped the lives of men and gods. His wife was Hinlil, goddess of grain, and wheat is reputed to have been given to humanity by these two.

6. The Kahuna are the indigenous medicine-men of the Hawaii Islands, possessing an advanced philosophy of life.

7. Megiddo is recognised by archaeologists to date back at least to Chalcolithic settlements around the 4000s BC (the time of Upper and Lower Egypt and the Sumerian city-states), and twenty occupation levels have been identified. It was attacked, re-peopled and re-built not only by the local peoples but also involving Phoenicians (1490s BC) Egyptians (1460s BC). When Joshua and the Israelites entered the area from Sinai (about 1250 BC), Megiddo, with Jericho, was one of the Canaanite strongholds and archaeological remains demonstrate a formidable level of civilisation there. It was completely re-built as a fortified city by Solomon (950s-940sBC), then destroyed and reconstructed by the Assyrians in 733 BC, and the Mesopotamians were involved around 730 BC. It went into terminal decline at the time of the defeat and death of Josiah in 609 BC.

8. Kingston-on-Thames has a landscape zodiac, miles wide, similar to the Glastonbury zodiac as was identified by Katherine Maltwood and Mary Caine in their work on landscape zodiacs and temples.

9. The Harmonic Convergence was held in August 1987. Thousands of people gathered together at different sacred sites to create a worldwide meditational link.

II: SCIENCE & ECOLOGY

10. Absolute zero, however, is super-cold only from our Earth

experience, and in relation to our dense physical existence, which survives within a narrow band of temperature parameters.

11. Matter and anti-matter are fundamentally dissociated kinds of energy and form which seek to neutralise each other.

12. Our neighbour star Sirius is seven light years away. The Pleiades are 410 light years away. All stars visible to the naked eye are from 4 to 1,000 light years away. The centre of our galaxy is 15,000 light years away. A light year is 63,240 times the distance between Sun and Earth. Local galaxies are over a million light years away from us.

13. In physics, when a moving or changing body of mass attains a certain impetus or intensity, it goes critical, while it gathers energy for a fundamental change into another form. An example of this is water approaching boiling-point, in which there is a pause in the heating process, as the water makes the conversion from liquid to steam-vapour.

14. Heavy water is a technology involved in the nuclear industry. If it is released into the environment, there is a risk that it would convert ordinary water into heavy water, thus rendering all water use imposs-ible.

15. According to the 'Hundredth Monkey principle' once some-thing new has been learned by a significant percentage of a species, others *of the same species* will adopt the new principle, even if they are not geographically connected to the orignal group. Rupert Sheldrake has written extensively about this and calls it Morphogenic Reson-ance.

16. In the last 150 years (the age of steam engines and cars), carbon dioxide levels in the atmosphere have increased by 30%, and continue to increase by 3% per year, or 0.4% of atmospheric composition. About half of the CO_2 we produce by fossil fuel burning is absorbed by carbon dioxide consumers like forests, wetlands and ocean plankton, which themselves continue to decline – the other half builds up in the atmosphere. If nothing changes, carbon dioxide levels are set to double between 1990 and 2030. Nitrogen and phosphorus output into the oceans also kills marine plant communities, taking oxygen out of the water and starving other marine life forms. The carbon dioxide factor is a major contributor to the Greenhouse Effect which is leading to rising temperatures and climatic change worldwide.

17. Dolphins: The Nine give special attention to dolphins, their work on Planet Earth is seen to be as significant as ours.

18. Chilean fishermen, who kill 5,000 dolphins per year for use as

crab-bait, call them 'tontitas' or 'silly ones' because they are friendly and easy to kill, and because their fellows mass around a captured dolphin to rescue it, thus becoming easy prey themselves. In a 13-year period, 4.8 million dolphins were killed by US-registered boats alone, and they are still permitted to kill up to 20,500 per year. The tuna industry kills 110,000 dolphins annually in the East Pacific. Commercial killing of dolphins is done mainly by Japan, Taiwan, Sri Lanka and Peru. (Data source: *WWF Environment Handbook,* Macdonald Optima, UK, 1990).

19. To feed our demand for meat and dairy products, we now have 15 billion cattle in the world, each of which contributes two litres of flatulence daily. Flatulence contains methane (also produced when land and water are disturbed), which absorbs oxygen. Additionally five billion people each produce 0.25 litres of flatulence daily.

20. Holes in the ionosphere relate to ozone-layer depletion, caused by CFCs and halon gases, which eat high-level ozone, and remove the ultra-violet filtering shield in Earth's atmosphere.

III: SPIRITUAL

21. The chakras are subtle energy centres within the body, traditionally seven in number: the root chakra between the legs; the sacral centre three finger-widths below the navel; the solar plexus, a handwidth above the navel; the heart chakra, in the centre of the breast bone; the throat chakra at the base of the throat; the brow chakra just above and between the eyebrows; and the crown chakra at the top of the head.

22. Karma is a Sanskrit (North Indian classical language) word, meaning action and its laws, often interpreted in the West as the law of cause-and-effect.

BIBLICAL QUOTES:
All quotes are from The Holy Bible, King James version.
GOSPEL ACCORDING TO SAINT MATTHEW, Chapter 7, v.15: Beware of false prophets, which come to you in sheep's clothing, but inwardly they are ravening wolves.
v.16: Ye shall know them by their fruits. Do men gather grapes of thorns, or figs of thistles?
v.17: Even so every good tree bringeth forth good fruit; but a corrupt tree bringeth forth evil fruit.
v.18: A good tree cannot bring forth evil fruit, nor can a corrupt tree

bring forth good fruit.

v.19: Every tree that bringeth not forth good fruit is hewn down and cast into the fire.

v.20: Wherefore by their fruits ye shall know them.

GOSPEL ACCORDING TO SAINT JOHN, Chapter 1, v.1: In the beginning was the Word, and the Word was with God, and the Word was God.

v.2: The same was in the beginning with God.

v.3: all things were made by him, and without him was not anything made that was made.

v.4: In him was life; and the life was the light of men.

v.5: And the light shineth in darkness; and the darkness comprehended it not.

GENESIS, Chapter 1, v.27: So God created man in his own image, in the image of God created he him; male and female created he them.

GENESIS, Chapter 6, v.2: And it came to pass, when men began to multiply upon the face of the earth, and daughters were born unto them,

v.2: That the sons of God saw the daughters of men that they were fair; and they took them wives of all which they chose.

v.3: And the Lord said, My spirit shall always strive with man, for that that he also is flesh: yet his days shall be an hundred and twenty years.

v.4: There were giants in the earth in those days; and also after that when the sons of God came in unto the daughters of men, and they bare children to them. The same became mighty men which were of old, the men of renown.

REVELATIONS, Chapter 4, v.1: After this I looked, and behold, a door was opened in heaven and the first voice which I heard was as it were of a trumpet talking with me; which said, Come up hither and I will shew thee things which must be hereafter.

v.2: And immediately I was in the spirit: and, behold, a throne was set in heaven, and one sat on the throne.

v.3: And he that sat was to look upon like a jasper and a sardine stone: and there was a rainbow round about the throne, in sight like unto an emerald.

v.4: And round the throne were four and twenty seats: and upon the seats I saw four and twenty elders sitting, clothed in white rainment; and they had on their heads crowns of gold

REVELATIONS, Chapter 7, v.13: And one of the elders answered saying unto me, What are these which are arrayed in white robes? And whence come they?

v.14: And I said unto him, Sir thou knowest. And he said unto me, These are they which came out of great tribulation and have washed their robes, and made them white in the blood of the Lamb.

v.15: Therefore are they before the throne of God, and serve him day and night in his temple: and he that sitteth on the throne shall dwell among them.

REVELATIONS, Chapter 8, v.1: And when he had [the Lamb] opened the seventh seal, there was silence in heaven about the space of half an hour.

v.2: And I saw the seven angels which stood before God; and to them were given seven trumpets.

v.3: And another angel came and stood at the altar having a golden censer; and there was given unto him much incense, that he should offer it with the prayers of all the saints, upon the golden altar which was before the throne.

v.4: And the smoke of the incense, which came with the prayers of the saints ascended up before God out of the angel's hand.

v.5: And the angel took the censer and filled it with fire of the altar and cast it into the Earth; and there were voices and thunderings and lightnings and an earthquake.

REVELATIONS, Chapter 20, v.4: And I saw thrones, and they sat upon them and judgement was given unto them: and I saw the souls of them that were beheaded for the witness of Jesus, and for the word of God, and which had not worshipped the beast, neither his image, neither had received his mark upon their foreheads nor in their hands; and they lived and reigned with Christ a thousand years.

v.5: But the rest of the dead lived not again until the thousand years were finished. This is the first resurrection.

v.6: Blessed and holy is he that hath part in the first resurrection; on such, the second death has no power, but they shall be priests of God and of Christ and shall reign with him a thousand years.

v.7: And when the thousand years are expired, Satan shall be loosed out of his prison.

Index